*Aristotle and Xunzi on Shame, Moral
Education, and the Good Life*

EMOTIONS OF THE PAST

Series Editors
Robert A. Kaster | David Konstan

This series investigates the history of the emotions in pre-modern societies, taking 1500 CE as the conventional threshold of modernity. In addition to new work on Greco-Roman and medieval European cultures, the series provides a home for studies on the emotions in Near Eastern and Asian societies, including pre-modern Egypt, India, China, and beyond.

The Elegiac Passion
Jealousy in Roman Love Elegy
Ruth Rothaus Caston

Envy and Jealousy in Classical Athens
A Socio-Psychological Approach
Ed Sanders

Hope, Joy, and Affection in the Classical World
Edited by Ruth R. Caston and Robert A. Kaster

The Ancient Emotion of Disgust
Edited by Donald Lateiner and Dimos Spatharas

The Emotions in Early Chinese Philosophy
Curie Virág

Feelings Transformed
Philosophical Theories of the Emotions, 1270–1670
Dominik Perler

Reading Roman Pride
Yelena Baraz

In the Mind, in the Body, and in the World
Emotions in Early China and Ancient Greece
Edited by Douglas Cairns and Curie Virág

Aristotle and Xunzi on Shame, Moral Education,
and the Good Life
Jingyi Jenny Zhao

Aristotle and Xunzi
on Shame, Moral Education, and
the Good Life

Jingyi Jenny Zhao

Oxford University Press is a department of the University of Oxford. It furthers
the University's objective of excellence in research, scholarship, and education
by publishing worldwide. Oxford is a registered trade mark of Oxford University
Press in the UK and certain other countries.

Published in the United States of America by Oxford University Press
198 Madison Avenue, New York, NY 10016, United States of America.

© Oxford University Press 2024

All rights reserved. No part of this publication may be reproduced, stored in
a retrieval system, or transmitted, in any form or by any means, without the
prior permission in writing of Oxford University Press, or as expressly permitted
by law, by license, or under terms agreed with the appropriate reproduction
rights organization. Inquiries concerning reproduction outside the scope of the
above should be sent to the Rights Department, Oxford University Press, at the
address above.

You must not circulate this work in any other form
and you must impose this same condition on any acquirer.

Library of Congress Control Number: 2023043770

ISBN 978–0–19–777316–1

DOI: 10.1093/oso/9780197773161.001.0001

Printed by Integrated Books International, United States of America

For my parents, Yu Bin and Zhao Yang

Contents

Acknowledgements   ix
Notes   xiii

Introduction   1

1. Aristotle and Xunzi: Their Times, Texts, and Audiences   25

2. Mapping the Vocabulary of 'Shame'   42

3. Human Nature and the Social Basis for Communities   61

4. Shame and the Path to Moral Goodness   93

5. Social Institutions and the Politics of Moral Education   116

Epilogue   139
Bibliography   149
Index   173

Acknowledgements

This book is a revised version of my PhD thesis completed at the Faculty of Classics at the University of Cambridge. It is incredible to think that more than a decade has passed since I started this project on Aristotle and Xunzi. It gives me great pleasure to thank the institutions, colleagues, and friends and family who have supported me on this journey.

I had the immense fortune of having been supervised by Geoffrey Lloyd, who provided sagely guidance throughout my studies and beyond. Geoffrey saw this project on Aristotle and Xunzi from its germination to fruition, having offered expert advice on the general direction of my research and provided astute and detailed comments throughout the different stages of its development. He also gently and very kindly reminded me when it was time to let go of the manuscript when I felt the need to cling on indefinitely. I could not have hoped for a better supervisor, and I remain grateful to Geoffrey, my mentor and now dear friend, for the countless inspiring discussions that we have had on comparative studies of Greece and China and for his unfailing belief in my research.

I had the privilege of having been supervised by David Sedley during the first year of my PhD. I am indebted to David for his perceptive comments, his guidance on detailed text-reading of Aristotle, and more generally for his kind encouragement and support. Robert Wardy acted as my secondary supervisor and I benefitted much from discussions with him on comparative methodology. My PhD examiners Roel Sterckx and Richard King made thorough observations on the thesis manuscript, which proved invaluable in the revisions process.

I am grateful to several institutions that generously supported this research. The Arts and Humanities Research Council (AHRC) UK provided a full scholarship for my PhD and granted me an AHRC Placement Scheme Award which allowed me to hold a happy and fruitful six-month fellowship at the Kluge Center in the Library of Congress, Washington, DC. I thank the director and the staff of

x *Acknowledgements*

the Library for their assistance, as well as the wonderful friends I made during my stay. During my studies, I benefitted from the Chinese Government Award for Outstanding Students Abroad, supported by the China Scholarship Council. In the final year of my PhD, I received financial support from the Great Britain-China Educational Trust and from the Faculty of Classics in Cambridge; the latter also funded several conference trips and a research trip to Beijing. I am grateful to the Distant Worlds Graduate School at the University of Munich for hosting me during my postdoctoral fellowship in 2015–16.

The Faculty of Classics, where I spent the best part of a decade as a student, played a vital role in my intellectual formation, and I have learnt much from all my teachers there. Seminars and reading groups at the Faculty of Asian and Middle Eastern Studies, many convened by Roel Sterckx, nicely complemented the Chinese side of my research. Several Cambridge colleges greatly enriched my intellectual and personal life. Trinity Hall witnessed my growth from a wide-eyed fresher to a PhD graduate; many happy days were spent in Bateman Street and the beautiful grounds of Wychfield and Central Site. Darwin College welcomed me as a research fellow, and I have many blissful memories of lunches, dinners, seminars, and garden parties with interesting and remarkable people. Clare Hall, where I currently hold the Needham Research Fellowship, has proven a wonderful place to be for its sense of community and family friendliness. My sincere thanks go to the Master, Fellows, and staff of these colleges. The Needham Research Institute has been a haven for me over the years. I had the good fortune of having held the Lloyd-Dan David Research Fellowship and subsequently the ISF Academy Research Fellowship at the institute, both of which provided me with invaluable opportunities to conduct research. My heartfelt thanks go to the Director Mei Jianjun, Chairman of the Trustees Martin Jones, and to friends and colleagues at the institute—in particular Sue Bennett, John Moffett, Sally Church, Wu Huiyi, and Arthur Harris—for their generous assistance and support. I could not have enjoyed a more collegial and convivial working environment and nicer colleagues.

I am grateful for the opportunity to share various aspects of this research in venues within the UK and across the globe, including the Needham Research Institute, the Kluge Center at the Library of Congress, Midwest Conference on Chinese Thought in Dayton, Classical Association Conference in Nottingham, the Annual Conference of the Pacific Division of the American Philosophical Association in San Francisco, the University of Munich, the University of Bern, King's College Cambridge, and the University of Swansea. Fellow classicists in Cambridge offered constructive comments on the Introduction at the Classics postdoc work-in-progress seminar. I am grateful to the organisers and

Acknowledgements xi

audiences of those events for their interest and feedback, and to Eric Hutton and David Machek for generously acting as commentators and offering constructive feedback during two of my talks. Chapter 4, 'Shame and the Path to Moral Goodness', is a modified version of my article 'Shame and Moral Education in Aristotle and Xunzi' in *Ancient Greece and China Compared* (2018). I thank Cambridge University Press for permission to reprint some of the materials in that article.

It has been a great delight to witness and contribute to the flourishing of Sino-Hellenic comparative studies in the recent decade or so, and I have learnt much from friends and colleagues. It is not possible to list them all; for their camaraderie and steadfast support, I wish to thank in particular Richard King, Michael Puett, Roger Ames, Yumi Suzuki, Jeremy Tanner, Xiaofan Amy Li, Lucia Prauscello, Yuan Boping, Katharine Carruthers, Teruo Mishima, Tao Tao, and Dong Qiaosheng. Roel Sterckx and Curie Virág read specific chapters of the manuscript, and Paul Williams proofread the entire text. I am grateful for their generosity and expert knowledge. I thank my editor at Oxford University Press, Stefan Vranka, for being ever so efficient and patient, and the series editors for their ongoing support. I was much encouraged by the two anonymous reviewers' reports and benefitted from their insightful feedback. It has not been possible to accommodate all the comments and suggestions that I received over the course of preparing this manuscript for publication, and I alone am responsible for my interpretations and for any errors that remain.

Great thanks are due to friends in Cambridge and beyond who have been a constant source of solidarity and comfort; life would have been a lot less fun and colourful without Casimir D'Angelo, Elisabeth Foster, Elena Giusti, Guo Yanyu, Guo Yuchen, Avital Rom, Qiu Yu, Laura Viidebaum, Emily Ward, Xu Daiqi, Zhang Lin, and Zhang Xi.

My family have showered me with love, help, and support in more ways than I can enumerate; indeed, this work has always felt like a joint effort rather than mine alone. I dedicate this book to my parents, who fostered in me the desire to learn and who sowed in me the seed for cross-cultural inquiry when they journeyed to Cambridge over 20 years ago. Their unconditional love and unfaltering support have afforded me much strength throughout the years. Deep thanks are due also to my in-laws in Shantou, and to my extended family in Beijing and Qinhuangdao, who have generously provided all sorts of moral and practical support. My husband Lu Meng has been my pillar and biggest cheerleader through these years—I thank him for his companionship and his intellectual and creative input. It had been my ambition to complete this manuscript far earlier than the present day, but two children later, I came upon the realisation

xii *Acknowledgements*

that one cannot have everything at once. My daughter Leonie (格格) and son Owen (原原) have given me immense joy and taught me so much about the important things in life. Though still little, they have started asking many philosophical questions; I am grateful to be the mother of such playful, inquisitive, and gentle souls.

Notes

Throughout the book, *pinyin* romanisation is adopted. When quoting works that use Wade-Giles romanisation, I have converted the relevant terms to *pinyin*, except where titles of the works are concerned.

In general, translations of Greek and Chinese passages are provided to make the study accessible to readers who may be unfamiliar with the classical languages. For key passages the original text is given in the footnotes.

For the works of Plato, I cite from Burnet's Oxford text; for Aristotle, from Bekker's Berlin edition. Unless otherwise stated, my translations are based on the following, with modifications: for Aristotle's *Nicomachean Ethics*, I use Sarah Broadie and Christopher Rowe (2002); for the *Eudemian Ethics*, the *Politics* and the *Rhetoric*, I use the translations of J. Solomon, B. Jowett, and Rhys Roberts, respectively, in Jonathan Barnes ed. (1984), *The Complete Works of Aristotle*. For the *Xunzi*, I consult the translations of John Knoblock (1988–94) and Eric L. Hutton (2014). My translation is based on Knoblock, though with moderate modifications where appropriate and with frequent reference to Hutton. I use Edward Slingerland's (2003) translation for the *Analects* and D. C. Lau's (2003) translation for the *Mencius*. For all other ancient texts, I give reference to the translation in the footnotes where applicable.

References to the *Xunzi* are based on *Concordance to Hsün Tzu* (*Xunzi Yinde*) in the Harvard-Yenching Institute Sinological Index Series. References to the *Analects*, the *Mencius* and the *Zhuangzi* follow the ICS concordances published by Commercial Press, Hong Kong. The *Xunzi* text that I cite is based on Wang Xianqian's *Xun zi ji jie*, Zhong hua shu ju edition (1988). The editions and commentaries used are included in the bibliography.

For ease of reference, I sometimes use locutions such as 'Xunzi says . . .' to refer to ideas in the text, without implying that Xunzi the historical figure necessarily composed the passages in question.

xiii

Introduction

'EMOTIONS AND FEELINGS ARE GUESTS WHO WERE INVITED LATE TO the banquet of history', write Piroska Nagy and Damien Bouquet in their article 'Historical Emotions, Historians' Emotion'.[1] Joanna Lewis offers one reason why emotions became one of the most elusive subjects in historical research: 'Emotions were considered suspect, irrational, something that stood in the way of proper scientific based historical enquiry, not hard-fact based, even embarrassing'.[2] The past two decades witnessed an 'emotional turn' taking place across several disciplines, including psychology, anthropology, history, philosophy, neuroscience, as well as classical studies. Centres for the History of Emotions have been set up in Queen Mary University of London, the Max Planck Institute for Human Development in Berlin, and by the Australian Research Council. The literature on the history of emotions has expanded significantly, featuring general works (e.g., Reddy 2001; Schnell 2015; Plamper 2015; Boddice 2018), studies on the emotions in the Greco-Roman traditions more generally (e.g., Sorabji 2000; Kaster 2005; Konstan 2006; Graver 2007; Chaniotis ed. 2012, 2021; Chaniotis & Ducrey eds. 2013; Sanders & Johncock eds. 2016; Cairns & Nelis eds. 2017; Cairns ed. 2019; Candiotto & Renaut eds. 2020), and works that focus on specific emotions in those traditions (e.g., 'shame', Cairns 1993, Jimenez 2020; 'pity', Konstan 2001; 'anger', Braund & Most eds. 2004, Kalimtzis 2012; 'forgiveness', Konstan 2010; 'envy and jealousy', Sanders 2014; 'hope, joy, and affection', Caston & Kaster eds. 2016; 'disgust', Lateiner & Spatharas eds. 2016; 'regret', Warren 2021). Furthermore, much has changed since Joel Marks' lament of the 'almost total lack of references to non-Western thought' in studies of the emotions.[3]

The 'emotional turn' coincided with the 'virtue turn' in contemporary philosophy, which saw renewed interest in Aristotelian and Confucian philosophy

---

1. Nagy & Bouquet 2011.

2. Lewis 2020, 122.

3. Marks 1995, 1. Recent books concerned with emotions in the Chinese tradition include Eifring ed. 2004, Santangelo & Guida eds. 2006; Santangelo & Middendorf eds. 2006; Lloyd 2007; Seok 2017; Virág 2017; Nylan 2018; Crone 2020; Lewis 2020. It is interesting to note that a significant proportion of these recent works concern topics relating to 'shame'.

Aristotle and Xunzi on Shame, Moral Education, and the Good Life. Jingyi Jenny Zhao, Oxford University Press.
© Oxford University Press 2024. DOI: 10.1093/oso/9780197773161.003.0001

2 *Aristotle and Xunzi on Shame*

through the lens of 'virtue ethics'.[4] This development should be viewed in the wider context of the globalising movement in the study of classics. Recent years have seen an exponential rise of interest in comparative approaches to the study of the ancient Greek and early Chinese traditions, reflecting a realisation of the enormous intellectual rewards that can be gained through a cross-cultural engagement. This can be seen in the burgeoning number of conferences and workshops, publications, as well as other initiatives that promote a cross-cultural comparative perspective.[5] The trend provides a sharp contrast with previous decades where debates raged as to whether non-Western traditions, broadly defined, had 'philosophy' at all, and even if they did, whether such traditions had anything to offer to the philosopher in the West. 'Is there 'philosophy' in China?' This question has been brought up again and again under various guises. As noted by Van Norden (2007) and others, the answer to that question necessarily depends upon what one takes 'philosophy' to be.[6] In the absence of the term 'philosophy' or 'philosopher' in early China, some have identified the corpus of works from the Spring and Autumn and Warring States periods as 'masters literature' in an attempt to avoid using 'philosophy' which is borrowed from the Western tradition.[7] Such an approach has the benefit of recognising the distinctive features of early Chinese literature without being constrained by Western categories and disciplines. However, I understand 'philosophy' in the broader sense of the word and assign the title 'philosopher' to Xunzi and other Chinese intellectuals of his time on the grounds that the subject matter of their discourse is similar to that of their ancient Greek counterparts, especially

4. See e.g., Russell ed. 2013 and Besser-Jones & Slote eds. 2015, both of which include chapters on the Greek and Chinese traditions as well as contemporary perspectives. See also Van Norden 2007; Yu 2010; Hutton 2015.

5. Conferences and workshops include: 'Ancient Greece and China Compared' (Needham Research Institute, Cambridge, January 2013); 'Globalising Classics' Summer School (Humboldt University, Berlin, August 2015); 'What Makes Us Human? Philosophical and Religious Perspectives in China and the West' (CEU Budapest, July 2016); 'Emotions in Ancient Greece and Early China' (Fondation Hardt, August 2019); 'Sino-Hellenic Environmental Philosophy' (University of Bern, December 2021), to name a few. Tanner 2009 and more recently Zhang 2023 provide helpful reviews of the different approaches taken in Sino-Hellenic comparative studies. Recent works in the form of monographs and volumes include: Shankman & Durrant 2000, ed. 2002; Lloyd & Sivin 2003; Reding 2004; Lloyd 2012, 2017, 2020; Sim 2007a; Beecroft 2010; Zhou 2010; King & Schilling eds. 2011; Chemla ed. 2012; Raphals 2013; King ed. 2015; Sun 2015; Lloyd & Zhao eds. 2018; Mutschler ed. 2018; Lai, Benitez & Kim eds. 2019; Angier & Raphals eds. 2021; Beck & Vankeerberghen eds. 2021; Konstan ed. 2022; Most & Puett eds. 2023; Cairns & Virág eds. (forthcoming). From this sequence, it is clear that there has been much development since 2010, with a clear upward trajectory in the number and breadth of relevant works.

6. This question has been addressed by, amongst others, Hatton 1987; Defoort 2001; Solomon 2001; Cheng ed. 2005.

7. Cf. in particular Denecke 2011. That is not to say, however, that 'philosophy' itself is uniformly understood and taught throughout the 'West', see Lloyd 2005.

Introduction 3

on the topic of how to live a good life.[8] We can say that in the current academic landscape, the starting points of enquiry have generally moved beyond such Eurocentric ideas; instead, there is a growing emphasis on taking all ancients on their own terms: not to justify the superiority in the modus operandi of a particular culture, but to arrive at a vantage point that allows for a deeper understanding of the 'Other'—as well as of oneself—through the comparative endeavour.

Despite recent developments in the history of emotions and in comparative studies, however, sustained cross-cultural comparative studies of the emotions remain few and far between.[9] As David Konstan recently remarked, 'the comparative study of the history of emotions is still in its infancy';[10] there remains much room for exploration. Needless to say, there already exists a vast body of literature on different aspects of Aristotle's and Xunzi's thought that have been objects of study over the past two millennia; recent years have also seen important works published on Greek and Chinese conceptions of the emotions.[11] However, no major work has been undertaken to date that adopts a comparative approach to the emotions, in particular shame, by offering a critical synoptic analysis of the key elements in ancient Greek and Chinese thought.[12] Indeed, few monographs exist in general that explore in detail the thoughts of two ancient thinkers or bodies of texts to show how philosophers from seemingly distant cultural traditions might usefully be brought together to raise fascinating new questions. Such questions might concern the relationship between the philosophers in question and their different social and political circumstances; a different kind of question is involved in the issue of the extent to which cross-cultural features are in play.

The present study is comparative at its core: it aims to use Aristotle and Xunzi to stimulate discussion of an interdisciplinary nature on the rich and complex topic of the emotions, and to effectively broaden our understanding

---

8. More will be said about Aristotle's and Xunzi's background in what follows, especially in the next chapter, and it will become apparent that while I call both 'philosopher', Aristotle and Xunzi served different roles in their own political settings.

9. So far as I am aware, there are very few book-length works that are dedicated to comparing major Chinese and Greek philosophers on the emotions. Konstan ed. 2022 features a collection of articles on the emotions in the Greek and Chinese traditions, though most articles focus on a single tradition. Cairns & Virág eds. (forthcoming) will contain articles on emotions in early China and ancient Greece.

10. Konstan 2022, 17.

11. Works most relevant to this study include Seok 2017; Virág 2017; Jimenez 2020; Crone 2020; Lewis 2020, all of which were published after the completion of the doctoral thesis upon which this book is based.

12. General works on 'shame' include Deonna et al. 2011, Stearns 2017, Flanagan 2021. Works specific to the Greek and Chinese traditions are outlined elsewhere.

4   Aristotle and Xunzi on Shame

of specific philosophical ideas as well as forms of philosophical enquiry.[13] It does so through (1) reflecting upon the comparative exercise itself and tackling directly the methodological problems that are relevant to anyone interested in cross-cultural comparisons, and (2) using 'shame' as a gateway to examining the values that are in play in these philosophers' ideas and in the societies to which they belonged. Given the approach of this book, readers will not find comprehensive accounts of Aristotle and Xunzi on topics as broad as human nature or the emotions. Furthermore, while I aim to maintain an overall balance, not all chapters will be equally divided in their discussions of the Greek and the Chinese sources. To keep its comparative focus, this book concentrates on the materials that are most relevant; discussions of the ancient sources are organised in such a way as to facilitate a thorough integration of perspectives from the two cultural traditions concerned. This approach provides sufficient focus to allow for detailed textual analysis of the two philosophers, while at the same time gives scope for making constant connections to the broader comparative questions at issue.

CROSS-CULTURAL COMPARISONS OF 'SHAME'

Just how might one bring together philosophers from disparate societies, each of whom has his own set of assumptions, to discuss the complex issue of the emotions and of shame in particular? My work is driven by three main questions of methodological and substantive interest:

1. We may have some provisional ideas about 'shame' and cognate terms, but are we entitled to suppose that other cultures will operate with anything like the same concepts?
2. How in particular do Aristotle and Xunzi deal with relevant phenomena and what can we learn by comparing their different approaches to, say, moral education and development?
3. What can we take away from (1) and (2) that is relevant to our own understanding of 'shame' and the emotions in general, as well as to issues pertaining to moral education?

---

13. To use the distinctions made in Smid (2009, 3), this book proposes to embrace two kinds of comparative philosophy—the 'comparison of philosophies', which is the 'comparison of ideas, texts, or aims of different philosophical traditions, where the primary focus is the comparisons themselves', and the 'philosophy of comparison', which is 'philosophical reflection on the nature of comparison itself, where the primary focus is the development of a philosophic account of what comparison is and how it is best carried out'.

Introduction 5

'Shame' has elicited much interest across the disciplines, from anthropology to psychology, philosophy to sociology, politics to neuroscience, each offering unique perspectives on what has commonly been termed a 'moral' and 'social' emotion. It is a difficult, if not virtually impossible task, to find a universal definition for the general term 'emotions', which is sometimes used to mean 'affect', 'feelings', or 'passions', and for the individual emotions themselves. Shame, for example, as John Kekes correctly observes, 'is not amenable to a precise definition. It shades into embarrassment, humiliation, chagrin, guilt, dishonor, regret, remorse, prudishness, disgrace, etc'. Kekes continues by concluding, 'to attempt to list necessary and sufficient conditions for shame is arbitrarily to simplify a naturally complex experience'.[14] 'Shame' is by no means short of near-synonyms, and the list that Kekes provides gives just some examples where each term has its own connotations and needs to be understood within the context of its usage. Robert Kaster in his work on the emotions of the ancient Romans calls for approaching the emotions in terms of 'narrative processes or scripts', so that one can 'more directly get at what a given form of emotion is about without becoming embroiled in the tedious regress of defining emotion-terms via other emotion-terms that in turn need definition'.[15] This approach has its benefits, as it acknowledges the trap of attempting to find strict definitions for emotion-terms, which is an impossible task in itself.[16]

According to the *Oxford English Dictionary*, shame as a noun connotes 'the painful emotion arising from the consciousness of something dishonouring, ridiculous, or indecorous in one's own conduct or circumstances (or in those of others whose honour or disgrace one regards as one's own), or from being in a situation which offends one's sense of modesty or decency'.[17] In the broadest terms I shall take it that shame signifies a painful reaction to being in a situation that reflects a violation of a social norm. Such a reaction involves feelings of inadequacy and discomfort, and possibly of remorse and regret, which might prompt one to take action to avoid being found in compromising situations of a similar nature in the future. In this study, I treat 'shame' as a *placeholder* to stand for a complex network of ideas concerning the self and its relationship with

---

14. Kekes 1988, 283.

15. Kaster 2005, 8ff.

16. As Konstan frames the question: 'Can a proper history of emotion simply treat individual sentiments, or ought it rather to consider the way that each is embedded in a network of emotional or quasi-emotional concepts, a matrix that is itself subject to transformation?' (Quoted with permission from Konstan's presentation "Appraisal Theory and the History of Emotion", Crete/Patras Digital International Workshop on Rethinking Ancient Emotions, 23 November 2021).

17. 'Shame, n.' *Oxford English Dictionary*, June 2022.

6   Aristotle and Xunzi on Shame

others, and acknowledge that it is a concept that is to be revised and reassessed on the basis of an analysis of the Greek and Chinese evidence.[18]

Shame has been the focus of much philosophical discussion, particularly for its relevance to moral psychology. As a complex and social emotion that is often highlighted as an attribute that separates human beings from animals, shame is not characteristic of young children or generally of animals,[19] but is acquired as a part of the moral education of the individual; it is therefore intricately connected to discourses on morality. A critical recognition of falling short of a certain standard, often one's own, but occasionally someone else's, suggests that the agent has acquired knowledge of the 'shameful' and the 'honourable', responds to those cues, and therefore has the capacity to make moral progress.[20] At the same time, shame is closely bound up with conceptions of the self in relation to other members of the same community, thereby reflecting the navigation of interpersonal relationships and the internalisation of societal values. In such a way, it is intricately woven into the sphere of political philosophy, taking on a role in maintaining social order and cohesion.

Shame has had a bad press in twentieth-century Western societies, in part due to being closely associated with 'shaming' and 'humiliation'[21] that lead to damage to the individual's self-esteem. The second half of the twentieth century was marked by an interest in the 'guilt culture' versus 'shame culture' debate, which was initially introduced by the anthropologist Ruth Benedict in her study of Japan.[22] The notion of a 'shame culture' was applied to early Greek society by E. R. Dodds,[23] and it came to be associated with the Chinese tradition as anthropologists and sociologists noted the prevalence of 'shame' and 'face' related ideas in China.[24] A 'shame culture' was identified as one that principally relied on inculcating a sense of 'shame' or 'loss of face in the agent' to maintain order

---

18. Quine and Davidson among many others have made important contributions to interpretation and translation through their debate on the indeterminacy of sense and reference and the indeterminacy of translation. However, space will not allow me to go into detail here on the general problems of the philosophy of language and meaning which have been extensively discussed in recent years, not just in philosophy but in social anthropology and linguistics.

19. The ancient philosophers studied here adopt different points of view in their arguments concerning how humans differ from animals as moral agents and are unique in their capacity to feel shame. In recent years, however, the emotional lives of animals and the idea of animal morality have come increasingly under scrutiny. The issue of animal morality will be taken up in Chapter 3.

20. In this way, 'shame' closely resembles 'regret' in being 'a self-directed negative evaluation accompanied by a painful affective state', and in revealing one's capacity for critical self-evaluation and for changing one's assessment of oneself over time. See Warren 2021, 2.

21. Frevert 2020.

22. Benedict 1946.

23. Dodds 1951.

24. E.g. Fung 1999; Li 2004. See the idea of 'face' discussed in Chapter 2.

Introduction 7

in society, while a 'guilt culture' was identified as one that relied on feelings of guilt, understood to be a true recognition of wrongful behaviour accompanied by repentance.[25] In other words, shame and guilt came to be seen as an antithetical pair whereby the former was associated with external sanctions, and the latter with internal reflection. For those concerned with moral development, shame came to have negative connotations as a result of its harmful impact on the individual.[26]

Contemporary society abounds in discussions and debates surrounding the role of shame in human lives. Mark Edward Lewis reviews a range of literature on 'honour' and 'shame' and discusses the implications of different groups and societies having different honour codes.[27] Others have pointed out the controversial nature of shame and shaming in the legal and the political contexts.[28] Shame has also been discussed at length in queer theory, which exposes its role in stigmatising society's sub-cultures and highlights the complex ways in which individual morals relate to societal expectations.[29] Li et al. (2004) has often been cited to illustrate the prevalence of 'shame' in Chinese culture, as contrasted with western cultures. In the study, the authors demonstrate that in the Chinese language, as many as 113 'shame terms' can be identified, a fact that serves as indication of the prominence of the concept of shame in Chinese culture. At first glance, the list seems excessively long. However, a closer examination of the 113 terms shows that the list contains many idioms and colloquial expressions which are not strictly 'terms' (e.g., 'so ashamed that the ancestors of eight generations can even feel it'), nor strictly speaking 'shame terms' (e.g., 'no filial piety for one's parents', 'an ugly toad dreams of eating a swan's flesh'). Such studies confound the concept of shame by 'overstretching' it and including expressions that have at most a peripheral association; as a result,

---

25. Benedict's distinctions are as follows: 'True shame cultures rely on external sanctions for good behavior, not, as true guilt cultures do, on an internalized conviction of sin. Shame is a reaction to other people's criticism. A man is shamed either by being openly ridiculed and rejected or by fantasying [*sic*] to himself that he has been made ridiculous. In either case it is a potent sanction. But it requires an audience or at least a man's fantasy of an audience. Guilt does not. In a nation where honor means living up to one's own picture of oneself, a man may suffer guilt though no man knows his misdeed and a man's feelings of guilt may actually be relieved by confessing his sin.' (ibid., 223)

26. In the context of political thought, shame has been regarded as 'negative' for contemporary democratic societies, as 'characteristic of more primitive stages of human development' (Tarnopolsky 2010, 174). See also Nussbaum 2004. For a survey of common claims against shame, see Deonna et al. 2011. That is not to say that 'guilt' has not suffered depreciation on the basis that it is a 'negative' emotion, as some see it. On the whole, however, 'shame' has been under more fervent attack because of its perceived associations with external evaluations. See also Tomkins 1963; Gilbert 2003.

27. Lewis 2020, 1–10.

28. Nussbaum 2004; Tarnopolsky 2010; Frevert 2020.

29. See Munt 2009; Halperin & Traub eds. 2009. I am grateful to Talitha Kearey for these suggestions.

8 *Aristotle and Xunzi on Shame*

they perpetuate the image of China as a 'shame culture'; one might say that with such lax criteria as to what counts as a term indicating 'shame', it is highly likely that other cultures would reveal just such a plethora of loosely related terms and expressions.

To give another example, Ute Frevert's 2016 article cites the 2008 BBC documentary *Chinese School* to illustrate how shaming practices are accepted in the Chinese educational system, in contrast to the West where they are generally denounced. Yet it is interesting to observe just how much opinion and practices have changed since the filming of the documentary, or indeed how the episode from the documentary cannot be taken as representative of Chinese views of shaming. In December 2021, a primary school pupil in Beijing, China, was publicly shamed by her two teachers for covering her ears with her hands during another pupil's performance. She was reprimanded with abusive language and told to stand at the back of the classroom as punishment. A video of the incident became viral online, which led to its being reported across major news outlets in China, causing public uproar and triggering an outpouring of criticism of the teachers.[30] As a result, the school issued a public apology, citing violations of *shide* ("teaching ethics") and confirming the suspension of the two teachers responsible. It was indicated that the local education authority had been involved in the establishment of an investigative committee and appropriate measures have been taken to attend to the affected pupil's mental health and to ensure that this episode will not be repeated. Ironically, overnight, the teachers involved in shaming the pupil became themselves objects of shame and humiliation for their alleged moral violations, their misconduct being made public on an extraordinarily large scale due to the power of social media. From this episode, it would seem that China, which has often been contrasted with the West for its acceptance of shaming practices, takes a zero-tolerance attitude towards shaming in an educational context; simultaneously, much stigma now surrounds the teachers for their behaviour, viewed as shameful by the public. This episode serves as a stark reminder that social attitudes are liable to rapid change; furthermore, making generalisations about an entire society's take on shame and shaming can be problematic when different views and practices co-exist. Some have remarked that in the current digital age, public shaming has evolved, taking on an even more destructive form than before, even if no physical punishment is involved. As Jennifer Jacquet (2015) observes, digital technologies have made it possible for each of us to instigate online shaming—and

---

30. Zou, S. (2022, January 4). *Two teachers suspended for berating first-grade girl*. China Daily. http://global.chinadaily.com.cn/a/202201/04/WS61d3a3afa310cdd39bc7ee20.html. Accessed 2022, January 7.

Introduction   9

each of us could become its victim, a fitting remark for the Chinese case in question.

The focus of the current work, however, lies in the relevance of shame (rather than 'shaming' per se), a major focus of my work being the relevance of this nexus of emotions for moral education and the good life. A number of works have emerged in recent years that seek to reinstate the importance of 'shame' in human lives. Some scholars have written in its defence, postulating the positive roles of shame and noting the crudeness of the 'guilt' versus 'shame' divide and in turn the 'guilt culture' versus 'shame culture' characterisation.[31] Once one recognises that feelings of shame include an element of internal self-reflection and are not simply concerned with external judgment, it becomes apparent that shame does have a positive role to play in moral lives. Bernard Williams is right in stating that the ancient Greeks clearly recognised internalised standards as well as public opinion, having a conception that 'brings (something like) guilt under a wider conception of (something more than) shame'.[32] Douglas Cairns, also critical of the 'shame' and 'guilt' polarisation, draws attention to the point that 'at all stages both shame and guilt possess an internalized component'.[33] He further notes that guilt is 'first of all narrowly and ethnocentrically conceived with reference to the Judaeo-Christian concept of "sin", and then linked with "honour" and "living up to one's own picture of oneself" in a way which indicates a readiness to represent in terms of guilt any form of shame which has reference to internalized standards'.[34] The concept of 'sin' is an integral part of Benedict's definitions of guilt and guilt culture, one that is loaded with religious meaning. In the Greek and Chinese sources, conceptual clusters of shame-related ideas do not rest on the 'guilt' vs. 'shame' antithesis.[35] Furthermore, the concept of 'sin' that dominates contemporary discourse on guilt is entirely absent.

In recent scholarship, alongside the rise of 'virtue ethics' as a major area of philosophical interest, scholars have begun to recognise that ancient philosophers

---

31. E.g., Piers and Singer 1953; Taylor 1985; Williams 1993. More recently Deonna et al. 2011.

32. Williams 1993, 92.

33. Cairns 1993, 27. Cf. ibid, 27–47 for Cairns' critique of the shame culture vs. guilt culture divide.

34. Ibid., 27.

35. Rosaldo (1984, 149) cautions that 'shame' and 'guilt' are social constructs that guide behaviour. She notes that 'the error of the classic "guilt and shame" account is that it tends to universalise our culture's view of a desiring inner self without realizing that such selves—and so, the things they feel—are, in important ways, social creations. "Shames" differ as much cross-culturally as our notions of "shame" and "guilt". [. . .] Thus, whereas the affect "shame" may everywhere concern investments of the individual in a particular image of the self, the way that this emotion works depends on socially dictated ways of reckoning the claims of selves and the demands of situations.'

10 *Aristotle and Xunzi on Shame*

such as Aristotle and the 'Confucians'[36] attribute a significant role to shame on a person's path to moral goodness,[37] in contrast to the tendency in contemporary western societies to treat 'shame' as negative and undesirable. The relevant ancient accounts suggest that experiencing shame in an appropriate way is conducive to leading a good life, since the notion of a good life is contingent upon making the right kind of moral choices and cultivating a moral character that allows one to exercise one's full human potential. The current study illuminates the ongoing debates on this topic across the disciplines by juxtaposing the moral agenda of Aristotle and Xunzi with contemporary thought, leading to a discussion about the ideas of a 'positive' or a 'negative' emotion, problematic notions that are repeatedly employed in current discourses on the emotions. Shame can be said to be 'negative' in the sense that it is an unpleasant feeling that makes one feel uncomfortable and unworthy. However, if one focuses on its longer-term impact, an argument can be made for its 'positivity'—feeling shame and having the urge to rectify one's shortcomings can lead to improvement in one's moral disposition, which is a desirable and thus 'positive' outcome. Locating an emotion in either the 'positive' or the 'negative' camp and treating it in its singular aspects, therefore, is an oversimplification. Furthermore, it is an anachronism when the ancient Greeks and Chinese are concerned, since the sources concerned do not formulate the discourses in such a way. The same can be said for the distinction made between 'prospective' and 'retrospective' shame, which is problematic since such a distinction was not made by the ancient authors themselves.[38]

Important as it is to recognise the nuances of related terms in the English language, it will ultimately be the conceptual maps of the ancient Greeks and Chinese themselves that will be of predominant concern for the present study. At this point, complexities in the comparison of emotion terms in a cross-cultural context need further elaboration. To give an example, in his article 'The ethical significance of shame: insights of Aristotle and Xunzi', Antonio Cua aims

---

36. The terms 'Confucian' and 'Confucianism' are sometimes used much too liberally in regard to the pre-Qin period, when 'schools of thought' did not exist on a formal level. That is not to say that affiliations cannot be identified between thinkers who had shared views. However, the use of the terms 'Confucian' and 'Confucianism' can be problematic in some contexts. I follow up this point below.

37. See, e.g., Jimenez 2011, 2020; Fussi 2015; Raymond 2017 on Aristotle; Van Norden 2002; Seok 2017; and Hu 2022 on the Confucian tradition. Tarnopolsky 2010 endorses a Platonic notion of respectful shame, which 'can offer us a model of civility that incorporates the kind of painful recognitions that are necessarily involved in trying to come to an agreement with others who may be quite different from ourselves' (172).

38. I am in agreement with Jimenez 2020, contra Irwin 1999 and Gottlieb 2021, on the point that Aristotle treats shame as a whole rather than making explicit distinctions between prospective and retrospective shame. See Chapter 2 for a detailed discussion of 'prospective' and 'retrospective' shame.

to use Aristotle's conception of shame 'as a sort of catalyst, an opening for appreciating Xunzi's complementary insights'.[39] However, Cua's study suffers from certain methodological oversights. Relevant terms in the *Xunzi* are clearly identified (*xiu* 羞, *chi* 恥, *ru* 辱), yet the English word 'shame' is adopted for discussions on Aristotle; only in the notes section are the terms *aidōs* and *aischunē* briefly mentioned. According to Cua, 'for both Aristotle and Xunzi, shame is not a moral virtue'.[40] However, statements of this kind are fraught with problems, for neither does Cua explain what, precisely, 'shame' entails here, nor what he means by 'moral virtue', especially when no equivalent idea can be identified in the Chinese sources. In stark contrast, Bongrae Seok claims that 'shame is a major moral virtue in Confucian philosophy'.[41] The divergence between Cua and Seok is indicative of the problems that arise when one uses terms such as 'moral virtue' in the context of Chinese philosophy, which does not lend itself easily to Western categorisations.[42]

What, then, does it mean to compare Aristotle and Xunzi on 'shame-related ideas'? Undeniably one of the first questions is whether we are dealing with the same phenomenon or feeling in both cases. As English is used as a medium to discuss ideas from two ancient traditions that are far removed from our own, there are in effect *three* different linguistic systems at stake. In the Greek and Chinese societies, different conceptual clusters can be identified that relate in some ways to the English notions of 'shame', 'disgrace' and 'guilt', etc. Translations of the texts matter, for how one renders into English *aidōs* and *aischunē* and their cognates in Aristotle and similarly *xiu*, *chi*, *ru* and their binomes in Xunzi necessarily affects interpretation. A concept has its particular connotations in every culture, time period and indeed in the work of every author, therefore concepts and terms from the ancient Greeks, the Chinese, and the modern era do not simply 'map onto' one another exactly. Furthermore, authors sometimes change their usage of a particular term at different points in the text, or employ a term in a way that does not agree with their own definition of it. I show in Chapter 2, for example, that *aidōs* and *aischunē*, both of which are terms employed by Aristotle in association with ideas of 'shame' and 'disgrace', are not

---

39. Cua 2003, 147.

40. Ibid., 147.

41. Seok 2015, 24.

42. As I will discuss in Chapter 4, *de* 德 has often been translated as 'virtue', yet that term has wide connotations and cannot be said to be equivalent to the Greek *aretē*, nor to the English 'virtue'. We cannot therefore responsibly say that anything in the *Xunzi* is a 'virtue' in the Aristotelian sense of *aretē*, nor should we discuss these two philosophers as though they had the same concept of 'moral virtue', as Cua seems to suggest. For a discussion of 'virtue' in a cross-cultural context, cf. King 2011, 9–13. See also King (2012) for a discussion of the problems that arise in categorizing *ren* as 'virtue' in the *Analects*.

exactly identical in their usage, despite some commentators' claims that they are interchangeable. For Xunzi, *xiu*, *chi*, and *ru* each has its own semantic range, further complicated by the fact that they are liable to form binomes between themselves and with other characters, resulting in different shades of meaning. For instance, *chi* 恥 on its own can be used as a verb to mean 'to consider a source of shame', while a combination with the character *lian* makes *lianchi* 廉恥, which has a very different set of connotations and carries the meaning of 'a sense of integrity or shame'. Rather than comparing *aischunē* with *ru*, for example, which cannot be thought of as exact parallels, I take clusters of related terms, which include all the vocabulary that Aristotle and Xunzi employ in talking about what we might associate with ideas such as 'shame', 'disgrace' and 'guilt'. Furthermore, when necessary I also consider cases whereby the text conveys such ideas without adopting the conventional vocabulary of 'shame'.[43]

Here, one may ask, if *aidōs* and *aischunē* for Aristotle altogether mean something different from what *xiu*, *chi*, *ru* mean for Xunzi, how are we to compare the terms and translate from one set to the other? Aaron Stalnaker in his comparative study of Xunzi and Augustine calls for the use of 'bridge concepts', defined as 'general ideas [. . .] which can be given enough content to be meaningful and guide comparative inquiry and yet are still *open to greater specification* in particular cases' (italics my own). These concepts are viewed as a way to overcome the two fundamental challenges which face any comparative ethical study, namely, to 'bring distant ethical statements into interrelation and conversation' and 'simultaneously preserve their distinctiveness within the interrelation'.[44] This definition is helpful, since it highlights the fact that just because we utilise certain concepts to allow for intelligibility across distinctive traditions, the concepts under question need to be problematised given that the philosophers do not make the same assumptions. For purposes of this study, in the absence of a common vocabulary, 'shame', 'human nature' and 'moral education' are used as 'bridge concepts' in discussing a recognisably similar set of ideas found in the Greek and Chinese traditions. Having drawn up networks of ideas that can be

---

43. See Zhao (forthcoming) on 'humility' in Greece and China. The article considers scenarios that convey a person's humility without explicitly using terms commonly associated with 'humility'.

44. Stalnaker 2006, 17. The idea of a 'bridge concept' can be assimilated to the 'thin description' as advanced by a number of scholars. The thin description can be understood as a rather general account that can be shared by the various investigators, while the thick description is a detailed account that is specific to the assumptions of just one group of investigators. The distinction between thick and thin descriptions was originally employed by Ryle 1968. Geertz 1973 adopted the term in his descriptions of the role of an ethnographer, whereby the ethnographer is expected to give a thick description of a culture by providing the details, including conceptual meanings and the context, which facilitate genuine understanding of that culture. Van Norden 2007 advocates it as a useful tool in cross-cultural studies. For a critique of Stalnaker's use of 'bridge concepts' as a methodological tool, see Cline 2013, 64–68.

Introduction   13

compared across cultures, the more complicated task is then to explain the distinct ways in which Aristotle and Xunzi go about their enquiries. Indeed, it is important to revise one's assumptions about the very terms under investigation as one proceeds with the comparisons.[45]

The problem of conceptual maps in a cross-cultural context takes me to another debate that has sparked much of the discussion about the emotions: is there a set of emotions that is universal to humankind or are emotions culturally determined, hence relative to each culture?[46] The question of just how far 'shame' itself is a cross-cultural universal is elusive; after all, the very concept of 'shame' requires unpacking, its associations being context-dependent. However, comparison allows us to see the level of abstraction at which we could speak of what cultures have in common and where they differ. What is evident in both the Greek and the Chinese contexts is that moral agents are expected to reflect upon their own actions and situations, and to take into consideration how they relate to other members of society in their conduct. Anyone who lives in a community is therefore bound by certain social expectations of how to behave; a person who fails to conform to the social norms risks being treated as an outcast. Therefore, while it can be problematic to consider 'shame' a universal, the historian of emotions can attempt to unpack the broader contexts that shape the social construction and representation of the emotions in the texts and material culture that have come down to us.[47] Discourses on the emotions reflect the values of the philosophers and their societies, especially where interpersonal relationships are involved.[48] Therefore, ideas of shame and disgrace in Aristotle and Xunzi need to be understood in relation to the philosophers' ethical frameworks as a whole. Robert Solomon illustrates the importance of the 'bigger picture', using Aristotle as an example: 'Perhaps the most important single point to make about Aristotle's view of emotion is that his analyses [of the emotions] make sense only in the context of a broader ethical concern. Anger was of interest to him because it is a natural reaction to offence and it is a moral force,

45. As Lloyd (2012, 38) remarks: 'To comprehend a radically different ontology does not mean reducing it to our own (whatever that is), provided [. . .] we allow the revisability of our own assumptions and the possible multidimensionality of what is there to be understood.'

46. Further discussions on this question can be found in Solomon (1995, 258–62) and Lloyd (2007).

47. Then there is the hotly contested question of the extent to which historians are capable of accessing emotions of the past, when emotions are generally regarded as subjective experiences (Schnell 2015, Cairns 2022). I do not regard this as a challenge to the present endeavour, since the aim of my study is not to claim any kind of knowledge of the subjective experiences of the ancients but to investigate the ways in which shame related ideas are presented in normative discourse.

48. Stearns 2017, 1: 'Shame, as an emotion, has a core meaning, in relating individuals to wider social groups and norms—real or imagined.'

14 *Aristotle and Xunzi on Shame*

which can be cultivated and provoked by reason and rhetoric.'[49] In a similar vein, Frevert remarks that

> The history of emotions is not so much a history of words and concepts, but of practices (Scheer 2012). Words and concepts are interesting only to the extent that they inform, guide, and frame emotional practices, be it in art, prayer, and meditation, or in the diverse kinds of economic, political, and social communication. It is those practices that give emotion words their historically precise meaning.[50]

Concepts of shame and disgrace, then, are studied not purely out of philological interest, but more importantly to help one gain a better understanding of Aristotle's and Xunzi's ethical and political frameworks of thought.

GENERALISATION AND OTHER ISSUES IN COMPARATIVE METHODOLOGY

Is it possible to draw conclusions about the traditions under investigation without running the risk of generalisation? Indeed, does the *goal* of comparison lie in reaching some meta-truths about the civilisations under study? These are some of the questions pertinent to comparative cross-cultural studies. The issue of generalisation has been discussed by a number of scholars. G. E. R. Lloyd calls for the 'anti-generalisation' and 'anti-piecemeal' approach to comparison, since any grandiose generalisation about ancient Greek or Chinese thought unjustifiably assumes uniformity within a tradition, in the relevant characteristics and across different domains and time periods.[51] In *Demystifying Mentalities*, Lloyd considers the problem of generalisation in his critique of French sociologist Lévy-Bruhl's concept of collective mentalities, whereby a shared mentality is attributed to a social group or a society as a whole. As Lloyd notes, such attribution 'always risks ignoring or playing down individual variations [. . .]. Collectivities do not think, only individuals do [. . .] but it is not that any group, any society consists of individuals with entirely uniform mental characteristics.'[52] Zhang Longxi argues along similar lines and illustrates the problems associated with making sweeping generalisations and believing in collective mentalities.[53] He takes Richard Nisbett's work *The Geography of Thought—How*

49. Solomon 2008, 5.
50. Frevert 2016, 56.
51. Lloyd 1996, 3.
52. Lloyd 1990, 5.
53. Zhang 2015, 374f.

Asians and Westerners Think Differently and Why, to challenge some of the remarks made in the book. Nisbett's polarisation of 'Asians' and 'Europeans' is criticised since both categories encompass people of various ethnicities and backgrounds; the assumption that little or no variation in thought processes and beliefs exists *within* each of the categories is problematic. Zhang also takes issue with some of the specific remarks made in the book, for example Nisbett's claim that the Greeks, 'more than any other ancient peoples, and in fact more than most people on the planet today, had a remarkable sense of personal agency'. Nisbett's claims about the Greeks' emphasis on personal agency and freedom from constraints might hold true up to a point when applied to certain philosophical accounts. However, by citing evidence from tragedy, a different genre from the philosophical works, Zhang exposes the limitations of Nisbett's universalising observations about the Greeks.

On the issue of genre, Michael Puett, citing Lloyd's earlier work, points to the danger of coming to conclusions about cultural mentalities on the basis of surveying different genres of evidence. Puett cautions against the tendency to take statements—made either in ritual contexts or in philosophical literature—as assumptions, which has led to the use of comparative frameworks in which 'Greece and China are contrasted for having "tragic" and "harmonious" cosmologies respectively'.[54] Puett gives the example of statements about Greek tragedy being contrasted with statements about Chinese political theory that are of a normative nature. According to Puett, because these texts had very different functions and served different purposes, the contrasts made in such a way say a great deal about the different genres, but very little about the larger comparative questions under discussion. Other scholars such as Paul Goldin[55] and Anne Cheng[56] have cautioned against the pitfall of cultural essentialism, which tends to see China as an alien other that is diametrically opposed to almost everything in the West. In his article 'The myth that China has no creation myth', Goldin memorably comments: "If there is one valid generalization about China, it is that China defies generalization. Chinese civilization is simply too huge, too diverse, and too old for neat maxims. For every China-is-this or China-does-not-have-that thesis, one can always find a devastating counterexample, and usually more than one."[57] Goldin further claims, 'comparing world cultures does not mean identifying something purportedly essential about the West and then poking around to see whether the same thing exists somewhere else'. The

---

54. Puett 2018, 162.
55. Goldin 2008.
56. Cheng 2013.
57. Goldin 2008, 21.

16   *Aristotle and Xunzi on Shame*

claim that 'China has no creation myth' for Goldin typifies one of the worst fallacies in comparative study', where certain evidence has been ignored on the account that it conflicts with the imagined view of China as this Other that stands in opposition to Europe. To treat China in such a way still remains part of an Orientalist perspective (Cheng) or an updated Orientalism (Goldin).

Making generalisations is a way of identifying patterns in the evidence encountered, an act which helps one organise and make sense of that evidence, hence it is not to be discarded altogether. After detailed analysis of particular ideas and features of texts, there will inevitably be a return to the 'broader picture questions' where patterns and trends are identified and explanations offered for them. Conclusions about, say, the ancient Greeks and the Chinese *can* be drawn, provided that precautions are taken: first, by ensuring that observations are drawn on the basis of detailed study of texts or material culture rather than through reliance upon superficial impressions or assumptions; second, by being aware of the limitations of the range of evidence at hand and qualifying the claims made, for example by specifying the time period and the sub-group referred to. Indeed, cross-cultural comparisons do not need to reach some kind of meta-truth about those cultural traditions as a whole in order to be fruitful. They can simply be case studies of materials that, when compared, yield fresh understanding of a particular concept or idea.

Is there any way generalisations can be helpful? Paradoxically, one way in which they can be put to use is by taking commonly-held generalisations as the starting point of an enquiry: not by assuming their validity, but by putting them under scrutiny, to see the extent to which they need to be challenged and one's assumptions revised. The topic of 'shame' provides just such an example. Assumptions about 'shame cultures' and 'guilt cultures', of course, partly rest on one's understanding of the concepts of 'shame' and 'guilt' themselves. In reality, as mentioned above, the difference between 'shame' and 'guilt' is not always easy to draw, and the modern, western-oriented conception of the primacy or ethical superiority of 'guilt' over 'shame' is not uncontested. Instead of employing the 'shame' vs. 'guilt' model to analyse cultural traditions, I investigate the ways in which Aristotle and Xunzi speak about the motivations for actions that can be prompted by moral considerations or concern for external approval, thereby offering alternative ways of distinguishing between the 'internal' vs. the 'external'.

Evidently comparisons rest on the assumption that there are sufficient features on each side to provide a basis for comparison. For example, Aristotle and Xunzi both give recommendations on how to live, both have their own value system which sets standards for what counts as good or bad, and both advocate notions of morality that dictate the right kinds of actions. *Aidōs* and *aischunē*, and *xiu*, *chi*, and *ru* are drawn up as terms relevant to the discussion

Introduction 17

in the first place since they are concerned with behaviour that is approved or disapproved of by the individual or other people, and so give us access to what we can identify as Aristotle's and Xunzi's notions of 'shame' and related ideas. While comparative studies have a strong component of establishing similarities and differences in the content, form and style of philosophical works, there is always a level of abstraction at which authors or texts can be said to be similar. The idiosyncrasies of Aristotle's and Xunzi's approaches open up rich grounds upon which we may re-evaluate the ideas of each philosopher by recognising their separate and distinct philosophical traditions and problem-contexts. My contextual approach in reading ancient texts, therefore, aligns more with that of Quentin Skinner[58] and G. E. R. Lloyd[59] than with Jonathan Barnes, who believes that 'philosophy lives a supracelestial life, beyond the confines of space and time'.[60] I seek to explain the phenomena encountered by asking why ethical theories are set forth as they are in terms of the authors' motivations, the overall aims of the works, and the social and political background. The role of persuasion is also discussed by way of an examination into the nature of discourse in the Greek and Chinese texts. Taking into account the factors cited above, my view of comparative philosophy is, after all, not simply 'comparative philosophy', but an endeavour that takes into account the various factors that shaped philosophical thought and its development, all the while probing the question of what shape 'philosophy' took in each case.

In summary, by drawing on two major philosophers from traditions that developed in virtual isolation, where the problem-contexts were different yet the discourses sufficiently similar for comparisons to be made, the present work identifies how reading Aristotle and Xunzi in parallel might complement and

---

58. Skinner talks about political life that 'sets the main problems for the political theorist, causing a certain range of issues to appear problematic, and a corresponding range of questions to become the leading subjects of debate' (1978, xi). Skinner also believes it essential to consider the intellectual context in which the major texts where conceived, i.e. 'the context of earlier writings and inherited assumptions about political society, and of more ephemeral contemporary contributions to social and political thought'. These give insights into the 'ideological context' from which we may be able to understand the ancients in their own right.

59. Lloyd and Sivin (2002, xi) in their comparative study of the ancient Greek and Chinese history of science speak of a 'cultural manifold' which takes into account the fact that ideas do not occur in a vacuum. Lane (2009, 592) agrees with this approach: 'We can learn from and with each other, but only by beginning with our most sophisticated understandings (not a pre-contextual textual surface), and without expecting that the texts we study will turn out to have been addressing the same questions in such a way that a bricolage of philosophical reflection will be either possible or illuminating.' Indeed, Lane (2009, 591) qualifies Yu and Bunnin's (2001) 'saving the phenomena' approach by noting that 'the phenomena available to comparative philosophy are always already *interpreted* phenomena, already understood as complex constellations marked by the questions they are asking and the purposes which they portend'.

60. Barnes 1979, I, x.

18   *Aristotle and Xunzi on Shame*

inform the study of each on topics such as the emotions, moral education and ideas of the good life. While methodological concerns pose considerable challenges to the making of comparisons between philosophical traditions, the very exercise of engaging in these methodological reflections is in fact one of the fruitful rewards of the enterprise.

Choosing the Comparanda

The historian E. H. Carr famously compares doing history to fishing in a vast and sometimes inaccessible ocean:

> what the historian catches will depend, partly on chance, but mainly on what part of the ocean he chooses to fish in and what tackle he chooses to use—these two factors being, of course, determined by the kind of fish he wants to catch. By and large, the historian will get the kind of facts he wants. History means interpretation.[61]

This analogy becomes particularly pertinent when read in the context of comparative studies. In each tradition, there exists a vast pool of sources that can be used as comparanda with those of another tradition. The outcome of a comparative study, therefore, will depend crucially upon the selection of sources (what part of the ocean the comparativist chooses to fish in), as well as the research question itself (the kind of fish he wants to catch), which can have certain biases and assumptions. If conclusions about the ancient Greek and Chinese traditions are drawn on the basis of a limited selection of sources, this necessarily leads one to question the validity of the conclusions reached. In other words, if different sets of sources were chosen for comparison, it is possible that different, or indeed, conflicting, conclusions could be reached. Given the difficulties, then, how should a comparativist navigate between texts within one tradition and across traditions so as to fully acknowledge the diversity of life in the 'ocean'? How could this be done within the constraints of a single study?

In the present case, I generally limit my discussion to Aristotle and Xunzi and do not generalise about Greek and Chinese societies, though I do provide wider contextualisation where needed since Aristotle and Xunzi cannot be read in isolation from the works of their predecessors and contemporaries. I have made the conscious decision to focus on two, rather than many 'bodies of texts', for the following methodological reasons. First, given the wealth of the materials and the limitations of a single study, there is not sufficient scope to analyse

---

61. Carr 1961. Chapter 1, 'The Historian and His Facts'.

Introduction   19

the views of many different philosophers and compare them without running the risk of being merely descriptive rather than analytical. Second, selections made within the entire corpus of sources would seem arbitrary. The wider the selection of authors and texts, the greater the justification required for the inclusion or exclusion of certain texts.[62] Finally, focusing on two philosophers allows for the undertaking of a detailed analysis of where 'shame' and related ideas fit into the overall map of emotions and values in Aristotle and Xunzi *without* neglecting their place in their respective traditions. While these philosophers cannot be viewed as representative of the societies in which they lived, it is possible to identify the focus and aims of their enquiries, which would shed light on the questions that they were seeking to address in the context of their societies and the concerns of the time. I investigate closely the ways arguments are presented in the writings of each so as to make progress by 'looking bottom up', that is, grounding the comparisons in the detailed analysis of the texts, rather than 'looking top down' which involves making a broad sketch of a vast amount of material.[63]

Why then are Aristotle and Xunzi chosen as the comparanda and in what ways are their works commensurable? Aristotle and Xunzi lived in societies which are not known to have come into direct contact with each other, therefore they belonged to cultural traditions that developed in virtual isolation.[64] Some might use this fact to argue that the two philosophers are incommensurable,[65] and that there is no basis for comparison due to the divergence in the conceptual frameworks and the foundations upon which they understood the world around them. But we might say that it is precisely because the Greeks and the Chinese are so different, and because our own conceptual frameworks are so different from the ancient Greeks and Chinese, that it becomes imperative for us to make comparisons, so that we can gradually create a framework for

62. For example, if I broaden the scope of comparison to 'Confucian' views of 'shame', I shall have to justify my inclusion or exclusion of a number of works in the large, so-called 'Confucian' corpus. As Yu (2007, 57) correctly observes in setting out the differences between Confucius, Mencius and Xunzi on human nature, 'in a comparison between Aristotle and Confucianism, if we just pick out one or two passages, all sorts of conclusions can be drawn'. That is not to say, however, that Yu himself does not commit the same errors that he cautions against, for he frequently shifts from Confucius to 'Confucianism' in his comparisons with Aristotle.

63. In this way, my aim is to engage in 'deep comparisons' as suggested by Denecke (2014, 295–96).

64. Contact can take many forms, and trade would have brought with it various foreign influences that cannot usually be traced to a specific point in time. The question of contact is a complex one which cannot be explored further here. What is to be noted is that at present there exists no persuasive evidence that exchange of philosophical ideas between ancient Greece and early China took place during the time that Aristotle and Xunzi lived. For more on the point of contact, see, e.g., Shankman & Durrant 2000, 2.

65. On the issue of incommensurability, see MacIntyre (1984, 1991), who adapts the term from the philosophy of science.

20 *Aristotle and Xunzi on Shame*

discussion that goes beyond what is specific to one culture. The Chinese philosopher Zhuangzi uses the analogy of a frog stuck at the bottom of a well to illustrate the ignorance of those who are restricted in their worldview: the frog assumes that the well is all there is, until a turtle confronts him with stories of the great sea. By extension, we might say that, in some senses we all resemble the frog, limited by our own viewpoints: looking up, it is easy to assume that the skies we see are separate, incompatible spaces. But when one emerges from the well, one realises that the sky is one, and that there is an urgent need to find a form of discourse enabling us to go beyond the framework of a particular culture, and to reach a comprehensive understanding of what we see above our heads. David Konstan compares attending to the meanings and contexts of ancient terms and expanding our awareness of how the emotions function to gaining 'in visual sensitivity by learning to apprehend an alternative colour system'.[66] In his book *Cognitive Variations: Reflections on the Unity and Diversity of the Human Mind*, Lloyd remarks on the purpose of referencing ancient attitudes in the study of the emotions: "First, like the fieldwork of contemporary anthropologists, it helps us to appreciate the possibility of alternative maps of the emotions, not just including those we easily recognize, but some that enlarge our conception of the possible world of the emotions themselves . . . Secondly [. . .] each society developed a range of different ideas—including some sophisticated explicit theories—concerning the emotions and advocated different policies about how to cope with them. The very fact of this diversity, within ancient Greek and within ancient Chinese, shows that they were not prisoners of their natural languages either, any more than we are of English."[67]

Among the existing comparative works that directly engage with ancient Greek and early Chinese philosophical texts, the Confucian *Analects* was traditionally seen as an obvious choice for comparison with Aristotle,[68] that is, until recently, when newfound interest in the *Xunzi* prompted scholars to notice ways in which Aristotle and Xunzi could be seen as a complementary pair. Xunzi, alongside Confucius and Mencius, is regarded as one of the foundational figures of 'Confucianism'. However, he was downgraded during the Song dynasty as unorthodox thanks to his apparently anomalous and often misinterpreted view that 'human nature is bad'.[69] It is only comparatively recently, during the past two or three decades or so, that a revived interest in Xunzi outside and within

---

66. Konstan 2003, 1049. Emotions have frequently been compared to colours due to the subjective elements in their nature. See discussion in Reddy 2001, 3ff.

67. Lloyd 2007, 82.

68. See, e.g., Sim 2007a, 2007b; Yu 2007.

69. On the early reception history of Xunzi, see Nylan 2016.

China has led to a recognition of the philosophical richness of the text. Unlike the aphoristic *Analects* attributed to Confucius, the *Xunzi* has the distinct advantage, for comparative purposes, of taking the form of largely a treatise. But the similarity in the form of the text is not the only reason why the *Xunzi* is chosen as comparanda:[70] Aristotle and Xunzi open up a rich field for comparative explorations on the topic of shame, for the following reasons:

(1) Shame-related ideas tie in directly with Aristotle's and Xunzi's conceptions of human nature, moral development, interpersonal relationships, and the individual's place in society—all of which occupy important roles in the two philosophers' ethical and political frameworks, allowing meaningful comparisons to be made.

(2) Aristotle and Xunzi are not the only philosophers from their respective cultural traditions to attribute an importance to the role of shame in the moral education of the individual. Indeed, *aidōs* features as an important idea in several Platonic dialogues; as for Xunzi's predecessors Confucius and Mencius, *xiu*, *chi*, *ru*, and related terms occur not infrequently in the *Analects* and the *Mencius*. Yet Aristotle and Xunzi provide an account of the role of 'shame' in moral education and in social cohesion that can be seen as a development from that of their respective predecessors, and as more sophisticated in nature than anything on offer previously in their distinct cultures. For example, Xunzi is the first to have introduced the distinction between disgrace that derives from force of circumstances (*shiru* 勢辱) and disgrace that derives from inner disposition (*yiru* 義辱). Similarly, although Aristotle inherits the discourse of *aidōs* from his predecessors, he discusses the idea in greater detail in terms of how it plays a part in the moral education of the individual and serves a social purpose.[71] In the *Rhetoric*, *aischunē* is treated at length as one of the *pathē*.

(3) Fourth-century classical Greece and Warring States period China are hugely fascinating periods in history, both having experienced a social and an intellectual upheaval. As I shall show, however, they present two different examples of political circumstances. Aristotle lived in Athens for much of his life and witnessed the change in power politics with the onset of Macedonian imperialism. Xunzi lived at a time when the arrival of a universal monarch seemed imminent and the political world was likewise in flux. Taking into account the differences in political institutions, we might

70. Indeed, such assimilation overlooks fundamental *differences* in the written form of the texts and problems of genre, as I shall explain in Chapter 1.

71. Aristotle's and Xunzi's debt to their predecessors is traced in Chapters 1 and 2 and throughout other chapters where relevant.

22 *Aristotle and Xunzi on Shame*

usefully compare how Aristotle and Xunzi went about persuading other elite members of their societies, how they reflected upon their own political situation and what took priority for them.

Despite being separated in space, both Aristotle and Xunzi came to be recognised as important philosophers and left a deep imprint on future thought (though many aspects of their influence cannot be treated here). Indeed, given the fundamental differences in their sociohistorical and intellectual backgrounds, it is all the more striking just how similar Aristotle and Xunzi are in many respects: their concept of humans as essentially members of communities, as having a unique set of characteristics that distinguish them from other living things, and as in need of moral training in order to fulfil their potential and become integrated into a well-ordered society. Xunzi has been hailed by some as the 'Aristotle of the East', though often in a cursory manner without substantial discussion.[72] Of course, any claims of 'similarity' must be qualified to a certain extent. Studying Aristotle and Xunzi through detailed textual analysis will enable us to bypass hopelessly general claims of 'similarity' and 'difference'.

CHAPTER OUTLINE

What are perceived as 'philosophical texts' were read in specific ways that reflected the literary practices of the time. Chapter 1, 'Aristotle and Xunzi: Their Times, Texts, and Audiences', locates Aristotle and Xunzi in their socio-historical and intellectual backgrounds and notes the factors that would have played a role in shaping the two philosophers' thought and influenced the way they 'philosophised', thereby setting the background for the detailed textual analysis in the subsequent chapters. Through identifying the particular features of classical Greek and Warring States Chinese societies and reconstructing the literary culture and context of persuasion, it reveals that within apparent similarities there are significant differences providing the backdrop to Aristotle's and Xunzi's philosophical formulations.

Chapter 2, 'Mapping the Vocabulary of "Shame"', lays out conceptual maps of shame-related ideas in Aristotle and Xunzi. Through a comparison of the different sets of shame-related vocabulary and their usage, it illustrates how these ideas were conceived by each philosopher and the contexts in which they were employed. The chapter is therefore philological in nature, paying close attention to how particular terms and phrases were used and laying the foundation for

---

72. See discussion in Hutton 2002. Xunzi is hailed as a 'Chinese Aristotle' in Spalding 1937. Examples where Xunzi and Aristotle are compared in passing include, among others, Dubs 1927, xix, 50, 150, 157; Spalding 1947, 168; Fung 1983, 106; Knoblock 1994; III, *Preface*.

the later chapters that are more philosophically focused. It first examines *pathos* and *qing* 情, both of which have been rendered as emotions, feelings or affections in English, although each has a wide semantic range. It then moves onto the use and connotations of *aidōs* and *aischunē* in Aristotle's works, including the important question of the interchangeability of the two terms, and *xiu*, *chi*, *ru* and their related binomes in Xunzi. The chapter shows that in both cases, shame-related vocabulary is employed in the context of upholding standards of behaviour and maintaining interpersonal relationships, though differences can be identified in their usage.

Both Aristotle and Xunzi dedicate substantial attention to the question of human nature; thus, to a great extent, they base their theories of moral education on an understanding of human capacities and expected ways of conduct. An investigation into human nature therefore forms a necessary part of identifying the significance of 'shame'. Chapter 3, 'Human Nature and the Social Basis for Communities' deals with a complex set of questions such as: what according to Aristotle and Xunzi are the distinctive characteristics of human beings as compared with nonhuman animals and other living things, and how do Aristotle and Xunzi reinforce those distinctions? How is the capacity to feel 'shame' construed as a uniquely human characteristic, vital for fulfilling human functions? At what level of abstraction might we say that Aristotle and Xunzi are 'similar' or 'different' in their view that humans are social beings and members of communities, and what is the relevance of 'shame' in community life? The chapter investigates in turn Aristotle's and Xunzi's taxonomies in which humans, animals and other living things are defined, paying particular attention to how human and animal characteristics are set apart in the two philosophers' discussions of different types of 'courage', which suggest that a sense of shame is unique to humans. It then explores Aristotle's and Xunzi's points of commonality and difference by focusing the discussion on their definitions of humans as social beings. This is done through a comparison of the ideas of *logos* in Aristotle and *bian* 辨/辯 (differentiation, argumentation) in Xunzi, both of which involve discriminating between sets of opposite values so as to enable members of society to communicate and collectively strive for what is good.

Chapter 4, 'Shame and the Path to Moral Goodness' addresses the issue of the relationship between shame and morality, illustrating the crucial role that Aristotle and Xunzi attribute to shame in an individual's moral self-cultivation and showing how ancient discourses can provoke fresh ways of thinking about the relevance of 'shame' in a person's education and upbringing. It starts by outlining the different ways in which Aristotle and Xunzi use shame-related ideas to 'rank' the position of the various goods in life and place an unmistakable emphasis on the moral self-cultivation of the individual over concerns

24 *Aristotle and Xunzi on Shame*

about external judgment. Both philosophers display a clear awareness that one's behaviour is not to be judged solely through external factors, i.e. by honour and status, but more importantly through moral disposition. However, they differ in how they distinguish between one's inner disposition and one's concern about external sanctions. For both, the morally mature person not only conducts himself in the right way, but also desires to behave in such a way on the basis of his moral disposition.

Shame has long been identified as a 'social emotion', an experience that reflects an individual's awareness of social values and of his adherence to particular codes of social conduct. For both Aristotle and Xunzi, shame-related ideas play an important role not only in shaping a person's path to moral goodness but also in the development of order in society. Chapter 5, 'Shame and the Politics of Moral Education', focuses on the politics of moral education and discusses the implications of shame-related ideas for social solidarity and for the integration of the individual into society. It further addresses the question of women and the politics of shame and seeks to explain the relative lack of concern for women in Aristotle's and Xunzi's discussion. For Xunzi, it is only by learning to reform one's nature through prioritising a sense of propriety over personal profit that one can cohabit with others in harmony, avoid disgrace, and allow one's own desires to be fulfilled. Furthermore, the topic of shame and disgrace is frequently discussed in the context of ruling, so that the moral disposition of the ruler and the ministers has a direct impact on social stability. For Aristotle, good constitutions are dependent upon the success of the legislators in habituating people to practise the right kinds of actions, setting standards for people, especially the young, to follow. In each case, certain social institutions are necessary to control people's behaviour which involve, on the part of Xunzi, *li* 禮 and *fa* 法 and on the part of Aristotle, *nomos* in the first instance. By showing the multi-faceted ways in which Aristotle and Xunzi project the individual's role within society, this chapter calls into question certain cultural stereotypes, such as the 'shame culture' vs. 'guilt culture' dichotomy, as well as the commonly accepted 'individualism' of the ancient Greeks and the 'collectivism' of the Chinese.

The Epilogue draws conclusions in three main areas. First, it summarises the insights that the study has provided into cross-cultural comparative research and its methodology; second, it reflects on the distinctive features of Aristotle and Xunzi that have emerged from studying them in parallel; third, it returns to the relevance of these ancient texts to current understandings of the emotions. Certainly, both ancient philosophers were clear about the essential role that training individuals to become more sensitive to shame plays in moral education and, beyond that, in political stability. This is a striking result given that their ideas on that stability differ so profoundly.

1

Aristotle and Xunzi

Their Times, Texts, and Audiences

THE SOCIOHISTORICAL BACKGROUND

The German intellectual Karl Jaspers famously introduced the idea of the 'Axial Age' in his 1949 publication *Vom Ursprung und Ziel der Geschichte* to refer to what he claimed to be similar striking developments in philosophical and religious thought across different parts of the world, including ancient Greece, China, and India around the eighth to the third centuries BCE. To what extent the 'Axial Age' is a valid concept that can be used to apply to phenomena that took place across a wide range of time and space has been called into question. Nonetheless, this concept has stimulated much discussion of a comparative nature about the socioeconomic and intellectual developments across civilisations, as well as about the very methodology that can be adopted when framing questions of such scale. Where Aristotle and Xunzi are concerned, the fourth and third century BCE Greece and China that they lived in respectively present us with the two very different backdrops against which their ideas were formulated. The political situation marks one of the major points of departure between the societies that Aristotle and Xunzi lived in, though on a point of similarity, both philosophers witnessed periods of significant social change and intellectual flourishing that reflected diverse trends in early philosophical thinking.[1] Each of them in turn had a profound effect on the development of their respective philosophical traditions. Investigations into 'shame' in the periods of classical Greece and Warring States (*Zhanguo* 戰國) China, therefore, allow us to delve into some of the earliest debates 'East' and 'West' surrounding the role of shame in the life of the individual and in society, before the dominance of the Confucian tradition in China and of Christianity in the West.

---

1. A link, not without reason, has sometimes been drawn between political fragmentation and intellectual creativity, the idea being that a centralised empire with established ideology prioritises uniformity, control and orthodoxy, while political fragmentation accommodates—and indeed, fosters—intellectual diversity. See for example Mokyr (2018) with respect to Europe; Scheidel (2019) contains comparative perspectives on ancient empires, attributing the initial breakthroughs to 'competitive fragmentation of power'.

Aristotle and Xunzi on Shame, Moral Education, and the Good Life. Jingyi Jenny Zhao, Oxford University Press.
© Oxford University Press 2024. DOI: 10.1093/oso/9780197773161.003.0002

Aristotle, though originally from Stagira, lived for many years as a metic in Athens. The city-states in ancient Greece could number over a thousand at any one time, with constitutions that involved varying degrees of oligarchic or democratic rule. Throughout his life, Aristotle witnessed different constitutions at work, in particular that of democracy in Athens and that of kingship in Macedonia under Philip II and his son Alexander the Great. The fact that Aristotle was well aware of the existence of different kinds of constitutions is corroborated by his travels to different parts of Greece. In addition, alongside his students, Aristotle launched a 'research project' on the constitutions of over a hundred city-states, which resulted in the now incomplete *Constitution of Athens*, thought to have been compiled by a student or a colleague. Unlike the vast majority of Chinese Warring States thinkers whose ideal was a universal monarch, for Aristotle, the question of the best kind of constitution was open to debate. In the *Politics*, Aristotle defines constitution (*politeia*) as 'an arrangement of the inhabitants of a state'[2] and assesses the different kinds in turn, setting down kingship, aristocracy and polity (*politeia*, here referring to a particular form of government) as the correct forms and tyranny, oligarchy, and democracy as deviants.[3] Robin Osborne comments on the shift in the discourse of political theory between the fifth and fourth centuries, noting that fourth century thinkers 'Plato and Aristotle, and also Isocrates in his own way, engaged in far more wide-ranging and far more open-minded investigation of the varieties of constitution and their various strengths'.[4] Indeed, Aristotle outlines the advantages and disadvantages of each kind of constitution, despite polity being offered as the ideal form in Books VII and VIII of the *Politics*.

Nevertheless, Aristotle had strong associations with monarchical rule. According to ancient sources, shortly after Plato's death, Aristotle spent three years at the court of Hermias, the controversial tyrant of Atarneus. The friendship between Aristotle and the tyrant is testified in Aristotle's so-called *Hymn to Hermias*, though the extent of Aristotle's political associations with Hermias' court, if any, is a matter of debate. Subsequently, Aristotle was involved with the Macedonian court, where at the request of King Philip, he famously served for more than two years as tutor to the young Alexander. While ancient authors such as Quintilian and Dio Chrysostom speak of the relationship between Aristotle and Alexander, some modern scholars caution that these sources are

---

2. ἡ δὲ πολιτεία τῶν τὴν πόλιν οἰκούντων ἐστὶ τάξις τις (*Pol.* 1274b38).

3. Aristotle's categorisation was much influenced by Plato's *Statesman* 302c–d.

4. Osborne 2010, 287. It is worth noting that fifth century authors such as Herodotus already has discussions of different institutions, for instance in the account of the imagined debate between the three Persian nobles preceding Darius' accession regarding the advantages and disadvantages of democracy, oligarchy and monarchy in *Hdt.* 3.80–88.

by and large 'the product of fantasy'.[5] Indeed, the enigma surrounding the relationship between Aristotle and Alexander has aroused much fantasy and speculation; due to the scarcity of information on the interaction between teacher and pupil, it is unclear how much impact the Macedonian associations had on Aristotle's political philosophy and how much Aristotle's teachings influenced Alexander's political career. The fact that Aristotle never mentions any major events during the reign of Alexander, particularly where we might expect him to do so, shows that it is doubtful that he has Alexander in mind anywhere in the *Politics*.[6] While the fragmentary pieces of evidence that we have about Aristotle's involvement with the courts do not allow for extended comparisons with the political engagements of Xunzi, they do point to the fact that in both societies, intellectuals had the privilege of associating directly with influential statesmen who were in a position to communicate their ideas to those high up in the social hierarchy.

Unlike the Chinese thinkers who were influential around Xunzi's time, none of whom set up their own schools despite having followers,[7] Aristotle settled, upon his return to Athens, in the Lyceum as a place to transmit his teachings. Like Plato's Academy, it was not known to have had a formal curriculum, though it was driven by empirical and collaborative research and without the extensive focus on the study of mathematics that came to be associated with the Academy. Aristotle's students would have consisted of well-to-do men who had political aspirations, with the capacity to become legislators in their own states.[8] In many places in his ethics and in the *Politics* especially, Aristotle evidently writes with the legislator in mind, showing awareness of the importance of setting up a strict legislative system which might serve to deal out appropriate

5. Natali 2013, 43, 163n84.

6. Natali (ibid., 47) notes the missing examples of Thebes, the expedition into Asia and the destruction of the Persian Empire. One might add that when Aristotle speaks of the justified rule by an absolute monarch who is superior to all other human beings, he does not mention Alexander. For a detailed discussion of Aristotle's relationship with the Macedonian court and with Alexander in particular, see Natali (ibid., 42–52).

7. Confucius, frequently hailed as 'the first teacher in China', reportedly had an entourage of three thousand disciples who followed him as he journeyed across the different states in search of a ruler worthy of his advice. Regardless of the truth or otherwise of this claim, we find no evidence of a formal procedure that is involved in the acceptance of a disciple in the *Analects*, nor records of a specific space that was known as Confucius' school. The *Analects* gives the impression that Confucius readily accepted anyone who wished to learn: 'Confucius said: "I have never denied instruction to anyone who, of his own accord, offered up as little as a bundle of cured meat."' (7.7/15/5) The nearest equivalent to a formal school of learning in pre-Qin China would be the so-called Jixia Academy in the state of Qi, which I explore below.

8. On the political nature of Aristotle's students, see Hutchinson & Johnson 2014; Scott, D. 2020, 122–24.

28 *Aristotle and Xunzi on Shame*

measures. While the Greeks often refer to legendary lawgivers such as Lycurgus and Solon, law-giving in the classical Greek city was the work of citizens in assembly, which differed vastly from the political set-up of their Chinese counterparts. Furthermore, as Morgens Hansen notes, when considering the political system of classical Athens, it is important to keep in mind the different kinds of political institutions involved, including 'the Assembly, the *nomothetai*, the People's Court, the boards of magistrates, the Council of Five Hundred (which was the most important of the boards), the Areopagos, and *ho boulomenos*, i.e. "any citizen who wishes"'.[9] Women and slaves were excluded from the citizen body and denied the full human capabilities by Aristotle as far as deliberation is concerned.

While Aristotle entertained the idea of having one, a few, or a multitude of people ruling and assessed each situation in turn, the Warring States thinkers were almost unanimous in their support for a universal monarchy that would bring welfare to 'all under heaven' (*tianxia* 天下), which markedly differentiated them from their Greek counterparts.[10] The Warring States period was a time of political turmoil. The King of Zhou no longer exercised real authority as dukes and lords sought to usurp power for themselves; their actions led them to be accused by some of violating rituals (*li* 禮) that prescribed the correct codes of social conduct.[11] One section in the last chapter of the *Xunzi*, thought to have been compiled by one of Xunzi's disciples, firmly states this fact: 'Sun Qing [Xunzi] had no recourse but to live in a chaotic world [. . .] propriety and the rites could not be implemented, moral cultivation was not successful, the benevolent were repressed, all under heaven turned dark [. . .].'[12] During the Warring States period, seven major states had formed, each with a similar political structure whereby one lord ruled over all. It had probably become evident during Xunzi's time that the constant power struggle between the states would lead to one supreme state that would supersede the others and unify China, though that would have required the orchestrated efforts of an elite population.[13]

---

9. Hansen 1991, 71.

10. Cf. Pines 2009, 220: 'The concept of a universal monarchy, shared by all the known thinkers—with the major exception of Zhuangzi—was the single most important outcome of Zhanguo ideological disputes.'

11. The *Analects* contains passages that express a deep concern for the violation of ritual and the transgression of social norms (e.g., 3.1/4/25, 9.30/20/10–11). These phenomena escalated during the Warring States period.

12. 孫卿迫於亂世 [. . .] 禮義不行，教化不成，仁者絀約，天下冥冥[. . .] (109/32/28–29).

13. Xunzi's dates are uncertain, and it is a matter of debate whether he lived long enough to see the unification of the Warring States by the ruler of the Qin state, who was to become the first emperor of China and lay down its imperial foundations. Nonetheless, Xunzi would certainly have witnessed the rise of the Qin in becoming a supreme power.

As well as being a time of political change, much like the Spring and Autumn (*Chunqiu* 春秋) period that preceded it, the Warring States also marked a time of extraordinary intellectual activity that was unparalleled in Chinese history. These periods are frequently referred to as the time of the 'Hundred Schools of Thought' that saw considerable movement and exchange of ideas between the different states, despite the constant interstate warfare. The phenomena could be understood with reference to the increased accessibility to private education during the late Warring States period with the rise of the *shi* 士 stratum.[14] While previously only the most aristocratic families had access to education in the arts, during Xunzi's time this had changed, the courts in the various states having become more open to those from less favourable backgrounds so long as they had the potential to contribute to the running of the state.[15]

It was in this context and with the expectation of a universal monarch that intellectuals of the Warring States era sought to be of service to a state. Erica Brindley sees the rhetorical abilities and intellectual expertise of fourth and fifth century persuaders as factors contributing to an increased sense of individual agency and control.[16] The same, and perhaps a stronger statement, could be applied to the third century, when there was an ever-impending sense that a capable monarch could unify 'all under heaven'. The courts served as arenas or intellectual 'marketplaces'[17] in which advisers, sometimes referred to as 'itinerant scholars' (*youshi* 遊士), competed for the attention of their lords by offering advice on government. Rhetoric became politically important in this context; the reception of a discourse such as the *Xunzi* could play a decisive

---

14. The physically mobile and socially mobile nature of the *shi* stratum is commented upon in Brindley 2010, xxii; and more extensively in Pines 2009, 115ff., and Wang 2012, 477ff. I generally adopt 'scholar-official' in my translation of *shi*, though it is important to note the broad semantic field of this term. Pines (2009, 117) remarks that *shi* can refer to a warrior, a husband, a retainer, or a petty official depending on context, variously translated into 'gentleman', 'scholar', 'scholar-official', etc., in English. He further notes 'the changing content of the term *shi* from the Chunqiu period, when it referred to a well-defined but politically insignificant social stratum, to the Zhanguo period *shi* as a loose appellation of both acting and aspiring elite members.'

15. Indeed there is evidence of the presence of people from all walks of life in the Warring States courts, examples of whom include Fan Ju 范雎 who came from a humble background and eventually worked his way up to being the minister of Qin, Su Qin 蘇秦 who was advisor in the Zhao, Qin and Qi courts despite having suffered from poverty and humiliation in the earlier stages of his career, and Lü Buwei 呂不韋 who became the minister of Qin after leading the life of a merchant.

16. Brindley 2010, xxii: 'The notion that individuals could decisively affect the general state of order and well-being of a state through official appointment, as well as the idea that they could gain significant personal and material benefits by using their rhetorical abilities and intellectual expertise to gain the ear of an important leader, no doubt contributed to an increased sense of individual agency and control in this period.'

17. Goldin (2022, 112) refers to the 'philosophical marketplace' of the *Zhanguo* period, and Scheidel (2019, 396) speaks of the 'vibrant marketplace of ideas'.

30 *Aristotle and Xunzi on Shame*

role in determining the fate of the author, and, on a grander level, the very way the state was run. Advising the ruler on far-ranging topics, from the choice of ministers to personal moral cultivation to the education and disciplining of the people, would have been part and parcel of the counsels provided to the court. Xunzi had a direct role in government, not in his original state of Zhao but in the state of Chu where he was appointed governor of Lanling by Lord Chunshen, the prime minister of Chu, and by whom he was later dismissed. Historical records show that Xunzi participated in the activities of the Jixia Academy of the Qi state, where discussions and debates over a wide range of issues took place among celebrated intellectuals under the patronage of the Duke of Qi. Few details can be ascertained in the historical sources regarding the precise activities of the Academy. We do know, however, that as opposed to the schools in Athens, the Jixia Academy did not serve to represent the views of one particular 'school' of thought; instead, it reputedly fostered intellectual diversity and accommodated philosophers or 'masters' from different states who held different opinions. According to the second century BCE historian Sima Qian 司馬遷, Xunzi was known as 'the most revered of teachers' and three times 'master of sacrifices' in the state of Qi,[18] which suggest that Xunzi was already well recognised for his teachings during his lifetime and held significant influence among fellow intellectuals.[19]

Text, Genre, Audience

Unlike some other texts from the Spring and Autumn and Warring States periods, the *Xunzi* is primarily written in the form of a treatise, which allows for sustained and rigorous argumentation. This has led some to see the form of the *Xunzi* as comparable to that of Aristotle's works. While there are some resemblances, we are ultimately dealing with two bodies of texts that are remarkably different in style, genre, and composition, a fact that needs to be taken into consideration when the philosophical ideas themselves are compared.

The first thing to notice is the disparity in the size and composition of the two corpuses: on the one hand, there is the Aristotelian corpus, with the *Nicomachean Ethics*, *Eudemian Ethics*, *Politics*, and the *Rhetoric* being the most relevant to the current topic of shame; on the other hand, the *Xunzi* consists of

---

18. As Sivin (1995, 23) and Weingarten (2015, 286n25) note, Sima Qian does not refer explicitly to the Jixia Academy in this instance.

19. The precise age of Xunzi when he made the journey to the Jixia Academy is open to debate, mainly due to conflicting sources, e.g., the *Shiji* and Liu Xiang's preface state fifty, while others such as the *Fengsu tongyi* 風俗通義 say fifteen. For a detailed discussion on chronology, see Knoblock 1988, I, 33ff.

Aristotle and Xunzi: Their Times, Texts, and Audiences   31

a single work divided into thirty-two chapters. Compared with texts such as the *Daodejing, Zhuangzi*, and the *Analects* that are beset with textual disputes, the received *Xunzi* is considered to be in a comparatively good state. Nonetheless, the question of the historical identity of the author remains, since some of the chapters were almost certainly written by Xunzi's disciples,[20] while others, to a greater or lesser extent, contain interpolations.[21] Furthermore, as Martin Kern (2012) notes, the composite nature of the text cannot be underestimated. The written style of the *Xunzi*, such as that found in the chapters *Human Nature is Bad* and *An Exhortation to Learning*, for example, is by no means consistent. The Western Han dynasty scholar Liu Xiang 劉向 is known to have edited the *Xunzi* and reduced the number of chapters from 322 to 32, ridding the text of duplicates (though the question remains of how the thirty two chapters came to be decided upon).[22] Due to Liu Xiang's involvement, the order and content of chapters do not reflect the author's original intention. Furthermore, chapter titles are often not indicative of the content. Yet despite Han editorial work, the chapters could nonetheless be read as an organic whole, as a 'body of ideas' that does not contain major inconsistencies.[23] Problems of transmission certainly exist also for the Aristotelian corpus: for one thing, we do not know how much control Aristotle exercised in determining the form of the texts that have been passed down to us; it is a matter of debate to what extent later editors had a role in organising the texts. The *Politics* is one example of a work that is beset with textual problems: the order of the chapters has been much contested, and we are left with an incomplete chapter on education. As critics have noted, Aristotle's texts are largely in the form of lecture notes that were probably presented to the students of the Lyceum.[24] This means that Aristotle probably envisaged revisions to be possible at a later date, which is one explanation for the terse style of writing for which he is known.

The concepts of *aidōs* and *aischunē* are significant in Aristotle's ethical theory, as can be seen from the *Nicomachean Ethics* and the *Eudemian Ethics* where they

---

20. For example, in the chapter *Yao Asks*, Xunzi is spoken about in the text as the master who is lauded by his disciples. Yang Liang 楊倞, the author of the oldest extant commentary on the *Xunzi*, believes that the last five chapters of the *Xunzi* were compiled by disciples of the master.

21. This study does not preoccupy itself extensively with identifying interpolated chapters or sections, though in close textual analysis, corrupted or contested sections inviting various interpretations are noted and discussed where relevant. For works that discuss textual issues of the *Xunzi*, see Loewe 1993; Gao 2010.

22. Loewe 1993, 178.

23. Pines 2009, 6: 'Nowhere can we discern traces of the Han redactors having significantly modified or expurgated politically problematic statements of the Warring States' thinkers.'

24. Those that have survived, at least—Aristotle is known to have written dialogues which are now lost, including the *Politicus* which is documented in Diogenes Laertius.

are discussed in relation to *aretē* and in terms of their role in moral development. The fullest account of *aischunē*, however, is found in II.6 of the *Rhetoric*, a work that can be viewed as a handbook for teaching a (presumably aristocratic, or at least, well-off) Athenian how to speak persuasively in public. *Aischunē* features as a *pathos* that is discussed alongside many other emotions, including anger, fear and pity. Scholars such as Gisela Striker have commented on the oddity that one should find extended discussions of the *pathē* in Aristotle's *Rhetoric*, a work that teaches methods of persuasion, rather than in the *De Anima* and his ethical treatises.[25] It is worth noting, however, that the other works mentioned above do contain discussions of *pathē*, even if not in extended form. Aristotle's accounts complement one another by presenting the *pathē* in ways that reflect the wider concerns of each individual work: the *De Anima* examines affections such as anger from a physiological and psychological perspective, for example, while the *EN* and the *EE* are primarily concerned with the attainment of *aretē*. For Aristotle, an orator is expected to understand the nature of the emotions so as to be able to manipulate them when he is trying to persuade, hence the extended discussions of the various emotions in the *Rhetoric*. Knowledge of the emotions is not to be misused, however, as Aristotle makes it clear towards the beginning of his treatise that rhetoric is concerned with distinguishing between true and apparent proofs and seeing clearly what the facts are. In practice, the orator ought never persuade people [to do or believe] what is wrong (*Rhet*. 1355a31). For Aristotle, therefore, the *pathē* are studied in order that the true and the just might prevail.[26]

Throughout Aristotle's ethical writings, one detects a concern for addressing the 'right kind of audience', the protreptic tone especially prominent in some books of the *Nicomachean Ethics*. Towards the beginning of the *EN*, Aristotle says:

> the young are not an appropriate audience for the political expert, for they are inexperienced in the actions that constitute life, and what is said will start from and will be about these actions. What is more, because the young have a tendency to be led by the emotions (*pathē*), there will be no point or use in their listening, and no advantage to them if they do, since the end is not knowing things but doing them. (*EN* 1095a2–6)

Aristotle thus specifies an audience that has the capacity and maturity to receive his teachings and to identify with the viewpoints expressed. In terms of *aidōs*,

---

25. Striker 1996, 286.

26. One point of contrast between Aristotle and Plato is that for the former, rhetorical technique itself is morally neutral, while in Plato's *Gorgias*, rhetoric without philosophy is not a moral endeavour.

even though it is said to be fitting only for the young, discourses on *aidōs* are not addressed to the young *directly*, since they are not ready for political discourse and have not habituated themselves properly. The target audience for the *EN* (and one might infer, for Aristotle's other ethical and political works as well) consists of people who have already habituated themselves to upholding the fine (*to kalon*) and avoiding the disgraceful (*to aischron*), and who are capable of associating pleasure and pain with the correct things.[27] In this way, the *EN* provides guidance for the early stages of moral education and expounds on the necessity of *aidōs* in education without serving the protreptic purpose of persuading the young themselves. To qualify to be on the receiving end of Aristotle's lectures, then, one has to have followed a certain path and to have learnt successfully to identify *to kalon* and *to aischron*.[28] As many commentators have noted, for Aristotle, the ethical and the political are intricately connected: while the *Nicomachean Ethics* focuses on the human good, it forms a natural prelude to the *Politics*, given that knowledge of the good life provides one with the first principles of political science.[29] Therefore, even though Aristotle's ethical and political discourses are presented in separate works, to understand their broader concerns, one needs to read these works as an organic whole.

In contrast to the *Rhetoric*, where Aristotle directly addresses the nature of each *pathos* and offers explanations of the circumstances that give rise to them, no 'systematic' treatment of the emotions can be found in the *Xunzi*. While Xunzi is concerned with discrimination and the correct kinds of argumentation, his work, unlike Aristotle's *Rhetoric*, is far from a 'handbook' that teaches one to succeed in persuasion. The *Xunzi* does not seek to teach ways of persuasion for persuasion's sake; rather, one of the ideas that the text conveys is that the ability to persuade is a reflection of the speaker's moral disposition. While Xunzi does recognise 'liking and disliking, delight and anger, sorrow and joy' as belonging to *qing*[30]—what we might categorise as the 'emotions', there is no sign of his having any interest in defining an emotion for its own sake and identifying its characteristics: the idea of *qing* is discussed in relation to human nature and

---

27. To what extent Aristotle's expectations were realistic or even made in earnest, however, is debatable.

28. Burnyeat (1980, 81) observes: 'He [Aristotle] is not attempting the task so many moralists have undertaken of recommending virtue even to those who despise it: his lectures are not sermons, nor even protreptic argument, urging the wicked to mend their ways. From x.9 it is clear that he did not think that sort of thing to be of much use; some, perhaps most, people's basic desires are already so corrupted that no amount of argument will bring them to see that virtue is desirable in and for itself (cf. iii.5, 1114a19–21). Rather, he is giving a course in practical thinking to enable someone who already wants to be virtuous to understand better what he should do and why.'

29. Scott D. 2020, 121. See also Frede 2013; Kamtekar 2014.

30. 性之好、惡、喜、怒、哀、樂謂之情。(83/22/3)

34 *Aristotle and Xunzi on Shame*

moral deliberation rather than in its own right.[31] On the whole, emotions are not discussed in terms of physiological changes to the body, but the focus lies more in the ways in which they reflect human tendencies and relationships. For this reason, unlike Plato and Aristotle, Xunzi does not discuss the physical signs of shame, for example, blushing, as such. Shame-related concepts such as *xiu*, *chi*, *ru*, and their binomes can be found scattered throughout the whole corpus of the work in relation to different topics, though the chapter *Of Honour and Disgrace* is particularly relevant in that it contains discussions on the distinctions between honourable and disgraceful actions.

While the *Analects* and the *Mencius* are replete with lively dialogues through which opinions are voiced and debated, the *Xunzi* is largely in essay form. Instead of dialogues that purport to be a record of conversations between historical characters, the *Xunzi* contains hypothetical exchanges that come to a climax in the chapter *Human Nature is Bad*, where Xunzi frames his arguments in response to Mencius (the historical figure then already dead). Even though Xunzi generally does not appear as a character in the text, a strong authorial voice presents itself through the employment of rhetorical questions, repetition, hyperbole and metaphors, which serve to reinforce arguments.[32] The *Xunzi* places 'more emphasis on teacher-disciple relations than any other Warring States text',[33] it has been observed, yet ironically the third-person essay suggests 'a further suppression of the teaching scene and the dominance of texts as the model form of instruction'.[34] Where the *Xunzi* is concerned, one might say that the teaching scene has shifted from dialogues between the master and the disciple or other interlocutor to the author's more direct form of address to the audience. Xunzi emphasises the importance of receiving education from a teacher, yet the text itself could be regarded as a 'form of instruction' and a transmission of proper teaching.

Xunzi does not explicitly identify what specific group should receive his teachings, though undoubtedly he would have had an elite audience who were sufficiently influential politically as to be able to implement his ideas. The text carried an ideology that was likely disseminated to the higher officials and potentially to the ruler of a state, who had power over ritual, education and the military, all of which are important concerns of the text itself. It can be rightly assumed that Xunzi's work was targeted at a ruler whom he hoped might become

---

31. For a discussion of *qing* in the *Xunzi*, see Virág 2017, 163–98.

32. Cf. Denecke 2011, 181: 'The master's physical aura is replaced by his voice, which is no longer framed and reported but is disembodied and direct.'

33. Ibid., 118.

34. Lewis 1999, 91.

influenced by the ideas and, as a result, seek to perfect his own character and exert a positive influence on his people. The *Xunzi*, then, like many other texts of the period, can be regarded as a heavily political treatise; its primary aim lay in assisting a ruler to achieve success in government so as ultimately to become the universal monarch. Viewed in this way, Xunzi's treatment of music, human nature, heaven, and even naming and rhetoric is just as political as his treatment of military matters and government; the ethical and the political are for him inseparable. Xunzi does not specify that his audience should be a particular sort of people, either in terms of age or moral standing; in contrast to Aristotle, he does not make the point that his audience should *already* be practising the right kinds of things. Indeed, Xunzi's discourse can very much be seen in the light of the kind that Burnyeat claims *not* to be Aristotle's, that is, protreptic arguments recommending virtue even to those who despise it, 'urging the wicked to mend their ways'.[35] Given the fact that Xunzi does not assume forthright that his audience will have a grasp of what constitutes right or wrong behaviour, as well as the fact that he was probably addressing those in power directly (rather than aspiring legislators in the Aristotelian context), the text shows an altogether rather more explicit kind of persuasion than is found in the texts of Aristotle where shame-related ideas are discussed. In this respect, Xunzi can be seen as following in the footsteps of Confucius and Mencius, both of whom are recorded as having advised those who practised the kinds of behaviour that they despised, attempting to persuade them to turn to virtue and benevolent rule.

PREDECESSORS AND CONTEMPORARIES

I now turn more closely to the intellectual background of Aristotle and Xunzi by looking at the ideas of the predecessors to whom the two philosophers sought to respond while owing them an intellectual debt, particularly concerning shame and its role in moral education.

Taking into account the fact that Xunzi was active at a time of exceptional intellectual flourishing that saw intense debates taking place between proponents of diverse views, it is no surprise that he, like many other contemporary thinkers, produced arguments that not only closely referenced well-known doctrines of the time, but also syncretised different strands of thought.[36] Throughout history, Xunzi has occupied a somewhat controversial position: he has long been

---

35. Burnyeat 1980, 81.

36. For example, Xunzi's focus on the role of ritual (*li*) in moral development distinguishes him from Confucius and Mencius, while his discussions on *xin* (心), the heart-mind, are highly reminiscent of ideas in the *Zhuangzi*.

36 *Aristotle and Xunzi on Shame*

held, along with Confucius and Mencius, as one of the great early 'Confucian' masters; on the other hand, his views have at times been associated with the so-called 'Legalist' School (*fajia*)[37] of thought. His alleged best-known disciples—Li Si 李斯 and Han Fei 韓非—both became extremely influential ministers in the Qin court and were seen in history as representative figures of Legalism. In recent years, scholars have increasingly begun to recognise the problematic nature of demarcating Spring and Autumn and Warring States thinkers to schools such as 'Confucianism' (*rujia*) and 'Legalism' (*fajia*). These terms are anachronistic and potentially misleading when applied to the periods in question, the notion of the existence of well-defined sets of theories within well-defined sects being something of an illusion given that the division of pre-Qin thinkers into distinctive 'schools' was a Han convention.[38] For sure, Xunzi places Confucius in high regard and attaches great importance to learning and self-cultivation by following ritual and acting in accordance with propriety, all of which are reminiscent of Confucius' teachings in the *Analects*. Yet clearly Xunzi does not approve of just anyone who claims to be a follower of Confucius; indeed, his heavy criticisms of Mencius and of Zi Si (grandson of Confucius who allegedly taught Mencius) reflect the fierce competition that took place at the time, even within a group of people who professed to uphold the authority of one master (in this case, Confucius). At the same time, Xunzi's discourses on the necessity of external restraints to control and regulate human behaviour depart from what was seen as the conventional 'Confucian' approach and are more reminiscent of so-called 'Legalism'. Xunzi's repeated proclamations that 'human nature is bad' is a notable polemic against the Mencian view—which later became the orthodox Confucian position—that 'human nature is good'.[39]

While one needs to exercise caution in attaching philosophers to 'schools' in the early period, it is evident that texts which were later perceived as 'Confucian' generally put far more weight on topics relating to 'shame' than those that were associated with other 'schools'. While Xunzi navigates his position with reference to a diverse range of thinkers, it is undeniable that his greatest intellectual debts are to the *Analects* and the *Mencius* where 'shame' and moral education are concerned. In the *Analects*, Confucius states the kinds of things that one

---

37. See Goldin 2011 on persistent misconceptions about Chinese 'Legalism'. Indeed, the term *fa* itself, as Goldin notes, can prove difficult to translate because of its broad semantic range. More will be said about *fa* in the *Xunzi* in Chapter 5, where comparisons will be made with social institutions in Aristotle.

38. Csikszentmihalyi & Nylan 2003; Pines 2009. For sure, one can identify thinkers that shared similar views, just as the ancients themselves made associations between certain groups. For example, Xunzi in the chapter *Against the Twelve* groups together in his criticisms pairs such as Zi Si 子思 and Meng Ke 孟軻 (Mencius), Hui Shi 惠施 and Deng Xi 鄧析, and Mo Di (Mozi) 墨翟 and Song Xing 宋鈃, which indicates that such people were sometimes perceived to have adopted somewhat similar positions.

39. To what extent Xunzi and Mencius are at odds with each other is discussed in later chapters.

Aristotle and Xunzi: Their Times, Texts, and Audiences 37

ought to be ashamed of, which include putting on a false display of one's intentions (5.25/11/15–16), accepting a salary when the state is without the Way (14.1/37/3–6), and not matching one's words with deeds (4.22/8/23). At the same time, Confucius comments on things that ought *not* to generate shame, with the understanding that these are likely to constitute sources of shame for the ordinary person:

> The Master said, 'A scholar-official who has set his heart upon the Way, but who is still ashamed of having shabby clothing or bad food, is not worth engaging in discussion.'[40]

> The Master said, 'Clad only in a shabby quilted gown, and yet unashamed to stand side-by-side with someone dressed in expensive furs—does this not describe You [i.e. Zilu]? "Not envious, not covetous, how could he not be good?" '[41]

Such statements suggest that for someone whose heart is set on the right kinds of things, an appearance that reflects his humble background ought not to be a source of shame. The underlying idea is that ostentatious wealth is not the measure of a good person, and that one's character and inner disposition are ultimately the things that are of importance. This idea of dispelling possible misconceptions about what counts as shameful certainly had an impact on Xunzi, who developed this notion by coining the terms *yirong* and *shirong*, *yiru* and *shiru*. Personal wealth and an elevated status, reflecting honour derived from force of circumstances (*shirong*), are contrasted with honour derived from inner disposition (*yirong*); poor clothing and food, reflecting disgrace by force of circumstances (*shiru*), contrasts with disgrace derived from inner disposition (*yiru*). Indeed, by making such distinctions, Xunzi effectively builds upon ideas in the *Analects* and offers far more elaborate accounts of reliable ways to assess one's moral standing and social status.

Besides the *Analects*, it is beyond doubt that Xunzi inherits much from Mencius, considering him to be his greatest rival. Fervently objecting to Mencius's views in the chapters *Against the Twelve* and *Human Nature is Bad*, the framework of Xunzi's discourse on human nature can be regarded as a response to Mencius.[42] Throughout *Human Nature is Bad*, Xunzi launches a

---

40. 子曰：“士志於道，而恥惡衣惡食者，未足與議也” (4.9/7/25).

41. 子曰：“衣敝縕袍，與衣狐貉者立，而不恥者，其由也與？不忮不求，何用不臧？” (9.27/22/11–12) See Wang's (2011, 214–17) discussions of these passages .

42. Brindley (2010, 87) comments upon how the idea of *xing* or human nature is crucial in Xunzi's polemic: 'By insisting on the detrimental, selfish forces of *xing*, these authors justify their opposition to the cultivation of one's personal agencies as a viable means of social control. They are thus inextricably

38 *Aristotle and Xunzi on Shame*

polemic against Mencius by making it clear that his thesis is in direct opposition to his predecessor's. He first lists formulations of Mencius' statement that human nature is good (*shan* 善), and then counters them one by one, arguing that human nature is bad (*e* 惡). Reading Xunzi with a view to the context of the debate, therefore, is essential if the modern reader is to understand the rhetoric that may be at play in the text and the particular ways in which questions are being formulated and answered. Despite his criticisms against Mencius, Xunzi inherits much from him in his definition of what it means to be human. In the chapter *On the Regulations of a King*, Xunzi observes that a sense of propriety (*yi* 義) is a capacity that is distinctive of human beings (28/9/69-70). This idea can be traced back to Mencius, who in his well-known idea of the 'four sprouts' of human nature states that the feelings of shame and dislike are the sprout of a sense of propriety (羞惡之心，義之端也), and that not to have such feelings is not to be human (3.6/18/7-9). Xunzi, therefore, takes one of the four sprouts from Mencius and establishes it as the defining feature of human beings that distinguishes them from other living things. Furthermore, Xunzi's assimilation of the shameless and selfish person with the dog and the boar conveys the idea that the lack of a feeling of shame renders one non-human, recalling Mencius's well-known statement that 'humans must not be without shame (*chi*), for the shame of being without shame is shamelessness indeed.'[43] This argument puts a sense of shame firmly on the map as one of the identifying traits of human beings. Xunzi's preoccupation with distinguishing humans from animals through their inborn capacity and moral training is reminiscent of passages in the *Mencius* where the untaught are compared with birds and beasts (5.4/29/9–10). According to both philosophers, then, acting in a shameless and uneducated way deprives one of fundamental human characteristics and casts one into the category of the beasts.[44]

While Xunzi boasted to be a true follower of Confucius, he was born some two hundred years after Confucius. Aristotle's intellectual lineage, however, was in a sense much more direct—he was a student at Plato's Academy. For all the disagreements between Aristotle and Plato, for example on the basic ontological questions such as the Form of the Good—both are anti-relativists

---

involved in debates on the power and authority of *xing* in human life and society, and their advocacy for institutionalized methods of control can be understood in terms of their opposition to individualistic trends and a discursive emphasis on private sources of authority that existed at the time.' I would not go so far as to say that *xing* for Xunzi is 'deterministic' (ibid., 90), since much emphasis is placed in the text on the powers of human agency. On 'agency' in the *Xunzi*, see essays in Kline & Ivanhoe eds. 2000.

43. 人不可以無恥。無恥之恥，無恥矣 (13.6/67/28).

44. This idea is discussed more extensively in Chapter 3, with reference to the *Mencius*.

Aristotle and Xunzi: Their Times, Texts, and Audiences 39

and objectivists in ethics. While the influence of Plato on many aspects of his thought cannot be underestimated, Aristotle was also reacting to other thinkers of his time. The different associations that Aristotle makes for *aidōs* or *aischunē*, despite the relatively similar definitions that he gives them, may be due to the influences of Homeric poetry, tragedy, Platonic writings, as well as contemporary usage in the fourth century, such as that of the orators. On the other hand, while Greek literature is full of references to occasions that give rise to *aidōs* or *aischunē*, Aristotle is the first in the Greek tradition to have treated these terms, and indeed, what we might more generally identify as 'emotions', in a systematic fashion.

It will not be possible to discuss the uses of *aidōs* and *aischunē* in Greek literature in any comprehensive manner.[45] However, a few paradigmatic examples from Homer, tragedy, Plato, and the orators will serve to bring out several interesting aspects of these terms that have ramifications in Aristotle's philosophy. In Homeric poetry, as in Hesiod,[46] *aidōs* is generally a positive term to mean awe, reverence and a sense of what is right[47] and *aischunē* a negative term suggesting dishonour and disgrace.[48] *Aidōs* is sometimes associated with heroism and honour. A prime example is provided by the Trojan hero Hector, who refuses his wife Andromache's plea to stay out of the fighting with the Greeks and, instead, on the basis of what he claims to be *aidōs* before the Trojans, launches himself into the battlefield, ultimately meeting his death, on the basis of what he claims to be *aidōs* before the Trojans. Hector's reason for fighting reflects his acute awareness of his social stature before his people, so that his action is propelled by a desire to avoid being viewed as cowardly by others belonging to the same community (*Il.* 6.463). This is one of the examples that Dodds gives for the 'shame-culture' of the ancient Greeks because Hector's motivation apparently comes from a concern about being viewed negatively by other people. The passage reveals the ways in which *aidōs* takes on the sense of 'honour', reflecting an individual's awareness of a social code that is shared by

---

45. For such a study, consult Cairns 1993.

46. Further discussion of *aidōs* in Hesiod can be found in Chapter 3.

47. E.g. *Il.* 15.128–129, 24.44–45; *Od.* 3.24. The use of *aidōs* in the Homeric sense of awe and respect is not much evident in Aristotle, one of the few exceptions being a passage in the *Politics* where Aristotle advises against youthful marriages on the grounds that the children would be lacking in respect (*aidōs*) for their parents, who would be too close to their age (*Pol.* 1335a1–4).

48. E.g. *Il.* 6.207–210, 22.74–76, *Od.* 2.85–86, 24.506–509. According to Grimaldi, what we find reflected in Aristotle's usages is 'very likely the historical development of *aidōs* toward a gradual fusion with *aischunē*' (1988, II, 106). Grimaldi agrees with Gauthier and Jolif in saying that 'the concept *aidōs* will become *aischunē* in Aristotle' (ibid., 107). In the next chapter, I address the question of the relationship between *aidōs* and *aischunē* and argue that in Aristotle, each of these terms has specific resonances.

40 Aristotle and Xunzi on Shame

members of the same group.[49] In Euripides' play *Hippolytus*, Phaedra, feeling ashamed of her sexual desire for her stepson, famously makes the statement that there are two kinds of *aidōs*, one good (i.e., a sense of shame), one bad (shame consequent upon bad actions), succinctly pointing to the double-edged nature of this concept—the fact that *aidōs* takes on both prospective and retrospective senses. Many references to *aidōs* can be found in the works of Plato, for example in the *Gorgias*, the *Phaedrus*, the *Protagoras* and the *Laws*.[50] Here I cite merely two examples, that of the *Protagoras* myth, where Zeus is said to have sent Hermes to bring upon humans *dikē* and *aidōs*—justice and a sense of shame, which are shared by all human beings, in order that they may preserve themselves and live in peace,[51] and the *Laws*, where *aidōs* is said to have acted as a kind of despot, making the Athenians live in willing subjection to the existing laws.[52] Both instances illustrate the social nature of *aidōs*, the idea of its bringing people together and enabling communities to survive and thrive on the basis of a shared social code. Words with the *aid-* root can be found taking on a positive resonance in the writings of the ancient orators. For example, Antiphon urges the jurors to respect (*aideisthai*) the piety (*eusebeia*) of those who have committed no crime,[53] while Democritus argues for the need for one to *aideisthai* oneself above all, so as to do nothing inappropriate, which suggests approval of the feeling of *aideisthai*.[54] In one speech, Antiphon claims that his answering the accusations will bestow honour and benefit on himself, while leaving his opponents with *aischunē*, which is clearly portrayed as negative and undesirable.[55] These examples generally highlight the conventional associations of *aidōs* with the positive sense of respect and the sense of shame that can be preservative, and *aischunē* with the negative sense of what is ugly and despicable. In Aristotle, as we shall see in the following chapter, similar resonances can be found.

---

49. In Aristotle, *aidōs* is associated with *timē*, honour, whereby actions taken on the basis of *aidōs* are contrasted with other motives. However, as I shall illustrate, in Aristotle the associations of *aidōs* are more complex. Despite being defined as 'a fear of loss of repute', in Aristotle *aidōs* bears resemblances to *aretē*, translated as 'virtue' or 'excellence', so that it has a peculiar relationship with the fine (*to kalon*), rather than being simply a concern for external recognition.

50. For emotions in Plato, see Candiotto & Renaut eds. 2020. On 'shame' in Plato, see for example Militello, Pfefforkorn and Scott in the same volume; Tarnopolsky 2010; Lin 2022.

51. Plato, *Prot.* 322bff.

52. *Leg.* 698b5–6. For a study of the idea of shame in the *Laws*, see Pfefferkorn 2020; Lin 2022.

53. *Antiph.* 2.d.11–12.

54. *DK* B 264.

55. *Antiph.* 6.8.

Similarities and Differences in the Sociohistorical Backgrounds

I have so far given a comparative overview of Aristotle's and Xunzi's background which sets the foundations for textual analysis in the chapters to follow. From an examination into the sociohistorical background, the nature of the texts, and finally the predecessors and contemporaries of Aristotle and Xunzi, I have been able to pinpoint certain similarities and differences. Main areas of difference include: (1) the political set-up and ideologies of the Greeks and the Chinese, as well as the very political roles that each philosopher assumed in his society; (2) the style, genre, and composition of the texts, as well as expectations held of the audience in terms of their being disposed in a certain way prior to receiving teaching; and (3) in each case, the intellectual context set the frameworks for discussion and provided different sets of questions to which Aristotle and Xunzi were responding.

Despite such differences, a number of similarities can be observed: (1) both philosophers' audience consisted of an elite who either held a certain amount of political influence or had the potential to do so in their respective societies; (2) for both, the ethical and the political are intricately connected; (3) both philosophers' works (the ethical ones at least for Aristotle) are protreptic in nature and discuss the cultivation of moral character that is expected of the audience. To a certain extent, the political elite would be expected to bring out those qualities in others. And finally, (4) neither Aristotle nor Xunzi is the first in their respective traditions to incorporate discussions of shame into their works, and both borrow extensively from their intellectual forefathers, even if they explicitly distance themselves from such figures. However, both philosophers provide a treatment of 'shame' that in many ways exceeds their predecessors' in sophistication, as I will seek to show in the following chapters.

2

Mapping the Vocabulary of 'Shame'

Pathos and *Qing* 情

This chapter offers a survey of shame-related vocabulary in Aristotle and Xunzi by noting its usage within the wider networks of relevant ideas and contexts. How is shame-related vocabulary mapped out in the two philosophers? How do the terms in question correspond to one another, and how do the ancient authors go about drawing distinctions between them? What can we make of the relationship between these and the wider discourses on the emotions (*pathos/ qing* respectively) in each case? The comparative study goes far beyond a comparison of terms; however, philological examination will serve to reveal the ways that discourses on shame are framed and explained.

Before undertaking a close examination of the vocabulary related to shame, a few words need to be said about the general terms *pathos* and *qing* 情, both of which encompass a wide spectrum of meanings and are relevant to discussions of feelings and emotions in the ancient Greek and early Chinese contexts.

H. Bonitz in the *Index Aristotelicus* outlines five distinctive usages of *pathos*, including (1) the process of being acted upon; (2) the underlying substrate, as a synonym of *sumbebēkos*; (3) qualitative change; (4) misfortunes and pains of considerable magnitude; and (5) affection or upheaval of the soul,[1] the last meaning being of primary relevance to the present study. In the *Rhetoric*, *pathē* are defined as all those feelings that so change people as to affect their judgments, and that are also attended by pleasure or pain, such as anger, pity, fear, and the like, with their opposites.[2] Aristotle identifies *pathē* as one of the three modes of proof, so that when the audience is roused to emotion the way the orator wishes, they will pass judgments the way the orator desired. *Aischunē* is discussed as a *pathos* among a list of emotions in Book II of the *Rhetoric* and is given a formulaic treatment in terms of the things that cause it, the persons before whom *aischunē* is felt, and the states of mind under which it is felt.

---

1. Bonitz 1955, 555–57. Summary based on Oele 2007, 3–5. For a discussion of the metaphysical status of *pathē* in Aristotle, see Rorty 1984.

2. ἔστι δὲ τὰ πάθη δι' ὅσα μεταβάλλοντες διαφέρουσι πρὸς τὰς κρίσεις οἷς ἕπεται λύπη καὶ ἡδονή, οἷον ὀργὴ ἔλεος φόβος καὶ ὅσα ἄλλα τοιαῦτα, καὶ τὰ τούτοις ἐναντία (*Rhet.* 1378a19–22).

Aristotle and Xunzi on Shame, Moral Education, and the Good Life. Jingyi Jenny Zhao, Oxford University Press.
© Oxford University Press 2024. DOI: 10.1093/oso/9780197773161.003.0003

Aristotle's list of the *pathē* bears undeniable resemblances to lists found in Plato. However, as has rightly been observed, there is no such thing as 'a concept of emotion' in Plato, nor is there a definition of what an 'emotion' is.[3] Plato is concerned with drawing up lists of states in the agent that might correspond to 'affections', 'sentiments', or 'emotions'. Instead of offering one definitive account of what the *pathē* are, he provides several lists with certain differences. His accounts of *pathē* go beyond what we might identify as 'emotions' to also include pleasures, pains and desire, which would typically not be included in a list of emotions in the contemporary anglophone context. Aristotle may be said to be the first in the Western tradition to have come up with a list of *pathē* that more or less resembles what one might categorise as emotions today, though it is important to bear in mind Aristotle's influence on subsequent conceptions of emotions.[4]

Unlike Aristotle who defines *pathos* itself and then goes on to define the *pathē* one by one in the *Rhetoric*, Xunzi does not give formal definitions for particular emotions such as shame. The text does contain glosses for the term *qing* 情, which features heavily in Xunzi's philosophy. When one searches for its appearances in the *Xunzi* and in other classical Chinese texts, on its own and with other characters as binomes, it soon becomes evident that, while *qing* is sometimes translated as 'emotions', it has a wide semantic range. Some scholars have attempted to render a single translation for all its appearances. For example, Chad Hansen proposes 'reality feedback' or 'reality input' for the meaning of *qing* in pre-Buddhist Chinese thought,[5] while A. C. Graham claims that it means 'the facts' as a noun and 'genuine' as an adjective.[6] Indeed, Graham goes so far as to claim that *qing* 'never means "passions" even in *Xunzi*'.[7] As Michael Puett rightly recognises, none of these definitions appears to account for all the meanings of *qing*.[8] For *qing*, even within the *Xunzi* itself, has a wide range of meanings that are to a great extent context-specific.[9] To demand a 'unified' meaning of

---

3. Candiotto & Renaut 2020, 1.

4. On the 'invention of emotion' in the Western tradition, see Konstan 2020. As Konstan notes (ibid., 379), 'the convergence of Aristotle's classification and later lists of basic emotions was not entirely a matter of chance, insofar as his selection of the sentiments that would count as πάθη indirectly influenced subsequent taxonomies of the passions, even when they were largely assumed to be noncognitive and indeed the very opposite of rationality'.

5. Hansen 1995, 201.

6. Graham 1990, 59.

7. Ibid.

8. Puett 2004, 41.

9. I agree, therefore, with Eifring (2004, 21): 'Because the reference of the word [*qing*] is much less readily identifiable than that of a more concrete term, much of its meaning is context-bound and derives from its position within one or more semantic fields, as well as its use in specific philosophical arguments or literary contexts.' For a reference to the various meanings of *qing* in pre-Buddhist Chinese texts, see Harbsmeier 2004, who also argues against finding any one plausible English equivalent for *qing*.

44 Aristotle and Xunzi on Shame

qing is to fail to recognise the semantic stretch of this complex term and to risk the danger of reductionism.

When not used in connection with *xing* 性 ('nature'), *qing* in the *Xunzi* can take on the meaning of 'basic facts' or 'situation'. For example, in the chapter *Against Physiognomy*, Xunzi uses *qing* to refer to the circumstances of the times: 'Fools say: "The *qing* of the past and the present are quite different, and the Way by which to bring order to the chaos of today must be different." '[10]. *Qing* could also mean the 'character' of a thing, for example in the chapter *On Music*: 'Exhausting the root of things and carrying change to its highest degree is the *qing* of music'.[11] More relevant to this study, *qing* occupies an important place in Xunzi's philosophy because of its close association with nature (*xing*)[12] and desire (*yu* 欲). Reading *xing* and *qing* with reference to the idea that 'human nature is bad' has led to speculation that *qing* is something to be suppressed or rejected.[13] In truth, in the *Xunzi*, it is not a clear matter of rejecting or embracing *qing* that is endowed by heaven (*tian* 天), and Puett is right to note that the term *qing* occupies an ambivalent place in Xunzi's thought.[14]

Contra Graham's statement that *qing* 'never means "passions" ' in the *Xunzi*, in certain passages of the text, it *would* make sense to understand *qing* to refer to something like the 'emotions'. Take the following two examples:

> (The feelings) of liking and disliking, of delight and anger, and of sorrow and joy of *xing* are called *qing*.[15]

> Love and hate, delight and anger, sorrow and joy, are stored within—these are called "one's heavenly *qing*".[16]

In these instances, *qing* appears in contexts that feature what we might identify as emotion terms, that is, love and hate, delight and anger, sorrow and joy. A question remains, however: in these passages, is Xunzi referring to *qing* qua 'basic instincts' or expressions of human nature, or is he referring to *qing* specifically qua 'feelings' or 'emotions'? *Qing* as basic instincts would of course *encompass* feelings and emotions, which makes what is being referred to here unclear—*qing* as the feelings of love and hate, delight and anger, sorrow and joy,

---

10. 夫妄人曰：“古今異情，其所以治亂者異道” (14/5/33).

11. 窮本極變，樂之情也 (77/20/34).

12. *Qing* and *xing* can form the binomes *qingxing* 情性 and *xingqing* 性情. Liu 2011 translates the terms respectively as 'emotional nature' and 'emotional disposition', but the precise meanings are difficult to draw out.

13. I discuss this further in relation to *yu*, desire, in Chapter 4.

14. Puett 2004, 58.

15. 性之好、惡、喜、怒、哀、樂謂之情 (83/22/3).

16. 好惡、喜怒、哀樂臧焉，夫是之謂天情 (62/17/11).

or the wider application of *qing* as basic instincts that belong to one's nature. There is perhaps no straightforward answer to this puzzle; however, the passages do suggest that the different ranges of the meaning of *qing* can sometimes overlap.

Unlike Aristotle who firmly situates his discussion of *aischunē* within the context of *pathē*, treating individual emotions in a similar fashion, there is no attempt in Xunzi to group 'shame' alongside other emotions, nor to discuss it within a wider context of emotions. Shame-related vocabulary is not included in Xunzi's glosses for *qing*; after all, Xunzi's glosses, like Plato's lists of *pathē*, are not meant to be exhaustive. The fact that Xunzi refrains from definition could be telling in itself: once a term is defined, some of its semantic elasticity is lost. This raises a number of interesting points relating to the issue of definition in the two traditions. While Greek philosophy is constantly preoccupied with finding the '*ti esti*' as posed by Socrates, the *Xunzi*, indeed classical Chinese texts as a whole, are not preoccupied with the same sort of definitions. So then, the very difference in approach between the Greek and Chinese philosophers constitutes a point of comparison, a topic that has already been noted and commented upon by scholars. According to Christoph Harbsmeier,

> The Chinese tended to be interested in definitions not in a Socratic way and for their own sake as descriptions of the essence of things, and they were rarely interested in definition as an abstract art in the Aristotelian manner. They were interested in clarifications of the meanings of terms in their literary contexts and as instrumental in controlling the physical and social environment. The Chinese were more concerned with finding useful distinctions than to find ingenious definitions.[17]

In a similar fashion, Yumi Suzuki discusses how the Chinese are more interested in making distinctions (e.g., the idea of regulation of naming, *zhiming* 制名 in *Xunzi* and the Mohist canon) rather than definitions of the Greek kind. She points to a similarity between the Chinese and the Greeks, for 'definition' in Greek (*horizesthai*) originally carried the meaning of 'drawing a special boundary', therefore it is similar in purpose to the making of distinctions in the Chinese context.[18] Roel Sterckx, using the example of animal taxonomies, discusses the absence of definitions in Chinese texts as providing a source of insight.[19] At the same time as delineating differences, one needs to be aware just whose definitions are being compared, for how Plato approaches

17. Harbsmeier 1998, 54.
18. Suzuki 2018, 31.
19. Sterckx 2002, 20–21.

46   *Aristotle and Xunzi on Shame*

the *pathē* certainly differs from how Aristotle does so, with the former's lists of *pathē* bearing a closer resemblance to Xunzi's lists of *qing*. The absence of an Aristotelian type of definition for *qing* and indeed for other terms relating to the emotions in the *Xunzi* should not pose any obstacles for the contemporary reader's understanding of how emotions fit in with Xunzi's ethical concerns. To be sure, even *with* definitions given, it may still be a challenge to distinguish clearly between terms, one obvious reason being that an author may define a term in one way but choose to use it in another. One therefore forms an understanding of terms and concepts with reference to the content and the context within which they are used rather than relying solely on definitions. While this study makes occasional references to other texts from classical Greece and early China, it does not attempt to compare 'shame' terms in the Chinese and Greek traditions overall; the focus lies in usages within Aristotle and Xunzi.

AIDŌS AND AISCHUNĒ IN ARISTOTLE

In my treatment of shame-related terms in Aristotle, I shall focus primarily on *aidōs* and *aischunē* and their cognates, though I recognise that other terms such as *sōphrosunē*,[20] *hubris* and *adoxia* can become relevant. Aristotle's fullest discussion of *aischunē* can be found in II.6 of the *Rhetoric*, amongst a list of other *pathē* such as anger, envy, pity, and fear. *Aidōs* is mentioned in *EN* II.7, III.8, and IV.9; in the *EE*, a brief note is made in passing in Book III.

Scholars have long debated the relation between *aidōs* and *aischunē* and offered various conjectures regarding their range of meaning. E. M. Cope and J. E. Sandys deny any distinctions made between *aidōs* and *aischunē* in *Rhetoric* II.6 and then go on to cite certain distinctions which 'may and may not be made between them': *aidōs* being 'a subjective feeling or principle of honour, Germ. *Scheu*', and *aischunē* 'as the fear of disgrace (from others, external) consequent on something already done, Germ. *Schaam* and *Schande*'.[21] According to David Konstan, Aristotle respects the distinct ranges of meaning between *aidōs* and *aischunē*, 'normally limiting *aidōs* to the prospective or inhibitory sense'.[22] By

---

20. Denyer (2008, 108) notes the close association—or sometimes even equation—of *aidōs* and *sōphrosunē* in several classical authors, for example in Plato's *Charmides* 160e, where Charmides equates *aidōs* with *sōphrosunē* because the latter is said to make people ashamed and bashful: Δοκεῖ τοίνυν μοι, ἔφη, αἰσχύνεσθαι ποιεῖν ἡ σωφροσύνη καὶ αἰσχυντηλὸν τὸν ἄνθρωπον, καὶ εἶναι ὅπερ αἰδὼς ἡ σωφροσύνη. In Aristotle's *EE* 1234a27–33, it is said that *aidōs* leads to *sōphrosunē*. Such a close association between *aidōs* and *sōphrosunē* in the works of Plato and Aristotle further encourages a positive reading of *aidōs*, for there is no doubt that *sōphrosunē* is always to be praised.

21. Cope & Sandys [1877] (2010, II, 71–72).

22. Konstan 2006, 95.

Mapping the Vocabulary of 'Shame' 47

contrast, William M. A. Grimaldi and R. A. Gauthier and J. Y. Jolif hold that *aidōs* and *aischunē* are interchangeable.[23] C. C. W. Taylor concurs that the two terms are interchangeable, though he goes on to agree with the Anonymous *EN* commentator on the distinction between *aidōs* as forward-looking and *aischunē* as backward looking and suggests that Aristotle fails to make such a distinction clear in his account.[24] Some commentators have separated Aristotelian shame into two kinds, with *aidōs* being 'prospective' shame that plays a guiding role in moral development, and *aischunē* being 'retrospective' shame that has a negative sense attached to it. In Jimenez's view, 'both terms denote the same emotion, although they do have different connotations',[25] which follows Cairn's position that the two terms 'refer to distinguishable aspects of a single emotional concept'.[26]

In what follows, I deal with the questions of whether *aidōs* and *aischunē* are interchangeable in Aristotle and whether it is appropriate to use 'prospective' and 'retrospective' shame to characterise *aidōs* and *aischunē* respectively. In short, I believe that the two terms should be viewed as two aspects of the same emotion in Aristotle, their difference being that *aischunē* is the generic term for 'shame', while *aidōs* generally denotes the inhibitory species of *aischunē*.

Let us begin with the definition of *aischunē* as found in the *Rhetoric*: 'Let shame (*aischunē*) then be defined as a kind of pain or disturbance in respect of bad things (*tōn kakōn*), present, past or future, which seem to tend to lead to disrepute (*adoxian*).'[27] Here, the temporal references to shame conflict with the Anonymous *EN* commentator's distinctions between *aidōs* as fear of disgrace at the thought of disgraceful deeds, and *aischunē* concerning bad things that have been done.[28] Nemesius, the Christian bishop of Emesa from the fourth century CE also makes such a distinction by defining *aidōs* as prospective and *aischunē* as retrospective.[29] The definition of *aidōs* as a fear of disrepute (*phobos tis adoxias*, *EN* 1128b11–12) is compatible with the definition of *aischunē* as a kind of pain or disturbance in respect of bad things, since the feeling of fear is

---

23. Grimaldi (1988, II, 105) claims that 'there is generally no discernible difference' between Aristotle's use of *aidōs—aischunē* in the ethical works and of *aischunē* in the *Rhetoric*. He concurs with R. A. Gauthier and J. Y. Jolif by saying that 'what we find reflected in A.'s [Aristotle's] usages is very likely the historical development of *aidōs* toward a gradual fusion with *aischunē*' (ibid., II, 106).

24. Taylor 2006, 235–36.

25. Jimenez 2020, 146. See Jimenez's review of this debate (ibid., 139–146).

26. Cairns 1993, 415.

27. ἔστω δὴ αἰσχύνη λύπη τις ἢ ταραχὴ περὶ τὰ εἰς ἀδοξίαν φαινόμενα φέρειν τῶν κακῶν, ἢ παρόντων ἢ γεγονότων ἢ μελλόντων (*Rhet.* 1383b12–14).

28. Anonymous 1892, 204, lines 7–11.

29. Nemesius, *De Nat. Hom.* 21, 231ff. Cf. Konstan's discussions of Nemesius (2006, 97ff).

48 Aristotle and Xunzi on Shame

characterised as being accompanied by pain elsewhere in the *Rhetoric*.[30] It is also worth noting that the idea of disrepute (*adoxia*) features in the definitions of both *aidōs* and *aischunē*. Despite such similarities, it is clear that already in the definition, *aidōs* is associated with the future, since fear is generally speaking forward-looking,[31] while *aischunē* encompasses past, present *and* future events, and is not limited to retrospective shame for Aristotle.

After establishing the topic to be *aidōs* in *EN* 1128b10, Aristotle goes on to speak about its effects: people who are ashamed blush, while those in fear of their lives turn pale.[32] One notes that the participle of *aischunomai* is used here rather than that of *aideomai*. The physiological effect of shame is placed in parallel to the fear of death; this follows from Aristotle's definition of *aidōs* as a fear of disrepute in the preceding line. Because the content of fear involves disadvantageous consequences for the future, it is possible that Aristotle is referring only to shame as a feeling that inhibits the commission of disgraceful actions. This is supported by a passage in the *Rhetoric* where it is said that people are ashamed not only of the disgraceful things mentioned, but also of the signs; for example, not only of the act of love but also of the signs of it.[33] On the other hand, it is much more common to associate blushing with bad things already done than with the hypothetical thought of doing them in the future. Aristotle has thus probably chosen the genus (*aischunomai*) rather than the future-looking species (*aideomai*) in order to embrace the three kinds of temporal possibilities—the *aischunomenos* person blushes either on account of a shameful deed that has been done, on account of something that is being done, or indeed because he is contemplating a deed in the future which is shame-inducing. The appearances of *aischunomai* in the *Rhetoric* and the *EN* passages just mentioned serve as evidence that *aischunē* and its cognates are not limited to retrospective use, but can indeed refer to past, present and future events.

Aristotle considers *aidōs* to be suitable and proper to the young but not to the *epieikēs*, the decent person, since *aidōs* is needed to keep the young in check due to their living by feeling (*pathē*) and often getting many things wrong.[34] Here, *aidōs* has the inhibitive function of preventing a young person from making

---

30. Cf. *Rhetoric* II.5, in which Aristotle defines fear as 'a pain or disturbance due to imagining some destructive or painful evil in the future'. ἔστω δὴ ὁ φόβος λύπη τις ἢ ταραχὴ ἐκ φαντασίας μέλλοντος κακοῦ φθαρτικοῦ ἢ λυπηροῦ (*Rhet.* 1382a21–22).

31. For sure, it is possible to experience fear for past events also, but only in terms of the future evils that they may bring, hence fear is always forward-looking.

32. ἐρυθραίνονται γὰρ οἱ αἰσχυνόμενοι, οἱ δὲ τὸν θάνατον φοβούμενοι ὠχριῶσιν (*EN* 1128b13–14).

33. αἰσχύνονται δὲ οὐ μόνον αὐτὰ τὰ ῥηθέντα αἰσχυντηλὰ ἀλλὰ καὶ τὰ σημεῖα, οἷον οὐ μόνον ἀφροδισιάζοντες ἀλλὰ καὶ τὰ σημεῖα αὐτοῦ (*Rhet.* 1384b17–19).

34. οὐ πάσῃ δ' ἡλικίᾳ τὸ πάθος ἁρμόζει, ἀλλὰ τῇ νέᾳ. οἰόμεθα γὰρ δεῖν τοὺς τηλικούτους αἰδήμονας εἶναι διὰ τὸ πάθει ζῶντας πολλὰ ἁμαρτάνειν, ὑπὸ τῆς αἰδοῦς δὲ κωλύεσθαι (*EN* 1128b15–18).

Mapping the Vocabulary of 'Shame' 49

mistakes, and hence appears to refer to events in the future. For example, a young man who has not been accustomed to performing good deeds and feeling pleasure and pain for the right kinds of things may be inclined to flee in battle. Upon recognising that fleeing constitutes cowardly behaviour that tends to lead to dispute, the young man experiences *aidōs* and chooses to stay firm in his position instead. In such a case, *aidōs* has an inhibitive effect and leads one to act in a way that will not cause disrepute. *Aidōs* here cannot be understood to mean a sense of shame at unseemly deeds, words or thoughts in the past because its inhibitory force cannot be applicable to actions that have already taken place. However, one might say that in shifting the course of an action, *aidōs* can be extended to present events. For example, the young man may already be on his way to retreat from battle when feelings of *aidōs* guide him to return to his proper position.[35]

In speaking of the role of shame for the young, Aristotle has so far limited himself to the term *aidōs* and used it specifically to indicate its positive value in preventing the young from making the many mistakes to which they are prone. In discussing the role of shame for the older man, however, both *aidōs* and *aischunē* are employed, which complicates the picture. *EN* 1128b19-20 features *aidēmonas* and *aischuntelōs* as parallels in one sentence: the first part involves praise for the young who are *aidēmonas*, while the latter suggests that no one would praise an older person for being prone to feeling shame (*aischuntēlos*).[36] Given the presence of *aidēmonas* in the first half of the sentence and the discussion in an earlier passage on the function of *aidōs* in preventing one from committing mistakes, we may be inclined to understand that *aischuntelos* has a similar inhibitive sense here. However, Aristotle then goes on to employ *aischunē* mostly in a retrospective sense in the rest of this passage: 'For we think he should not do anything that incurs shame (*aischunē*) in the first place. For shame is not something that belongs to the decent person at all, given that it is occasioned by bad actions.'[37] The phrases *eph' hois* and *ginetai epi tois phaulois* convey the idea that *aischunē* is consequent upon actions, and is thus retrospective. The following line glosses that idea and links *aischunē* with bad actions: 'One should not do them [. . .] and so one should not feel shame.'[38] This line implies that the experience of *aischunē* is a direct result of doing bad deeds, so that there is a strong emphasis on the link between *aischunē* and actions

---

35. See Fussi 2015, 117.

36. καὶ ἐπαινοῦμεν τῶν μὲν νέων τοὺς αἰδήμονας, πρεσβύτερον δ᾽ οὐδεὶς ἂν ἐπαινέσειεν ὅτι αἰσχυντηλός (*EN* 1128b18–20).

37. οὐδὲν γὰρ οἰόμεθα δεῖν αὐτὸν πράττειν ἐφ᾽ οἷς ἐστιν αἰσχύνη. οὐδὲ γὰρ ἐπιεικοῦς ἐστιν ἡ αἰσχύνη, εἴπερ γίνεται ἐπὶ τοῖς φαύλοις (*EN* 1128b20–22).

38. οὐ γὰρ πρακτέον τὰ τοιαῦτα [. . .] ὥστ᾽ οὐκ αἰσχυντέον (*EN* 1128b 22–25).

50 *Aristotle and Xunzi on Shame*

(words with the *prat-* stem). Indeed, further associations can be found in the rest of the IV.9 passage, where it is said that 'even being the kind of person to do anything shameful (*aischrōn*) is a sign of worthlessness'.[39] Such repeated associations emphasise the point that *aischunē* is very much concerned with actions that have already been done rather than 'intentions' or 'thoughts' about events in the future.

Towards the end of Book IV, Aristotle defines *aidōs* as a *pathos* rather than a *hexis*, disposition, and goes on to speak of *aidōs* as something that is hypothetically good for the decent person. The appearance of *aidōs* and *aischunē* in the same passage leads Grimaldi and Konstan to make very different claims regarding the meaning and interchangeability of those two terms. Grimaldi sees this as evidence for the lack of distinction between the two terms, pointing out that 'we find Aristotle speaking formally of *aidōs* in *EN* 1128b10–35 but interchanging *aischunē* with it and without qualification'.[40] Konstan, refuting Grimaldi, cites *EN* 1128b32–3 as an example that marks the distinction between *aidōs*, 'understood to inhibit bad behaviour', and *aischunē*, that 'reflects back on it with regret'.[41] More recently, Jimenez has argued that the frequent terminological back and forth in these lines 'speaks strongly against the two-kinds-of-shame interpretation' and indicates that 'Aristotle does not draw a sharp line between the two terms'.[42] I agree with Jimenez's claim that Aristotle treats *aidōs* and *aischunē* as one emotion, though I do not consider this passage to provide sufficient evidence for the interchangeability of the two terms, as I shall explain below.

Aristotle denies that it would be proper for someone to consider himself good on the basis of feeling shame (*aischunesthai*) when he does a shameful act, for shame (*aidōs*) comes from the voluntary, and a decent person would never voluntarily do base actions.[43] Having associated many words with the *aisch-* stem with bad actions, Aristotle finally comes back to *aidōs*, which is the term that he originally said he would discuss (*EN* 1128b10). He concludes by saying: '*aidōs* will indeed be hypothetically something decent—*if* one did such-and-such, one would be ashamed; but this is not a feature of the excellences. If shamelessness is something bad, and so is not being ashamed at doing shameful things, that

---

39. φαύλου δὲ καὶ τὸ εἶναι τοιοῦτον οἷον πράττειν τι τῶν αἰσχρῶν (*EN* 1128b25–26).

40. Grimaldi 1988, II, 106.

41. Konstan 2006, 95.

42. Jimenez 2020, 146.

43. τὸ δ᾽ οὕτως ἔχειν ὥστ᾽ εἰ πράξαι τι τῶν τοιούτων αἰσχύνεσθαι, καὶ διὰ τοῦτ᾽ οἴεσθαι ἐπιεικῆ εἶναι, ἄτοπον· ἐπὶ τοῖς ἑκουσίοις γὰρ ἡ αἰδώς, ἑκὼν δ᾽ ὁ ἐπιεικὴς οὐδέποτε πράξει τὰ φαῦλα (*EN* 1128b26–29).

Mapping the Vocabulary of 'Shame' 51

does not make it decent to do such things and be ashamed.'[44] Once again, a cognate of *aischunē* is associated with actions so that if one does something (bad), one would feel ashamed (*aischunoit'*, *EN* 1128b30), hence the word here has a retrospective sense. Further down the passage, however, *aideisthai*, which is a cognate of *aidōs*, is also associated with bad actions, when Aristotle says that it is base not to be ashamed of doing bad actions (*phaulon kai to mē aideisthai ta aischra prattein*, *EN* 1128b31–32). Contrary to Konstan's belief that *aidōs* plays an inhibitory role here,[45] I believe that this phrase leaves the question open as to whether Aristotle has the prospective, the retrospective or both significations in mind. Indeed, Aristotle may be referring to both: on the one hand, *aidōs* could be felt towards bad *intentions* (as suggested by its popular usage), which would not befit the decent person; on the one hand, the decent person should never find himself in a situation where he would experience shame on account of bad actions done. The last part of IV.9, then, complicates the relationship between *aidōs* and *aischunē*, making it unclear whether *aidōs* is referring to past or future events. However, in almost all the cases that have been examined so far, *aidōs* does appear to have a primarily inhibitory function.

The *Rhetoric* presents another example where *aischunē* and *aidōs* are employed in the same passage, which raises further questions about their interchangeability. Grimaldi points to an instance where Aristotle uses *aischunontai* for the feeling of shame that accompanies words, actions and intentions that are contrary to good deeds, and then goes on to cite two passages in verse that contain *aidōs*, where a sense of shame appears to inhibit disgraceful action.[46] In the case of Alcaeus, shame restrains him from saying something, while Sappho talks of shame filling up one's eyes when one is about to speak baseness. Clearly, the verse examples cited concern shame associated with bad *intentions* and present *aidōs* as a force that inhibits the agent from committing unseemly acts. Even though *aischunē* by its definition can refer to pain that is associated with future misdeeds, such as the ones that Alcaeus in the verses cited is contemplating,

---

44. εἴη δ᾽ ἂν ἡ αἰδὼς ἐξ ὑποθέσεως ἐπιεικές· εἰ γὰρ πράξαι, αἰσχύνοιτ᾽ ἄν· οὐκ ἔστι δὲ τοῦτο περὶ τὰς ἀρετάς. εἰ δ᾽ ἡ ἀναισχυντία φαῦλον καὶ τὸ μὴ αἰδεῖσθαι τὰ αἰσχρὰ πράττειν, οὐδὲν μᾶλλον τὸν τὰ τοιαῦτα πράττοντα αἰσχύνεσθαι ἐπιεικές (*EN* 1128b29–33).

45. Rackham's (1934, 251) translation of 'shrinking' from shameful actions' suggests that he also takes *aidōs* to have an inhibitory function here.

46. θέλω τι εἰπῆν, ἀλλά με κωλύει
αἰδώς, [Alcaeus fr. 55]
αἰ δ᾽ ἦχες ἐσθλῶν ἵμερον ἢ καλῶν
καὶ μή τι εἰπῆν γλῶσσ᾽ ἐκύκα κακόν
αἰδώς κέν σε οὐκ εἶχεν ὄμματ᾽,
ἀλλ᾽ ἔλεγες περὶ τῶ δικαίω [Sappho fr. 28]
(*Rhet.* 1367a10–15).

52 Aristotle and Xunzi on Shame

Aristotle chooses to use *aidōs*, which can be interpreted as one species of *aischunontai* that is primarily associated with bad intentions. Grimaldi cites this passage as evidence that for Aristotle, there is no discernible difference between these two terms. However, the fact that Aristotle chooses to use *aidōs* in giving examples of *aischunē* shows that he does have a tendency to employ *aidōs* in specific instances of shame that have an inhibitive function and are directed at future events. In this case, instances of *aidōs* towards bad intentions can be seen to represent a species of *aischunē*, *aischunē* being here the broader category of feelings that accompanies bad words, actions and intentions.

Even though Aristotle in his definition and use distinguishes between *aidōs* and *aischunē*, he usually does not explicitly point out whether the feeling of *aidōs* or *aischunē* in question refers to past, present or future events. He himself does not distinguish between those terms, hence drawing out differences between 'prospective' and 'retrospective' shame introduces a potentially artificial distinction.[47] One may experience shame for things that have not yet been performed but are being contemplated, for example, in the case of Alcaeus cited above, since contemplating bad actions also constitutes a source of shame; at the same time, feeling shame for things that have happened in the past may have the effect of inhibiting the performance of similar actions in the present and in the future. In both situations, the shame experienced is neither solely 'prospective' nor solely 'retrospective'. This seems to be a point that has not received due attention from commentators on Aristotle's concept of shame, where 'prospective' and 'retrospective' shame have often been regarded as mutually exclusive. Instead of characterising shame episodes in such ways, which can be misleading, it may be useful to use the term 'inhibitive' to refer to any shame that might have an inhibitive force on one's actions, whether it is directed at present, past, or future events.

With regard to the passages examined above, it is apparent that Aristotle does not limit *aischunē* to a retrospective sense, while he employs *aidōs* almost exclusively to suggest the inhibitive power of shame that stops one from acting badly, which is usually forward-looking. However, despite its definition, it is rare for us to find *aischunē* clearly associated with present or future events, and in some passages (e.g., *EN* 1128b28ff.), it is ambiguous whether *aidōs* refers to past or future deeds. One might say that Aristotle is, on the whole, often more prepared to praise shame (regardless of whether it is prospective or retrospective, as Aristotle himself does not distinguish explicitly between the two) using the

---

47. Konstan (2006, 98) is right to note that Aristotle in his definitions does not explicitly spell out the differences between prospective or restrictive shame on the one hand and retrospective or remorseful shame on the other.

term *aidōs* and its cognates because of their inhibitive force, emphasising the positive aspects of the emotion and its role in moral development (e.g., *EN* 1108a31–35, 1116a27–28, 1128b18–20, 1179b11–16).[48] Cairns' claim that *aidōs* is 'an inhibitory emotion based on sensitivity to and protectiveness of one's self-image'[49] appears to be generally correct. *Aischunē* and its cognates, on the other hand, are often—though not exclusively—used to denote the sense of shame that follows upon inappropriate action. This use probably comes from the etymology of the word, as *to aischron* implies the ugly and the disgraceful.[50]

RU, XIU, AND CHI IN THE XUNZI

The semantic field of 'shame' in classical Chinese involves a conglomeration of terms, including *xiu* 羞, *chi* 恥, *ru* 辱, *can* 慚, *kui* 愧, *zuo* 怍, and *jiu* 疚, several of which are liable to form compounds. Then there are terms such as *bei* 卑 and *jian* 賤 that translate to 'lowliness', which can be used to describe one's social status; however, in various parts of the text, Xunzi argues against the idea that being in a lowly position due to external factors necessarily constitutes a source of shame.[51] The term *jiu* 疚 is commonly translated as 'guilt', the phrase *neixing bu jiu* 內省不疚—'one does not have a guilty conscience upon self-reflection'— found in several texts in the early period to represent the internal state of the gentleman.[52] While the term *jiu* itself is not found in the *Xunzi*, the important

---

48. On this point I am in agreement with Jimenez (2020, 144).

49. Cairns 1993, 2.

50. In the previous chapter I cited examples from Antiphon to illustrate his uses of *aidōs* and *aischunē*. One passage in Antiphon's speeches deserves closer attention as it uses *aischunē* to suggest the sense of respect or reverence that is normally represented by *aidōs*: 'Involuntary accidents deserve such pity: not deliberately planned crimes and acts of wickedness. Just as this woman put her husband to death without respecting (*aischuntheisa*) or fearing god, hero, or human being, so she would in her turn reap her justest reward were she herself put to death by you and by justice, without finding consideration (*aidous*), sympathy (*eleou*), or respect (*aischunēs*)' (*Antiph.* 1.27, trans. Maidment). In addition, Antiphon pledges the judges not to display *aidōs*, *eleos*, or *aischunē*, which again suggests that *aidōs* and *aischunē* both carry the sense of respect and challenges the idea that *aischunē* refers only retrospectively to bad things done. The fact that Antiphon should feel the need to employ *aidōs* and *aischunē* in the same phrase provokes the question of the distinctions in connotation between these two words: they are similar enough to be included together yet may well have slightly different nuances (unless, of course, Antiphon is employing them merely for the sake of rhetorical flare).

51. On the related concepts of 'lowliness' and 'humility' in ancient Greece and China from a comparative perspective, see Zhao (forthcoming).

52. As Crone 2020 points out, in the early Zhou period, in works such as the *Book of Odes*, *jiu* (in the form of 咎 or 疚) appears to denote 'an extreme internal distress when referring to a feeling', thus signifying a physiological reaction. In later texts, at least by the time of the Han commentator Bao Xian, *jiu* came to be related to 'internal suffering related to past moral wrongdoings'. On a detailed examination of *jiu* in relation to moral guilt, see Crone (ibid., 153–61). Note the idea that in the ancient Greek context, *pathos* was sometimes interchangeable with the idea of disease.

54 *Aristotle and Xunzi on Shame*

concept of *neixing*, commonly translated 'introspection' or 'self-reflection', is; it can be assimilated to the idea of conscience, thus reflecting internal activity that is frequently associated with 'guilt' (discussed further in Chapter 4). The idea of 'face' (*mianzi* 面子, *mianmu* 面目, *lian* 臉, or *lianmian* 臉面), more commonly construed in the negative 'loss of face', has been identified as particularly prominent in Chinese culture in the context of social relations,[53] and indeed one of the reasons for which China has been labelled a 'shame culture'. While expressions of 'losing face' did exist in the pre-Qin and Han periods, usually in contexts where the agent feels unable to report to someone due to his own failure, they are by no means frequent occurrences.[54] In the present study, I focus on the terms *xiu*, *chi*, and *ru* since these are the main terms found in Xunzi's shame-related discourse.

The character *ru* 辱 is etymologically associated with farming. According to the Han dynasty dictionary of graphic etymology *Shuowen jiezi* 說文解字, failing to farm at the right opportunity leads to public disgrace.[55] *Ru* 辱 can function as a verb, a noun or an adjective. As a verb, it means to 'insult' or 'bring disgrace upon' someone; as a noun, it translates to 'disgrace'; as adjective, it carries the meaning of dirty or murky. In the *Xunzi*, It is frequently used as an antonym of *rong* 榮—honour (most prominently in the chapter *Of Honour and Disgrace*), and is associated with other deplorable states of human life. Disgrace can sometimes come about from no fault of the agent's own; nonetheless, there is no denying that public insult necessarily leads to disgrace of some kind. In two places in the text, Xunzi takes issue with Songzi's (Song Xing's 宋鈃) claim 'to be insulted is not to suffer disgrace' (*jian wu bu ru* 見侮不辱), believing that people like Song Xing are confusing names (*luanming* 亂名) when they make such a statement. In those contexts, Xunzi is not interested in insult and disgrace per se. Rather, he uses a number of examples to attach importance to the correct use of names and to criticise those who misuse them. Nonetheless,

---

53. Hu 1944; Hwang 1987.

54. *Mencius* (5.5/30/22–25) gives an account of people who perspire upon discovering their parents' corpses being devoured by wild animals as a result of their negligence. Their behaviour is said not to originate from external considerations (*wei ren* 為人, literally, 'for the sake of other people') but a natural response emanating from their heart to the faces (*mianmu* 面目, literally 'face and eyes'). In this case, the face manifests inner feelings rather than stands as a symbol for mere reputation. Warring States texts contain instances of people who commit suicide on account of shame or humiliation, though explicit references to the idea of lacking or losing face (*wu mian* 無面/*wu mianmu* 無面目) occur later, generally from the Han dynasty on, as found for example in the *Shiji* and the *Hanshu*. Stearns (2017, 23) speaks of the 'intense desire to preserve public face' in Confucianism, and Flanagan (2021, 152) describes the Chinese idea of 'saving face' as a 'virtue'. Those claims need qualification, given the minimal number of 'face-related' expressions in Warring States literature.

55. 辱，失耕時，於封畺上戮之也。(*Shuowen jiezi*, 745) *Lu* 戮, cognate with *lu* 僇, has the meaning of kill or disgrace, conveying the sense that corporal punishment leads to public disgrace.

Mapping the Vocabulary of 'Shame' 55

Xunzi's exposition of the distinctions between *different* types of *rong* and *ru* takes account of the fact that honour and disgrace can arise out of different kinds of contingencies that do not necessarily reflect the agent's moral disposition. This marks one significant way in which Xunzi's account surpasses that of his predecessors in its sophistication: Xunzi coins the terms *yirong* 義榮 (honour that derives from inner disposition), *shirong* 埶榮 (honour that derives from force of circumstances), *yiru* 義辱 (disgrace that derives from bad actions) and *shiru* 埶辱 (disgrace that derives from force of circumstances) to clarify the different associations that honour and disgrace can have depending on what causes them:

> There is honour that derives from inner disposition, and honour that derives from force of circumstances; there is disgrace that derives from inner disposition and disgrace that derives from force of circumstances. When a person is cultivated in will and purpose, accomplished in virtuous action, lucid in wisdom and thought, then there arises from within the cause of honour, and this is what is meant by honour that derives from inner disposition. Holding exalted rank and distinction, receiving substantial tribute or emolument, holding a position of overwhelming power and influence, being at the highest a son of heaven or a feudal lord or at the lowest a minister or prime minister, *shi* or grand officer—these are honours that arrive from without, and precisely these are what is meant by honours that derive from a person's circumstances. When a person is wayward and abandoned, base and reckless, when he offends against the divisions (*fen*) of society and brings principles to disorder, when he is arrogantly violent and cruel with a rapacious appetite for profit (*li* 利)[56]—these are the forms of disgrace that come from within, and these are precisely what is meant by the forms of disgrace that derive from a person's inner disposition. Vilified and insulted, dragged about by the hair and beaten, whipped and cudgelled, kneecaps shattered or legs amputated, decapitated, drawn and

---

56. *Li* 利 in the *Xunzi* may be translated as 'benefit' or 'profit', corresponding to that which brings advantage to the individual. It can take on either a positive or a negative sense. For example, when *li* is spoken of as the counterpart of 'harm' (*hai* 害), it is positive; yet as the counterpart of propriety (*yi*), in the sense of self-interest, it is almost always negative. I sometimes adopt 'profit', sometimes 'benefit' or 'self-interest' for *li* in order to render a translation that is most suited to the context (for example, animals are also said to *haoli* 好利, in which context 'love benefit' would be more suitable than 'love profit'). For Xunzi, *li*, even in the sense of self-interest, is not to be denounced in its entirety. It is something that all people desire by nature, and therefore necessarily occupies a place in people's everyday dealings. Nonetheless, it should only come after *yi*, a sense of propriety. For more discussions on the ambiguity of the term *li*, see Defoort 2008, especially 158, 160, 165n37, 177–178, 180 on occurrences of *li* in the *Xunzi*. See also Schumacher 1993 on the idea of *li* in the *Mencius*.

56 Aristotle and Xunzi on Shame

quartered, chained and destroyed, with the tongue unable to speak[57]—these are the forms of disgrace that come from without, and these are precisely what is meant by the forms of disgrace that derive from a person's circumstances. Such are the two principles of honour and disgrace.[58]

The distinctions between the types of honour and disgrace will be treated in greater detail in Chapter 4; for now, it is sufficient to note the existence of these sub-categories of *rong* and *ru*, which befit the gentleman and the petty man accordingly. Such categorisation is distinctive of Xunzi's usage, so that the prefixes attached to *rong* and *ru* help to identify the sources of one's honour and disgrace depending on context.

The terms *xiu* and *chi*, often used to form the compound *xiuchi* 羞恥 in modern Chinese to mean shame or a sense of shame, are sometimes synonymous, both carrying the sense 'to consider something shameful'. Unlike *xiu*, which is largely restricted to verbal usage in the context of shame, *chi* can also be taken as a noun to mean 'disgrace'; however, it is generally used in its verbal sense. Kwong-loi Shun regards *chi* as 'more like the attitude of regarding something as contemptible or as below oneself than like the emotion of shame'. He establishes that while '*chi* is focused more on the thing that taints oneself [i.e. someone], *xiu* is focused more on the way the self is tainted by that thing'.[59]

If one morning one should have to bury one's revered parent, and if in attending to the ceremonies of the funeral one shows neither grief nor respect, then one has conducted oneself in the manner of the birds and beasts. The gentleman (*junzi* 君子) would consider it shameful (*chi zhi*).[60]

Thus the gentleman is ashamed of (*chi*) the lack of cultivation but not ashamed of being insulted; ashamed of untrustworthiness but not ashamed of not being trusted; ashamed of lack of competence, but not ashamed of not being employed.[61]

---

57. The characters *ji mi she ju* 藉靡舌𦟱 present textual difficulties. Wang Xianqian's commentary refers to the *Zhuangzi* chapter *Autumn Floods*, where the phrase *she ju er bu xia* 舌舉而不下 is used to describe Gongsun Long 公孫龍 who is speechless. For an alternative reading, see Hutton (2014, 199, 370–71), who takes *she* 舌 as *hou* 后/後, going against traditional readings by rendering the phrase 'when one's family records are destroyed or one's descendants are eradicated'.

58. 有義榮者，有埶榮者；有義辱者，有埶辱者。志意修，德行厚，知慮明，是榮之由中出者也，夫是之謂義榮。爵列尊，貢祿厚，形埶勝，上為天子諸侯，下為卿相士大夫，是榮之從外至者也，夫是之謂埶榮。流淫、汙僈、犯分、亂理、驕暴、貪利，是辱之由中出者也，夫是之謂義辱。詈侮捽搏，捶笞、臏腳，斬、斷、枯、磔、藉、靡、舌𦟱，是辱之由外至者也，夫是之謂埶辱。是榮辱之兩端也 (69/18/104–108).

59. Shun 2001, 236.

60. 一朝而喪其嚴親，而所以送葬之者不哀不敬，則嫌於禽獸矣，君子恥之 (73/19/61–62).

61. 故君子恥不修，不恥見汙；恥不信，不恥不見信；恥不能，不恥不見用 (17/6/40–41).

Mapping the Vocabulary of 'Shame' 57

Nonetheless, the average lord would be ashamed (*xiu*) to have them as ministers, the average father to have them as sons, the average brother to have them as brothers, and the average man to have them as friends.[62]

If in serving the people, a minister does not care whether his actions are proper but is concerned only with personal benefit (*li*) whatever the cost, then his conduct is a case of 'using assault machines to go into a cave after profit'. Such behaviour is what the humane person would be ashamed of (*xiu*) and he will not act in this fashion.[63]

Both *xiu* and *chi* are at times used to contrast with scenarios involving *le* 樂— happiness, willingness or pleasure in undertaking an activity. For example, it is said that if the gentleman is capable of something, others consider it an honour to learn from him and if he lacks the ability to do something, others will be pleased (*le*) to inform him about things. The petty person (*xiaoren* 小人) receives a different treatment, however—if he is capable of doing something, others will consider it contemptible to learn from him and if he is not capable, they will be ashamed (*xiu*) to inform him about things.[64] In another passage, we find:

When all people from the *shi* above feel ashamed of (*xiu*) being eager for profit, they will not compete with the people for [material and non-material] goods[65]. Rather, they will find enjoyment (*le*) in sharing and making distributions, considering it disgraceful (*chi*) to engage in accumulating hoards.[66]

It is implied that (inappropriately) accumulating stores or competing for goods with others are unwelcome activities and are disapproved of, and that one would find enjoyment in doing things that are of an entirely different nature. *Le* is not an antonym for *xiu* and *chi*; it is merely that shame-inducing activities are contrasted with those that do not involve inhibitions but willingness on the part of the agent.

Chi in the *Xunzi* can form a compound with the character *lian* 廉 to make *lianchi* (廉恥), which can be broadly translated as 'a sense of integrity and

---

62. 然而中君羞以為臣，中父羞以為子，中兄羞以為弟，中人羞以為友 (13/5/17).

63. 為人臣者，不恤己行之不行，苟得利而已矣，是渠衝入穴而求利也，是仁人之所羞而不為也 (60/16/45–46).

64. 故曰：君子能則人榮學焉，不能則人樂告之；小人能則人賤學焉，不能則人羞告之 (6/3/9–10).

65. Knoblock's translation of *ye* 業 as 'goods' gives the impression that *ye* concerns material goods only, while Hutton's rendering of 'business' focuses on one aspect of *ye*. The scope of *ye* is much wider, extending to ideas of property, business and even one's studies.

66. 從士以上皆羞利而不與民爭業，樂分施而恥積藏 (98/27/69).

shame'.[67] While *lian* is common in Chinese texts of the early period to mean integrity and moral uprightness, occurrences of *lianchi* as a binome are uncommon before the Han dynasty; indeed they are more commonly found in the *Xunzi* than in other texts from a similar period.[68] In the *Xunzi*, *lianchi* is almost always used in the negative, that is, with *wu* 無 as a prefix to form *wu lianchi* 無廉恥, meaning 'a lack of integrity or shame'.[69] Examples include:

> Evasive, timorous and shirking from duties, lacking in integrity and a sense of shame and having an inordinate fondness for food and drink, that person is properly called a 'despicable youth'.[70]

> Fighting over food and drink, with no scruples nor sense of integrity and shame, not knowing right from wrong, not trying to avoid death nor injury, not fearful of the greater forces, greedily only seeking after profit and food and drink, that is the courage of the dog and the boar.[71]

> In those trying and bitter functions of official life, they become dispirited and passive, evasive, timorous, and irresolute, lacking integrity and a sense of shame and enduring insults. Such is the image of your scholars.[72]

The last passage cited shows that having a sense of shame is connected with the idea of responding to criticisms and insults, and thus marks an awareness of social values. If one lacks a sense of shame, insults from others will not have an impact on one's moral behaviour. Xunzi's repeated criticisms of a lack of shame (*wu lianchi*) form a strong contrast with Aristotle's comparative neglect of the idea of a lack of shame (*anaischuntia*). In the *Rhetoric*, Aristotle appears to deem it unnecessary to go into any lengths about shamelessness—indeed he moves

67. Lewis (2021, 12) identifies *lian* as a term pertaining to honour. Goldin 2021 believes that *lian* comes close to *aidōs*, though he points out that it is necessary to contextualise these terms. I would suggest that the binome *lianchi* bears a closer resemblance to *aidōs*, since it brings out the sense that *aidōs* has close associations with what is considered shameful. See Goldin's critique of Lewis regarding *lian* and *lianchi*, 482–83.

68. In the *Guanzi*, *lian* 廉 and *chi* 恥, alongside ritual (*li* 禮) and propriety (*yi* 義), are outlined as the 'Four Cords' (*siwei* 四維) of a state, necessary for the survival of a state (*Guanzi*, *Mumin* 牧民, 11).

69. I note here one exception to this where *lianchi* appears without *wu*: 'As to the mouth and stomach of humans, how are they to know ritual and propriety? How are they to know deference? Or know a sense of shame or the part and whole of something?' 今是人之口腹，安知禮義？安知辭讓？安知廉恥隅積？ (11/4/51–52) Wang (2011, 213) makes the remark that the ethical significance of *chi* in the *Xunzi* comes across principally through criticisms of *wuchi*, shamelessness.

70. 偷儒憚事，無廉恥而嗜乎飲食，則可謂惡少者矣。(5/2/42) Cf. 17/6/49 where there is an almost verbatim repetition of the idea.

71. 爭飲食，無廉恥，不知是非，不辟死傷，不畏眾彊，恈恈然唯利飲食之見，是狗彘之勇也 (9/4/17–18).

72. 勞苦事業之中，則儢儢然，離離然，偷儒而罔，無廉恥而忍謑詬。是學者之嵬也 (17/6/47–48).

Mapping the Vocabulary of 'Shame' 59

on to the next topic with a brief remark: 'So much for shame; to understand shamelessness, we need only consider the converse cases, and plainly we shall have all we need.'[73]

MAPS OF SHAME VOCABULARY COMPARED

Through a detailed examination of the shame-related vocabulary in Aristotle and Xunzi, I have shown that in both the ancient Greek and Chinese traditions, clusters of terms are employed to convey self-conscious reflections on one's own behaviour, often in relation to the opinions of others. Conceptual clusters of shame-related terms in Aristotle and Xunzi differ considerably from corresponding terms in English.

From a survey of the Greek and Chinese semantic fields of 'shame', certain noticeable differences between Aristotle's and Xunzi's accounts become apparent.

First, unlike *aidōs*, which can take on the meaning of respect, modesty or reverence, the Chinese shame-related terms generally do not have such a positive resonance. The compound *lianchi*—a sense of integrity or shame—can be said to be an exception, since this quality is considered praiseworthy, but it certainly does not have the wide semantic range associated with *aidōs* and it almost always has the negative *wu* 無 prefix.

Second, Aristotle and Xunzi differ in terms of setting out whether 'shame' is praiseworthy. Aristotle distinguishes between the age groups for which shame would be appropriate: while *aidōs* is praised in the young, it is considered not suitable for the older person. Furthermore, not much attention is given to the idea of 'shamelessness' (*anaischuntia*) in Aristotle. This contrasts with the *Xunzi* where even an exemplary person is expected to have a sense of shame, both on account of his own and others' misconduct, and the text is punctuated with disapprovals of a lack of a sense of shame (*wu lianchi*), which is pointed out as a vice. This difference can be explained by the fact that a far weaker link is drawn in the *Xunzi* between a sense of shame and personal misconduct; *lianchi* can be regarded more generally as a sense of knowing right and wrong, which Aristotle would also consider to be important for all stages of human life. Ultimately, the differences between Aristotle and Xunzi on the praiseworthiness of shame depends upon whether or not 'shame' is portrayed as being consequent on bad actions or intentions.

Third, in the *Xunzi* honour (*rong*) and shame (*ru*) appear as a pair frequently throughout the text. Even though in the Greek sources, the shameful

---

73. περὶ μὲν οὖν αἰσχύνης ταῦτα· περὶ δὲ ἀναισχυντίας δῆλον ὡς ἐκ τῶν ἐναντίων εὐπορήσομεν (*Rhet.* 1385a14–15).

60 Aristotle and Xunzi on Shame

or ugly—*to aischron*—is sometimes construed as the opposite of *to kalon*—the fine, and *adoxia* the opposite of *timē*, the link between *aidōs* and *aischunē* and their antonyms is not as strong.[74] For example, shame-related vocabulary does not feature in Aristotle's discussions of the vices that are in excess and in deficiency of the virtue of *megalopsuchia*, which is concerned with honour.

Fourth, Xunzi is keen to demarcate clearly the things for which one should feel ashamed and those things for which the sources of disgrace are external and, to a great extent, beyond one's control. Aristotle appears less concerned with making such distinctions. Even though in the *Rhetoric* (1383b-1384a) he distinguishes between shameful situations that (1) have come about as a result of one's own actions, (2) do not seem to be one's own fault, and (3) involve being on the receiving end of acts that bring dishonour and reproach,[75] elsewhere he says that if some actions are truly shameful and others only commonly thought to be shameful, it makes no difference, since neither kind of action should be undertaken, so that no shame should be felt.[76]

Finally, while Aristotle discusses the *pathē*, including *aischunē*, in both physiological and psychological terms, Xunzi is primarily interested in the ethical implications of shame.

While different clusters of terms are found in the texts of Aristotle and Xunzi, shame-related vocabulary is employed in each case in the context of upholding standards of behaviour and maintaining interpersonal relationships. Having sketched out the semantic fields of shame-related vocabulary found in Aristotle and Xunzi and the contexts in which they appear, the following chapters will analyse the relevant passages in relation to the broader ethical and political concerns of the two philosophers.

---

74. Cua (2003, 180) makes similar observations, noting 'the key role of honor in understanding shame as an ethical concept' in the *Xunzi*. See also Lewis (2021).

75. See Fussi 2015, 124ff.

76. εἰ δ᾽ ἐστὶ τὰ μὲν κατ᾽ ἀλήθειαν αἰσχρὰ τὰ δὲ κατὰ δόξαν, οὐδὲν διαφέρει· οὐδέτερα γὰρ πρακτέα, ὥστ᾽ οὐκ αἰσχυντέον (*EN* 1128b23–25).

3

Human Nature and the Social Basis for Communities

THE MULTIPLE DIMENSIONS OF 'HUMAN NATURE'

This chapter examines the concept of human nature in Aristotle and Xunzi, and in particular the role that the two philosophers attribute to 'shame' in shaping human identity. Aristotle and Xunzi are both known for articulating a taxonomy in which the human and the nonhuman are set apart in distinct ways. To a great extent, ideas about human nature set the context, on both accounts, for a discussion of human potential in moral cultivation. A general discussion about human nature falls beyond the objectives of this chapter; the focus, instead, will be on the ways in which ideas of 'shame' and 'morality' relate to ideas of what it is to be human. This involves examining a network of questions such as: How do Aristotle and Xunzi construe the capacity to feel 'shame' as a uniquely human characteristic, vital for fulfilling human functions? On what level of abstraction and in what respects might we say that the two philosophers are 'similar' or 'different' in their view that humans are social beings and members of communities? If humans are defined as social beings, and 'shame' is commonly thought to be a 'social emotion', what, then, is the relevance of 'shame' in community life?

Regardless of whether we are dealing with ancient or contemporary discourses, the fact that human nature is spoken of in a multiplicity of senses sometimes causes difficulties in interpretation. Lloyd stresses the difference between normative and descriptive uses of 'the natural': 'On the one hand the natural is equated with what is true always or for the most part. On the other, what is natural is the goal, the end, the ideal.'[1] With reference to Aristotle in particular, Richard Kraut distinguishes between multiple senses of 'nature' in his ethics and politics: (1) first nature—what is already present in us prior to habituation; (2) second nature—what grows into us, as a result of a process of habituation; and (3) perfected nature—the goal at which we should arrive when

---

1. Lloyd 1991, 428. *Cf.* also Annas 1996, 732–34.

Aristotle and Xunzi on Shame, Moral Education, and the Good Life. Jingyi Jenny Zhao, Oxford University Press.
© Oxford University Press 2024. DOI: 10.1093/oso/9780197773161.003.0004

62 Aristotle and Xunzi on Shame

the process of habituation has worked well and we achieve something that is good.[2] To give an example from classical Confucian thought, one of the most hotly debated issues is the question of what Xunzi and Mencius may have meant by *xing* (性), and whether in refuting Mencius' claim that *xing* is good (*xing shan* 性善) and arguing instead that *xing* is bad (*xing e* 性惡), Xunzi's disagreement with Mencius simply rests on their varying conceptions of how *xing* is to be defined. Some have claimed that Xunzi and Mencius understand the term 'xing' differently.[3] After all, Xunzi could not have reasonably argued that human nature is bad when he included the functions of the sense organs as *xing*, for we can hardly say that it is bad that the eyes are capable of seeing and the ears capable of hearing;[4] furthermore, Xunzi attributes to humans the capacity for a sense of propriety (*yi* 義), which reflects the positive aspects of their potential. To give another example, with regard to Aristotle's definition of humans as being 'by nature' a *politikon zōon* (*Pol.* 1253a1–3), there has been much debate as to what he may have meant,[5] as well as disputes as to whether Aristotle's teleology is anthropocentric.[6] Certainly, the issue is further complicated if we take into account complexities surrounding the general terms *phusis* and *xing*. The Greek noun *phusis* is derived from the verb *phuo*, meaning 'grow'; similarly, the Chinese term *xing* is etymologically related to *sheng* 生, meaning 'live' or 'grow'. In the Chinese case, *xing* in the *Xunzi* is sometimes contrasted with *wei* (偽), artifice or conscious effort, so that human potential is to be understood through the combination of nature and artifice. In the Greek tradition, *phusis* is often contrasted with *nomos* ('law' or 'custom'); Aristotle distinguishes between *phusis* and *technē* in that the former is its own source of motion, while the latter requires an external source of motion. It is worth noting that neither *phusis* nor *xing* is limited to human experience,[7] though in my discussion I focus on the idea of human nature. Taking stock of the complexity of the debate, we might say that any attempt to reduce 'nature' to one definition necessarily runs the risk of oversimplification. In the ancient philosophers' search for the best life for a

---

2. Kraut 2007, 213.

3. See for example Graham [1967] 1990; Lau [1970] 2003, xx. Goldin (2000a, 117), in agreement with Graham, summarises it thus: 'For Xunzi, *xing* means "what is so by birth" (生之所以然者), or everything which we possess without having exerted any effort to obtain it. For Mencius, on the other hand, *xing* represents the natural course of development which an organism may be expected to undergo given nourishing conditions'.

4. The relevant passage is from the chapter *Human Nature is Bad*, where it is said that 'it belongs to the nature of humans that the eye is able to see and the ear to hear' (87/23/13).

5. *Cf.* Miller 1995, Kraut 2007.

6. *Cf.* Sedley 1991, Wardy 1993, Osborne 2007.

7. The term *anthropeia phusis* is used in Herodotus and Thucydides to denote specifically 'human nature'.

human being, the multidimensional nature of *phusis* and *xing* highlights the very complexity of human existence. Taking a cross-cultural comparative approach brings in different viewpoints, not only in terms of the solutions offered, but also in terms of the questions themselves and the very perspectives through which we might probe into human capacity and purpose. To quote Lloyd on theories of nature in Greek philosophy: 'We have almost as many theories of nature as of . . . earthquakes. However, the value of those disputes is not diminished, but may if anything be increased, by the very range of disagreement—since that secured the exploration of the widest possible range of answers to the questions of the proper subject-matter of the study of nature, and the outer limits of its intelligibility.'[8]

In this chapter, I begin by investigating in turn Aristotle's and Xunzi's taxonomies in which humans, nonhuman animals (hereafter 'animals') and other living things are defined, focusing on their scales of nature. While that has proved the most obvious place to look in drawing comparisons between the two philosophers on the topic of human nature,[9] I suggest that fresh insights can be obtained by turning attention to discussions of different types of courage that feature in both philosophers' accounts. These discourses, for sure, are not *centred* upon an explanation of the differences between humans and animals; nonetheless, in delineating different types of courage, they do point to the idea that a sense of shame and, by extension, the capacity for morality, are unique to humans. I then go on to explore Aristotle's and Xunzi's expositions of humans as members of communities and leading social lives, which has been identified as a point the two philosophers have in common, though the level of abstraction upon which Aristotle and Xunzi can be said to be 'similar' or 'different' on this point has not been sufficiently addressed. I explore the social aspect of human life in these two philosophers' accounts through a comparison, previously unexplored, of the ideas of *logos* in Aristotle and *bian* 辨/辯 (differentiation, argumentation) in Xunzi, which allow humans to communicate and collectively strive for the good. Animals, by contrast, being devoid of *logos* or the ability for *bian*, are able neither to form nor to pass on value judgments, for whom, therefore, 'shame' and 'morality' are irrelevant. The 'social' aspect of human life bears particular significance in a discussion of shame because shame arises from interpersonal contact and involves a sense of the self as distinguished from 'other'. Finally, I draw some connections between ancient accounts of human/animal emotions and morality and contemporary discourses.

8. Lloyd 1991, 432.
9. See Needham 1956, 23; Sterckx 2002, 89–90; Raphals 2018, 146.

64 Aristotle and Xunzi on Shame

DEFINING THE HUMAN IN ARISTOTLE

In his taxonomy, Aristotle attributes to plants the nutritive faculty only, while animals are said to have sense perception and therefore also the appetitive faculty. This includes *epithumia*, which is said to be an appetite for what is pleasant. In addition to having the nutritive and sensory faculties, humans and anything else which is similar or superior (by which Aristotle means god) have thought (*to dianoētikon*) and intellect (*nous*), which make them more complex than plants and animals and that entails that they have a different function in life.[10] In the *Eudemian Ethics*, Aristotle stresses that if we were to speak of a human being *qua* human being, we ought to neglect the parts of the soul that are not distinctive to him but should look to the power of reasoning (*logismos*).[11] In the *Nicomachean Ethics*, *eudaimonia* is identified as the human good, the activity of the soul in accordance with excellence; or in accordance with the best and the most perfect among them, if there are several human excellences.[12] Animals are said not to share in *eudaimonia*, since they, unlike humans, do not partake in reason. Aristotle places god at the top of his taxonomy (which sets him in contrast with Xunzi, examined in the section below), who engages in *theōria*—pure contemplation—and from whose activity the human good comes to be defined. Human beings, then, are closer to god and to a supreme kind of being than plants and animals on account of their capacity to contemplate (what *theōria* covers, however, is controversial).[13] It is worth noting that Aristotle's definition

---

10. *DA* 414a29–b19.

11. 'We also neglect any other part of the soul that there may be, e.g. the vegetative, for the above-mentioned parts are peculiar to the human soul; therefore the excellences of the nutritive part and that concerned with growth are not those of the human. For, if we speak of him *qua* human, he must have the power of reasoning, a governing principle, and action; but reason governs not reason, but desire and the emotions; he must then have these parts.' ἀφήρηται δὲ καὶ εἴ τι ἄλλο ἐστὶ μέρος ψυχῆς, οἷον τὸ φυτικόν. ἀνθρωπίνης γὰρ ψυχῆς τὰ εἰρημένα μόρια ἴδια· διὸ οὐδ᾽ αἱ ἀρεταὶ αἱ τοῦ θρεπτικοῦ καὶ αὐξητικοῦ ἀνθρώπου· δεῖ γάρ, εἰ ἦ ἄνθρωπος, λογισμὸν ἐνεῖναι καὶ ἀρχὴν καὶ πρᾶξιν, ἄρχει δ᾽ ὁ λογισμὸς οὐ λογισμοῦ ἀλλ᾽ ὀρέξεως καὶ παθημάτων, ἀνάγκη ἄρα ταῦτ᾽ ἔχειν τὰ μέρη. (*EE* 1219b36–1220a2) *Cf.* also *EN* 1097b22–1098a20 on the function of human beings.

12. τὸ ἀνθρώπινον ἀγαθὸν ψυχῆς ἐνέργεια γίνεται κατ᾽ ἀρετήν, εἰ δὲ πλείους αἱ ἀρεταί, κατὰ τὴν ἀρίστην καὶ τελειοτάτην (*EN* 1098a16–18).

13. 'So then the activity of a god, superior as it is in blessedness, will be one of contemplation; and so too the human activity that has the greatest affinity to this one will be most productive of happiness. Another indication of this is that the other animals do not share in happiness, being completely deprived of this sort of activity.' ὥστε ἡ τοῦ θεοῦ ἐνέργεια, μακαριότητι διαφέρουσα, θεωρητικὴ ἂν εἴη· καὶ τῶν ἀνθρωπίνων δὴ ἡ ταύτῃ συγγενεστάτη εὐδαιμονικωτάτη. σημεῖον δὲ καὶ τὸ μὴ μετέχειν τὰ λοιπὰ ζῷα εὐδαιμονίας, τῆς τοιαύτης ἐνεργείας ἐστερημένα τελείως (*EN* 1178b21–25). Osborne (2007, 110) makes the remark that Aristotle's *scala naturae* is a cumulative sequence, but not a hierarchy, since 'Aristotle regards the complexity of one's activities as an indicator of one's inferiority and distance from perfection' (ibid., 118) and that 'success in each life is measured against a standard set by the aspirations of a species. There is no single purpose to which we all aspire, and no hierarchy of contributions towards each others' ends' (ibid., 127). While it is true that according to Aristotle there is no single goal to which all living

Human Nature and the Social Basis for Communities   65

for the function of human beings does not extend to all humans, as he notoriously excludes slaves from having the deliberative part of the soul and claims that the female has it, but without full authority, and the child has it, but in an undeveloped form (though that is not to deny that women, slaves and children are still *anthrōpoi*).[14] This contrasts with Xunzi who emphasises throughout that all humans have the same nature and are equally bad in terms of their natural tendencies, yet everybody has the same potential to become not only good, but to become even a sage king who is a model of excellence.[15] Xunzi's attribution of equal potential to human beings, then, invites reflection on the idea that the hierarchical society often associated with Confucian thought is on one level not a natural hierarchy, but a hierarchy based on merit.[16] While all humans have the capacity to achieve moral status, that is not to say that all manage to actualise that potential—only certain people are able to do so through personal effort, and it is those people that merit power.[17]

Aristotle distinguishes between different kinds of courage (the Greek word for which is *andreia*, implying 'manliness'), where true courage is delineated from five other types. In what follows, I shall focus on civic courage and spirited courage in particular, which form the first half of Aristotle's discussion,

beings aspire, and Osborne provides a refreshing alternative way of interpreting Aristotle's *scala naturae* compared to the widely accepted interpretation, I believe on the basis of humans' affinity to god who is at the top of the scale, Aristotle would consider humans to be on a higher level than other living beings. While no living being can aspire to the superior position of god, human beings at least have the capacity to engage in contemplation, despite having to fulfil their nutritive needs and engage in the active political life that is demanded of them. Plants and animals, on the other hand, cannot partake in contemplation at all and thereby cannot be blessed, even to the smallest extent. It is clear from the *EN* passage cited that the activity of god is used as a standard here for Aristotle's judgment of the best kind of life. It ought to be noted also that Aristotle's *scala naturae* is cumulative only up to the level of human beings.

14. καὶ πᾶσιν ἐνυπάρχει μὲν τὰ μόρια τῆς ψυχῆς, ἀλλ᾽ ἐνυπάρχει διαφερόντως. ὁ μὲν γὰρ δοῦλος ὅλως οὐκ ἔχει τὸ βουλευτικόν, τὸ δὲ θῆλυ ἔχει μέν, ἀλλ᾽ ἄκυρον, ὁ δὲ παῖς ἔχει μέν, ἀλλ᾽ ἀτελές (*Pol.* 1260a10–14).

15. For sure, Xunzi very rarely mentions women explicitly in his ethics, but women can be expected to be included in the category of humans, *ren*. In Chapter 5, I discuss the issue of women in relation to the sociopolitical implications of shame.

16. I disagree with Knoblock's remark that 'like all Ru thinkers ["Ru" being a term that represents the erudite members of society, which later became synonymous with "Confucians"], Xunzi advocated a hierarchical society. He believed that things are unequal by nature and that this inequality extends to people' (1990, II, 117). From a close analysis of the relevant passages, it is clear that Xunzi places emphasis on the fact that all humans are born with the same nature, and are hence equal in terms of their potential. Social hierarchy is only established on the basis of what people do with their nature, whether they indulge in inappropriate desires or whether they learn to refine their nature through moral self-cultivation. Therefore, Xunzi does not get entangled in arguments to justify slavery, as in Aristotle, nor in eugenic arguments as in Plato (cf. Rosemont 2000, 4).

17. Cf. Lloyd 2012, 15: 'The moral sense has often been used to suggest not what all humans share, but what many humans lack.'

66 Aristotle and Xunzi on Shame

and in the next section I shall then turn to examine Xunzi's distinctions, which are revealing in terms of human and animal nature. One might wonder why 'courage' is used in both philosophers' accounts to further delineate differences between animal and human nature. One reason may be that courage is an excellence apparently shared by humans and animals, which can manifest itself in easily observable behaviour (even though, as I shall show, both philosophers deny that animals have true courage, since that depends on a moral sense).[18]

Civic courage is not identical to true courage, though it is said to be most like it (*EN* 1116a17). While the truly courageous person acts for the sake of achieving the fine,[19] civic courage is said to come about from excellence (*di' aretēn ginetai*, *EN* 1116a27–28), that is, from *aidōs* and the desire for what is fine, namely honour (*EN* 1116a28–29).[20] The civically courageous person resembles someone who has true courage since he associates good actions with honour and bad actions with shame, thereby having at least some sense of what constitutes fine conduct, though without the correct motivation. The status of *aidōs* is complicated here, since in other parts of the *EN* (II.7 and IV.9), this affection is explicitly said not to be an excellence, yet in describing the civically courageous man, Aristotle draws connections between excellence and *aidōs*, and between honour and a desire for what is fine.[21]

In his account of spirited courage, by contrast, Aristotle likens human beings who act on such a basis to wild animals:

> People also count temper (*thumos*) as courage; for the courageous are thought also to include people who act through temper, like wild animals that rush at the people who have wounded them, because courageous people too are strong-tempered; for temper especially strains to go out and face dangers.[22]
>
> Courageous people act for the sake of the fine (*dia to kalon*), and temper cooperates with them; by contrast, the wild animals in question act

18. One must note, however, that Aristotle's discussion of *andreia* is primarily in a martial context while Xunzi's *yong* 勇 extends to a much wider range of ideas. For a discussion of Confucius' view of courage in comparison with Aristotle's and Neo-Confucians', see Jiang 2012.

19. καλοῦ δὴ ἕνεκα ὁ ἀνδρεῖος ὑπομένει καὶ πράττει τὰ κατὰ τὴν ἀνδρείαν (*EN* 1115b23–24).

20. δι' αἰδῶ γὰρ καὶ διὰ καλοῦ ὄρεξιν (τιμῆς γάρ) καὶ φυγὴν ὀνείδους, αἰσχροῦ ὄντος (*EN* 1116a28–29).

21. See also Chapter 4 where I discuss the ambivalent status of *aidōs* in Aristotle depending on the context.

22. καὶ τὸν θυμὸν δ' ἐπὶ τὴν ἀνδρείαν φέρουσιν· ἀνδρεῖοι γὰρ εἶναι δοκοῦσι καὶ οἱ διὰ θυμὸν ὥσπερ τὰ θηρία ἐπὶ τοὺς τρώσαντας φερόμενα, ὅτι καὶ οἱ ἀνδρεῖοι θυμοειδεῖς· ἰτητικώτατον γὰρ ὁ θυμὸς πρὸς τοὺς κινδύνους (*EN* 1116b23–27).

Human Nature and the Social Basis for Communities   67

because they are distressed—after all, it is because they have been hit by a weapon, or because they are frightened (since they do not approach if they have a wood for cover). That they are driven out by distress and temper and so impelled towards the danger, without seeing in advance any of the frightening aspects of the situation—that, then, does not make them courageous, since at that rate even donkeys would be brave when they are hungry; beating them does not stop them from feeding.[23]

It seems, then, that human beings who are driven by their *thumos* are swayed by emotion (*dia pathos*) and act without the operation of reason, and their behaviour resembles that of other animals. For such people, the factor that motivates their apparently courageous behaviour does not involve reasoned reflection upon the present situation, but rather comes about from distress or fear (of punishment) or, we might say, theirs is an impulsive action carried out on the spur of the moment.[24] Those who act on the basis of *thumos* resemble animals who have only *epithumia* and *thumos*, and who do not share in *prohairesis*—purposive choice,[25] for we are told in *EN* III.2 that 'appetitive desire (*epithumia*) concerns what is pleasant and what brings pain, whereas purposive choice is neither for what is painful nor for what is pleasant. Still less is purposive choice temper (*thumos*); for things we do because of temper seem furthest from purposive choice';[26] rather, it is reason combined with the right desire that gives rise to purposive choice. Taking action merely on the basis of *thumos* is not excellence, since purposive choice is said to be something that is most fitting (*oikeiotaton*) for excellence, and to be more of an indicator of the differences between people's characters than actions (*EN* 1111b5–6).

---

23. οἱ μὲν οὖν ἀνδρεῖοι διὰ τὸ καλὸν πράττουσιν, ὁ δὲ θυμὸς συνεργεῖ αὐτοῖς· τὰ θηρία δὲ διὰ λύπην· διὰ γὰρ τὸ πληγῆναι ἢ διὰ τὸ φοβεῖσθαι, ἐπεὶ ἐάν γε ἐν ὕλῃ [ἢ ἐν ἕλει] ᾖ, οὐ προσέρχονται. οὐ δή ἐστιν ἀνδρεῖα διὰ τὸ ὑπ᾽ ἀλγηδόνος καὶ θυμοῦ ἐξελαυνόμενα πρὸς τὸν κίνδυνον ὁρμᾶν, οὐθὲν τῶν δεινῶν προορῶντα, ἐπεὶ οὕτω γε κἂν οἱ ὄνοι ἀνδρεῖοι εἶεν πεινῶντες· τυπτόμενοι γὰρ οὐκ ἀφίστανται τῆς νομῆς (*EN* 1116b30–1117a1).

24. *Cf. EN* 1111b9–10.

25. 'Purposive choice is not something shared by non-rational creatures, whereas appetite and temper are.' οὐ γὰρ κοινὸν ἡ προαίρεσις καὶ τῶν ἀλόγων, ἐπιθυμία δὲ καὶ θυμός (*EN* 1111b12–13). See also the *EE* where it is said that animals do not possess reason and desire in opposition to it, but live by desire, while in human beings both forms of force are present. A child is compared to a wild animal because he is not yet capable of acting by rational calculation: (οὐ γὰρ ἔχει λόγον καὶ ὄρεξιν ἐναντίαν, ἀλλὰ τῇ ὀρέξει ζῇ)· ἐν δ᾽ ἀνθρώπῳ ἔνεστιν ἄμφω, καὶ ἔν τινι ἡλικίᾳ, ᾗ καὶ τὸ πράττειν ἀποδίδομεν. οὐ γάρ φαμεν τὸ παιδίον πράττειν, οὐδὲ τὸ θηρίον, ἀλλὰ τὸν ἤδη διὰ λογισμὸν πράττοντα (*EE* 1224a26–30). Scholars have noted the difficulties in capturing the meaning of *prohairesis* in an English translation; here I adopt Kenny's (2000) translation of 'purposive choice'. For an examination of the meaning of *prohairesis*, see for example Chamberlain 1984.

26. καὶ ἡ μὲν ἐπιθυμία ἡδέος καὶ ἐπιλύπου, ἡ προαίρεσις δ᾽ οὔτε λυπηροῦ οὔθ᾽ ἡδέος. θυμὸς δ᾽ ἔτι ἧττον· ἥκιστα γὰρ τὰ διὰ θυμὸν κατὰ προαίρεσιν εἶναι δοκεῖ (*EN* 1111b16–19).

68 *Aristotle and Xunzi on Shame*

Taking action on the basis of temper, then, is further from true courage than civic courage, for anyone who engages in such behaviour has not been properly brought up to take pleasure in the right things but merely acts on impulse. Aristotle calls this the most natural form of courage,[27] perhaps for the simple reason that without education and habituation, this is the form of courage that one is likely to experience, as evidenced by children's behaviour, which does not involve rational calculation.[28] Children and young people are rather like animals in the sense that they live by their emotions, temper, and desires; however, in contrast to animals that simply do not have the capacity for reason, humans do have it and are expected to habituate themselves to performing the right kinds of actions and using reason to guide their thoughts and behaviour. In order for humans to become dissociated from animals and fulfil the human function, it appears that *aidōs* (from which civic courage derives) becomes a bridge in helping people to make the right associations and to identify good and bad behaviour so that even if they do not act for the sake of what is fine in the early stages of moral development, they can at least exercise *aidōs* to stop themselves from following *thumos* alone and making many mistakes. In this way, we come to understand why civic courage stands closer to true courage than actions taken merely on the basis of temper. Learning to associate bad actions with *to aischron* and acquiring a sense of what constitutes the shameful and honourable (i.e., a sense of what constitutes good and bad behaviour) is a crucial step in early moral education and in becoming human.

Defining the Human in Xunzi

Arriving at an informed understanding of Xunzi's views on *xing*, (human) nature, requires navigating through the many apparent inconsistencies and conflicts across the text on this very topic, on which much ink has been spilt. Xunzi is famously known as an advocate of the idea that 'human nature is bad' (*xing e* 性惡),[29] a phrase that appears only in the chapter bearing that phrase as its title, and found nowhere else in the treatise. Is nature bad merely in terms of the

---

27. φυσικωτάτη δ' ἔοικεν ἡ διὰ τὸν θυμὸν εἶναι (*EN* 1117a4).

28. Broadie & Rowe 2002, 324: 'it owes less to culture or special experience (or lack of it) than the other types'.

29. Translators have opted to either render *e* 惡 as 'bad' or as 'evil'. The former is preferable, since 'evil' suggests serious moral shortcomings and carries with it a sense of 'original sin', while 'bad' could simply suggest something that is undesirable or negatively regarded. Another reason for this choice is that *e* often acts as the antithesis of *shan* 善 in classical Chinese, where *shan* carries the sense of something that is good or desirable, but is not necessarily to do with moral good. On this point see also Knoblock (1988: I, 99) 'translating *e* as "evil" often overstates its meaning since the Chinese does not carry the sinister and baleful overtones of the English word', and Ivanhoe (1994, 172).

Human Nature and the Social Basis for Communities **69**

bad consequences that indulging in it may bring (Chong 2008), or is it bad in that humans have a *tendency* to do bad things (Li 2011)? For sure, *haoli* 好利—possessing a liking for profit, suggests that humans are self-interested beings. However, self-interestedness alone does not entail bad deeds—humans can do good things that bring profit to themselves without harming others. The fact that humans have desires and a liking for profit, therefore, is not bad in itself, but bad with qualification: given that resources are limited, if one were to follow one's natural instincts without having regard for others, this would lead to undesirable consequences. The arguments in support of the line 'human nature is bad' need to be understood within the rhetorical context of that chapter, situated in the hypothetical debate that Xunzi is staging between himself and Mencius. While Mencius highlights human potential in cultivating a moral life, Xunzi chooses to emphasise the necessity of external teachings.

In the *Xunzi*, *xing*, 'nature', is described as 'what characterises a person from birth' (83/22/2), and 'that which cannot be learned and cannot be worked at, and that which depends on heaven (*tian* 天)'.[30] As *xing* is the product of heaven, and heaven according to Xunzi is neutral, neither rewarding people for good actions nor punishing them for bad, one could take *xing* to be neutral, or *pu*, that is, raw, plain, or unadulterated, as Xunzi appears to claim in the chapter *Discourses on Rites*:[31]

> Thus it is said: nature is the root and the beginning, unadorned in terms of material; conscious exertion (*wei* 偽) is what makes it patterned and exalted. If there were no nature, there would be nothing on which conscious exertion could work; if there were no conscious exertion, nature would not be able to beautify itself. Only when nature and conscious exertion combine, will the reputation of the sage be perfected, and the unification of all under Heaven be accomplished.[32]

Nature is said to be plain and unadulterated and set in opposition to *wei* 偽, which is responsible for what is adorned. *Wei*, in its sense of pretence and artifice, is a term that has negative connotations in works such as the *Mencius* and

---

30. 不可學、不可事而在人者謂之性 (87/23/12). Wang Xianqian (1988, 436) cites Gu Qianli 顧千里 who suggests that *er* 而 should be read as *zhi* 之, while *ren* 人 should be read as *tian* 天. I believe this to be a plausible reading and have translated the passage in this way since the phrase immediately following speaks of *wei* 偽, conscious exertion or artifice, which is said to depend on a person, and intended to form a contrast with *xing*.

31. Ivanhoe and Perkins are among those that take Xunzi's view of nature to be neutral. Ivanhoe (1994, 173) takes Xunzi to mean that humans 'begin life in a state of moral blindness', while for Perkins (2014, 200), Xunzi's *xing* is 'not really evil but amoral'.

32. 故曰：性者，本始材朴也；偽者，文理隆盛也。無性則偽之無所加，無偽則性不能自美。性偽合，然後成聖人之名，一天下之功於是就也 (73/19/75-76).

the *Zhuangzi*. Xunzi, however, directly opposes his predecessors' perspectives and turns *wei* into something that is to be celebrated.[33] *Xing* and *wei*, nonetheless, are not mutually exclusive, and Xunzi is not advocating that one should abandon one's *xing*, or that it is even possible. Rather, nature provides a template upon which conscious exertion can be made, and it is the combination of *xing* and *wei* that makes the ideal state. While Xunzi claims that 'nature cannot be learned and cannot be worked at', he also speaks of the sage as being capable of transforming his nature (*huaxing* 化性), thereby provoking the question of whether or not it is possible for one's nature to be altered. To resolve this potential conflict, it is helpful to consider Xunzi's views on desire. Xunzi favours the view that humans have many desires and argues against Song Xing's 宋鈃 view that human desires are few. If we were to grant that human nature cannot be learned and cannot be acquired by effort, then it is clear that desires cannot be reduced to a few in number, for it is simply human nature to have many desires. However, there is a way in which one can cultivate oneself so as to aspire to a better way of living rather than indulging all those desires. By following ritual practices and abiding by a sense of propriety, one gets accustomed to responding appropriately to those desires through the medium of the heart-mind (*xin*).[34] It is not the number of desires that is reduced; 'conscious exertion' involves the heart–mind deliberating whether a desire should be fulfilled and leading the body to act accordingly. So then, nature cannot be changed for better or for worse and one may still have a liking for personal benefit after receiving the appropriate education simply because that is one's natural inclination; nonetheless, through external teachings and conscious exertion, one acquires a liking for a sense of propriety and learns to prioritise that over one's liking for personal benefit.[35]

Just to what extent Xunzi chooses to set apart the differences between human nature and animal nature is subject to debate. Yu, who attempts to compare Mencius's and Xunzi's accounts of human nature 'in the light of Aristotle's approach to ethics', says,

> Whereas Aristotle identifies human function or humanity in order to ground his theory of happiness on it, Xunzi, while knowing what distinguishes humans from animals, chose not to pursue this line of thought. On the contrary, he based his ethics on the thesis that 'human nature is evil'. In other words, he starts from the aspect of human nature that

---

33. See Jiang 2021, 356–57.
34. 心慮而能為之動謂之偽 (83/22/4).
35. See the next chapter for a detailed treatment of the role of the heart-mind in deliberating desires.

Human Nature and the Social Basis for Communities   71

human beings share with other animals.[36] In Aristotle's view, Xunzi failed to appreciate the significance of humanity.[37]

Yu then goes on to conclude that 'Mencius and Aristotle shared the same general approach to ground ethics on humanity'.[38] Based on my reading and interpretation of the texts, Xunzi places as much emphasis as Mencius—if not more—on the differences between animal and human nature. Xunzi is in fact remarkably similar to Aristotle in recognising human beings' distinctive ability to differentiate between good and bad, and to habituate themselves to performing the right kinds of actions.

In the well-known passage from the chapter *On the Regulations of a King*, Xunzi sets out the differences between humans and other things:

> Water and fire possess life force (*qi*) but have no life (*sheng*). Grass and trees have life but no awareness (*zhi*). Birds and beasts have awareness but no sense of propriety (*yi*). Humans possess life force, life, awareness, as well as a sense of propriety, therefore they are the noblest under heaven.[39]

A sense of propriety, then, is established as the distinctive characteristic of human beings. Indeed, human beings' capacity for a sense of propriety need not conflict with the claim that human nature is bad. It is not the case that human beings, left to mature independently of education, have an innate tendency to follow a sense of propriety in their conduct; following their inborn tendency would lead them to seek only their own profit. Rather, human beings have a sense of propriety in that they have the *capacity* to attain it, but they can only exercise it if they receive education and cultivate themselves accordingly. Xunzi makes the very explicit remark that those who engage in learning (*xue* 學) count as humans, while those who dismiss learning count as mere birds and beasts.[40]

The key to solving any potential conflict between the claims that 'human nature is bad' and 'humans alone possess propriety' lies in the chapter *Human Nature is Bad*. Much of this chapter takes the form of hypothetical dialogues whereby the authorial voice directly addresses a series of questions posed by the imaginary interlocutor. Such questions include what it means for any ordinary person to become a Yu, a legendary king, and why it is possible for the sage to

---

36. By saying so, Yu is implying that animals are 'evil' which cannot be right.

37. Yu 2005, 28.

38. Ibid., 29.

39. 水火有氣而無生，草木有生而無知，禽獸有知而無義，人有氣、有生、有知，亦且有義，故最為天下貴也 (28/9/69–29/9/70).

40. 2/1/27–28.

72   *Aristotle and Xunzi on Shame*

reach a cultivated state through accumulated effort while the rest of humankind cannot. In answer to these questions, Xunzi distinguishes between something being permissible (*keyi* 可以) and something that can (*neng* 能) be done:

> Something's being permissible (*keyi*) does not guarantee that it can be done (*neng*). Even though one is unable (*buneng*) to do something, this does not make it any less permissible (*keyi*). This being the case, whether something has the ability (*neng*) or not (*buneng*) is entirely dissimilar from something being permissible (*ke*) or not (*buke*).[41]

Furthermore, it is said that the petty man and the gentleman are unwilling to become the other person, even though it is permissible for them to do so.[42] Even though everyone is born of the same nature and it is permissible for each person to become a sage, not everybody is *capable* of cultivating himself to reach that state. Cultivation requires focused learning and the accumulation of efforts in following ritual practices and adhering to a sense of propriety in one's conduct. The gentleman succeeds in cultivating his abilities and fulfils his potential to become a sage, while the unwillingness on the part of the petty man prevents him from doing so.[43]

In the chapter *Of Honour and Disgrace* Xunzi views humans in relation to animals and compares the courage (*yong* 勇) of various groups of beings. Unlike the taxonomy in the chapter *On the Regulations of a King* where human beings are spoken of as a collective group, Xunzi now places the dog and the boar at the bottom and distinguishes between *different* groups of people, with the peddler, the robber and the petty man in the middle of that hierarchy, and the scholar-official (*shi*) and the gentleman on top:

> There is the courage of the dog and the boar, that of the peddler and the robber, that of the petty man, and that of the scholar-official and the gentleman. Fighting over food and drink, with no scruples and no sense of shame (*wu lianchi* 無廉恥), not knowing right from wrong, not trying to avoid death nor injury, not fearful of the greater forces, only greedily seeking benefit (*li* 利) and food and drink, that is the courage of the dog and the boar.[44] Dealing in transactions of profit, fighting over goods and

41. 90/23/74–75.

42. 89/23/70–71.

43. For a fuller treatment of Xunzi's distinctions between *keyi* and *neng*, see Chong (2003), who discusses these terms in relation to Xunzi's critique of Mencius.

44. Knoblock (1988, I, 287), following Wang Yinzhi and Kuobo Ai, believes *li* 利 in this line to have been miscopied from a parallel expression in the next sentence. However, I am inclined to keep it in the text precisely for the parallel with the next sentence, so that descriptions of the courage of the dog and boar are formulated in a similar way to those of the peddler and robber.

valuables, with no concern for deference, being audacious and daring, ferociously greedy and perverse, greedily only seeking after profit (*li* 利), that is the courage of the peddler and the robber. Scorning death and vicious in behaviour, that is the courage of the petty man. Grounded in a sense of propriety, not swayed by power, not minding his own profit, even when granted power over the whole state, he does not change his behaviour, weighing the threat of death and upholding a sense of propriety, not backing away from it—such is the courage of the scholar-official and the gentleman.[45]

There are several interesting points about this passage. First, it would seem that only the scholar-official and the gentleman stand by a sense of propriety, which further illustrates the fact that while the quality is attributed to human beings on a general level, only those who are morally cultivated can be said to act consistently in accordance with it. Second, those who stand between the lowest animals and the highest exemplary humans bear remarkable resemblances to the dog and the boar. The peddler and the robber fight over material goods just like animals that fight over their basic needs—food and drink. Their point of similarity is highlighted when Xunzi applies the same phrase 'greedily only seeking after *li* (benefit/ profit)' to both, repeated within a short space.[46] While the dog and the boar are said not to avoid death and injury, the petty man is described as scorning death or regarding death lightly. Such behaviour in Xunzi's view is not true courage, but simply rashness that reflects a lack of thought and knowledge of what is in one's best interest. A further point that brings out the animalistic nature of the peddler's and the robber's behaviour lies in the phrase *meng tan er li* 猛貪而戾, which can be translated as 'ferociously greedy and perverse'. Appropriately, *li* 戾, while taking on the meanings of 'perverse' and 'ferocious', is a character composed of a dog under a roof. The Chinese character shows a dog exiting a door (understandably in a lowly manner);[47] hence ascribing this description to the peddler and the robber has the effect of further downgrading them to the animal realm.

Further in the same chapter, we are told that all humans are born petty and that without teaching and regulation they would seek only their own profit.[48] The real difference between the gentleman and the petty man does not lie in

45. 9/4/16–20.

46. The phrase *mou mou ran wei li*恈恈然唯利 appears to be a unique form of expression found only in the *Xunzi*.

47. *Cf.* its description in the *Shuowen jiezi*, 475.

48. 11/4/49–50.

74   *Aristotle and Xunzi on Shame*

their nature and in terms of the capacity with which they are born, but in the actions that they choose to take and the habits instilled by their customs.[49] While animals do not know right from wrong and do not have the capacity to distinguish between them, human beings do have such a capacity, their potential realised through constant good practice, as exemplified by the gentleman. In Xunzi's discussions of different types of courage, animals are placed on the very bottom rung of the ladder because their courage can best be interpreted as rashness and recklessness. They are said not to have a sense of *lianchi*, shame. Certain groups of people are likened to animals in their behaviour, forming a strong contrast with the scholar-official and the gentleman who uphold a sense of propriety. When Xunzi criticises the debauched and says that they are without scruples and a sense of shame, having a particular liking for food and drink,[50] he is in fact drawing implicit parallels between those people and animals whose moral status is dubious. In the examples shown, a sense of shame acts as a defining feature of human beings—an attribute that is comparable to humans' sense of propriety in that it must be cultivated and exercised to prevent humans from being relegated to the lower status of animals. While animals by nature do not have this quality, humans are expected to have a sense of shame and therefore should be ashamed of shameless behaviour.[51] In *Human Nature Is Bad*, Xunzi offers another account of different kinds of courage—this time between that of the best kind (*shangyong* 上勇), middle kind (*zhongyong* 中勇) and the worst kind (*xiayong* 下勇) (90/23/82–86). In that passage, resonances of the courage of the dog and boar can be found in the description of people who have the worst kind of courage, for they are said to 'disregard matters of right and wrong and the essential characteristics of what is so and what is not so', to take their own character lightly and to consider material wealth to be important.[52] Even though no explicit links are drawn, such people resemble Xunzi's description of animals that fight for whatever brings them benefit, without having a regard for what is right or wrong.

Elsewhere Xunzi compares those who engage in belligerent behaviour with the dog and the boar, this time claiming that such people are inferior to animals because while belligerent people have no regard for their own life, their kin, and for their ruler, even animals are shown to be capable of caring for their

---

49. 10/4/40–41.

50. The phrase often used is 'having no scruples and no sense of shame and indulging in food and drink' (無廉恥而嗜飲食), which can be found in the chapters *On Self-Cultivation* and *Against the Twelve*.

51. See *Mencius* 13.6/67/28.

52. 90/23/85–6.

Human Nature and the Social Basis for Communities   75

own kin.[53] Xunzi considers putting these people into the category of beasts, but recognises that that cannot be done because they have the form and substance of human beings and their likes and dislikes are in large measure the same as humans'.[54] In a similar vein, in the chapter *Discourse on Rituals* a list of examples is given of animals that show grief at the loss of their family, which is evidence of their possessing awareness and hence love of their own kind. Since no creature supposedly has more awareness than humans,[55] human beings who do not care for their kin is relegated to a position below that of animals. Xunzi's attribution of 'moral' behaviour to animals at certain points appears to contradict the idea that humans alone have a sense of propriety. Mark Csikszentmihalyi cites a passage in the *Mencius* where it is said that what separates human beings from birds and beasts is minuscule and that the common people dispense with it, while the gentleman preserves it. He remarks that 'the actions of animals may be conventionally described as "benevolent" and "righteous", but genuine moral motivation is something they cannot achieve.'[56] While it is difficult to define precisely what 'genuine moral motivation' might be, I believe that Csikszentmihalyi is right in recognising that animal action can fall within our categories of what might constitute 'proper' behaviour, though that is to be distinguished from 'moral' behaviour since animals do not possess awareness of the moral implications of their actions.[57]

In another passage from *Discourse on Rituals*, an altogether different picture of animal morality is presented, where Xunzi now employs 'birds and beasts' as purely negative examples. The gentleman considers shameful those that do not show grief or respect at their parents' funeral, whose manners are compared to birds and beasts.[58] Jane Geaney points to this passage as an example of Xunzi repeatedly picking shame 'as the human characteristic, or one of the human characteristics, that marks the difference between human and nonhuman.'[59] Yet I believe the main point made in this passage is that entirely different kinds of

---

53. 'A nursing sow will charge a tiger, and a nursing dog will not wander far away. They are not neglectful of their kin. A human being who is neglectful of their own safety, neglectful of their kin, and neglectful of their ruler above is not even as good as the dog and the boar' (9/4/9–11). Cf. *Analects* 2.7/3/ 11–12, where Confucius, in speaking about filial piety (*xiao* 孝), refers to dogs and horses that are capable of caring for their parents.

54. 9/4/15.

55. 74/19/97–75/19/100.

56. Csikszentmihalyi 2004, 109n18.

57. I follow up this debate in the final section of this chapter.

58. 73/19/61–62.

59. Geaney 2004, 121, 139n53. A better example of Xunzi's identification of shame as a human characteristic would be the passage from *Of Honour and Disgrace*, where the dog and the boar are said not to have scruples or a sense of shame.

76　Aristotle and Xunzi on Shame

moral expectations are held of humans and of animals: human beings, unlike animals, are expected to show grief and reverence at the death of their kin, and when they fail to do so, they are considered to have done something shameful since their failure evokes the subhuman. Referring to Warring States and Han sources, Roel Sterckx remarks: 'As signifying living creatures surrounding the human observer, the animal kingdom provided models for authority in human society and functioned as a catalytic medium for the conception of human morality.'[60] A survey of the discussions of animals in the *Xunzi* certainly reveals the 'sociocentric' nature of Xunzi's models: as I have illustrated, at times animals are portrayed as living things that resemble humans in their conduct and at other times they are presented as counterexamples, the very opposites of human morality. What we find in the *Xunzi*, therefore, is that unlike Aristotle's approach, there is little if any systematic investigation of animal behaviour, so that Xunzi does not discuss animal behaviour for its own sake. Rather, the focus is always on using examples from the animal world for the construction of a model of behaviour for human beings, assimilating and at times contrasting these two groups to advance protreptic arguments.

We now come to see that Xunzi in many ways shares his predecessor Mencius' views in distinguishing human nature from animal nature. Indeed, Xunzi develops his account of human nature based on Mencius' 'four sprouts of goodness' as found in the well-known passage:

> From this it can be seen that whoever is devoid of the heart of compassion is not human, whoever is devoid of the heart of shame and dislike is not human, whoever is devoid of the heart of courtesy and modesty is not human, and whoever is devoid of the heart of right and wrong is not human. The heart of compassion is the germ of humaneness; the heart of shame, of propriety; the heart of courtesy and modesty, of observance of the rites; the heart of right and wrong, of wisdom.[61]

Without these qualities, one is said not to be a human being, *ren* 人. With reference to Xunzi's discussions of courage, we can see that except for the feeling of compassion, Xunzi touches upon the feelings of right and wrong and of deference and complaisance, all of which are distinctly human characteristics (when the peddler and the robber are said to have no concern for deference, the underlying line is that human beings ought to have this quality and that

---

60. Sterckx 2002, 240.

61. 由是觀之，無惻隱之心，非人也；無羞惡之心，非人也；無辭讓之心，非人也；無是非之心，非人也。惻隱之心，仁之端也；羞惡之心，義之端也；辭讓之心，禮之端也；是非之心，智之端也 (*Mencius* 3.6/18/7–9).

they should not fight over goods as animals do). The Mencian statement that the feeling of shame and dislike is essential to humans resonates strongly with Xunzi's views of human nature; we see that Xunzi appears to have deliberately chosen the sprout of a sense of propriety as the defining characteristic of human beings over all the other qualities. We may conjecture that cultivating the appropriate feelings of shame and dislike will lead to a sense of propriety on the basis that it requires a sense of awareness of what constitutes rightful and wrongful conduct. The Mencian reference helpfully illustrates how the idea of propriety springs from feelings of shame and dislike, and is therefore associated with discriminating between what is good and bad.

Read with these observations, Yu's criticism that 'Xunzi failed to appreciate the significance of humanity' on the basis of his claim that 'human nature is bad' can be said to be far from valid. Furthermore, I hope to have shown that despite what some scholars have claimed, there do not appear to be significant inconsistencies in Xunzi's accounts of human nature, and that parallels drawn between human and animal behaviour in the various contexts serve the very purpose of highlighting just how *different* humans and animals are in terms of their capacities.

HUMAN COMMUNITIES AND THE MAKING OF SOCIAL DISTINCTIONS

Having examined Aristotle's and Xunzi's taxonomy, where we find each attributing a unique set of qualities to human beings including the capacity for 'shame', I now investigate an idea that is shared by the two philosophers, that is, human beings' nature to live in communities. A discussion of 'human nature' implies speaking of humans as a group with a certain degree of *shared* attributes and capabilities. Both Aristotle and Xunzi recognise engagement in community life to be one of the defining features of human beings, whereby certain expectations exist for those that partake in community life. Taking stock of the fundamental differences in the social-historical background of the two philosophers and the kinds of political situations that they have in mind, it is perhaps all the more striking just how similar Aristotle and Xunzi are in their conceptions of humans as members of communities, and in their emphasis upon the essential role of habituation and moral training in allowing humans to fulfil their functions and become integrated into a well-ordered society.

How and why are humans more community-oriented than other animals, and what does community life entail for Aristotle and Xunzi? Answering these questions involves investigating the subtleties of Aristotle's claim that a human being is a *politikon zōon* and Xunzi's claim that humans alone can form

78   *Aristotle and Xunzi on Shame*

communities (*qun* 群).[62] Zooming in on the previously unexplored comparison of *logos* in Aristotle and *bian* 辨/辯 (differentiation, argumentation) in Xunzi, I argue for two main points: first, that in both philosophers' accounts, the idea of making distinctions is intricately connected with the idea of reasoned speech; second, that discriminating between sets of opposite values and voicing them go hand in hand in providing a political as well as a moral context for human lives, with significant implications for social cohesion. Such actions allow humans to communicate and collectively strive for the good. Aristotle's and Xunzi's shared vision of humans as participants in community life has significant implications for our understanding of the role that a sense of shame occupies in their ethical and political schemes, for shame and related ideas are closely associated with interpersonal relationships and with how one is regarded by others in a society. We might say that for both, the capacity to be aware of one's wrongdoings and to correct them is not only commendable, but an indispensable part in becoming integrated into the social and political lives demanded of human beings.

In classical Greek literature, certain features are commonly associated with humankind and serve as defining characteristics of humans' collective identity. For example, in Plato's *Protagoras*, humans are said to be the only creatures that worship gods, and to articulate speech and words. Furthermore, humans possess *aidōs* and *dikē*, conventionally translated as 'shame' and 'justice', which allows them to preserve themselves and live in peace.[63] *Aidōs* and *dikē* are also found as a pair in Hesiod and Theognis, qualities that are commendable in a collective sense, enabling humans to engage in community life without violence and strife.[64] It is essential that all humans share them, since if only some had them, violence and strife would follow upon shamelessness and lawlessness, and the human species would struggle to survive.[65] We can say that in Hesiod, Theognis, and Plato, *aidōs* is often portrayed as a commendable collective quality in the sense that it is particularly commended for preserving the

---

62. Animals can be *social*, certainly, and neither Xunzi nor Aristotle denies this. However, what is at stake is how and why humans are *more* community-oriented than other animals, in the context of what Xunzi and Aristotle discuss.

63. *Prot.* 322aff.

64. In Hesiod, *aidōs* is personified and sometimes paired with the goddess *Dikē*, sometimes with the goddess Nemesis ('retribution', 'indignation'). If nemesis is to be understood as a sociological or psychological deterrent to committing actions that do not accord with *aidōs* and *dikē*, then this pairing brings out the connection between shame and the fear of reprisal. In this case, Aristotle's emphasis on the role of *aidōs* in moral education, discussed in detail in Chapter 4, can be viewed as a divergent model from the Archaic paradigm. I thank an anonymous reviewer for bringing the point of nemesis to my attention.

65. *Cf.* αἰδὼς μὲν γὰρ ὄλωλεν, ἀναιδείη δὲ καὶ ὕβρις νικήσασα δίκην γῆν κατὰ πᾶσαν ἔχει (*Thgn.* 291–92).

Human Nature and the Social Basis for Communities 79

human species and enabling human beings to engage in community life without violence and strife.

Following that tradition, Aristotle, too, sees human beings as members of communities and attributes to them certain features that allow them to live in a *koinōnia*. Just what Aristotle may have meant by the claim that 'a human being is by nature a *politikon zōon*' (*Pol.* 1253a2–3) has been subject to debate, largely because of the semantic range of the word *politikon* itself. As is well known, *politika* is not limited to mean life in a *polis*, for animals certainly do not live in *poleis*, and nor do many humans. Indeed, in the *History of Animals*, some animals are also described as *politika* (although to a lesser extent than humans). In Book I, Aristotle places animals into categories according to their way of life and their activities. Some are said to be gregarious (*agelaia*), some solitary (*monadika*). Of the gregarious animals, some are social (*politika*) and some are more dispersed (*sporadika*).[66] The social animals have one common activity (*koinon to ergon*), which is not true of all the gregarious animals.[67] I wish to set aside, for now, the argument for the naturalness of the city, and focus on a passage from Book I of the *Politics* which offers an explanation for humans' political nature by virtue of their possession of *logos*, speech:

> Now, that a human being is more of a political animal (*politikon zōon*) than a bee or any other gregarious animal is evident. Nature, as we often say, makes nothing in vain, and the human being is the only animal that has the gift of speech (*logos*). And whereas mere voice (*phōnē*) is but an indication of pleasure or pain, and is therefore found in other animals (for their nature attains to the perception of pleasure and pain and the intimation of them to one another, and no further), the power of speech is intended to set forth the advantageous and the harmful, and therefore likewise the just and the unjust. And it is a characteristic of the human being that he alone has any sense of good and bad, of just and unjust and the like, and the association of living beings who have this sense makes a family and a state.[68]

---

66. *HA* 487b33–488a7.
67. *HA* 488a9–10.
68. διότι δὲ πολιτικὸν ὁ ἄνθρωπος ζῷον πάσης μελίττης καὶ παντὸς ἀγελαίου ζῴου μᾶλλον, δῆλον. οὐθὲν γάρ, ὡς φαμέν, μάτην ἡ φύσις ποιεῖ· λόγον δὲ μόνον ἄνθρωπος ἔχει τῶν ζῴων· ἡ μὲν οὖν φωνὴ τοῦ λυπηροῦ καὶ ἡδέος ἐστὶ σημεῖον, διὸ καὶ τοῖς ἄλλοις ὑπάρχει ζῴοις (μέχρι γὰρ τούτου ἡ φύσις αὐτῶν ἐλήλυθε, τοῦ ἔχειν αἴσθησιν λυπηροῦ καὶ ἡδέος καὶ ταῦτα σημαίνειν ἀλλήλοις), ὁ δὲ λόγος ἐπὶ τῷ δηλοῦν ἐστι τὸ συμφέρον καὶ τὸ βλαβερόν, ὥστε καὶ τὸ δίκαιον καὶ τὸ ἄδικον· τοῦτο γὰρ πρὸς τὰ ἄλλα ζῷα τοῖς ἀνθρώποις ἴδιον, τὸ μόνον ἀγαθοῦ καὶ κακοῦ καὶ δικαίου καὶ ἀδίκου καὶ τῶν ἄλλων αἴσθησιν ἔχειν· ἡ δὲ τούτων κοινωνία ποιεῖ οἰκίαν καὶ πόλιν (*Pol.* 1253a7–18). A similar idea can be found in the *Rhetoric*,

80 Aristotle and Xunzi on Shame

Logos is a term that has a notoriously wide semantic range, covering the ideas of account, speech, reason, and so forth. As is well known, it derives from the verbal noun *legein*, meaning to gather, say, or speak, which is its basic meaning.[69] Its broad semantic range can make finding the most apt translation for it in a given passage difficult. In the passage cited, however, *logos* is clearly used in its basic sense of 'speech' in order to contrast with *phōnē*, 'voice'. Animals are said to have voice, which allows them to indicate sensations of pleasure and pain. It is on the basis of those sensations, it is implied, that they take action. Humans, on the other hand, possess *logos* or speech, which enables them to indicate things that animals cannot, namely the advantageous (*to sumpheron*) and the harmful (*to blaberon*), leading to the just (*to dikaion*) and the unjust (*to adikon*). The perception (*aisthēsis*) and indication of the pleasurable and the painful, which are characteristic of animals, can be understood to be automatic responses to external stimuli that do not involve judgment or calculation. Yet the morally refined person should not take action on the basis of pleasure, as Aristotle cautions in the *EN*:

> For each disposition has its own corresponding range of fine things and pleasant things, and presumably what most distinguishes the good person is his ability to see what is true in every set of circumstances, (this ability) being like a carpenter's rule or measure for them. But most people are deceived, and the deception seems to come about because of pleasure; for pleasure appears to be a good thing when it is not. So they choose what is pleasant as (though it were) something good, and they avoid pain as (though it were) something bad.[70]

Aristotle contrasts the good man with the bad by saying that the life of the former is directed towards the fine, allowing *logos* to govern him, while the latter's desire is for pleasure, which needs forcible constraint by pain like a yoked animal (*EN* 1180a10–12). It is not sufficient, then, to choose on the basis of pleasure and pain, which may lead one to the apparent but not to the true good. The perception and indication of the advantageous and the harmful, the just and the unjust, and the good and bad, by contrast, are capacities of a more sophisticated sort which

---

where it is said that the use of *logos*, rather than that of the body, is more characteristic of humans (*Rhet.* 1355b1–2). The cited passage does not explicitly comment on the political nature of *logos*, though rhetoric is necessarily political when practised in a social and political setting.

69. On the transformative use of *logos* in Greek literature, see for example Heath 2005; Moss 2014.

70. καθ᾽ ἑκάστην γὰρ ἕξιν ἴδιά ἐστι καλὰ καὶ ἡδέα, καὶ διαφέρει πλεῖστον ἴσως ὁ σπουδαῖος τῷ τἀληθὲς ἐν ἑκάστοις ὁρᾶν, ὥσπερ κανὼν καὶ μέτρον αὐτῶν ὤν. ἐν τοῖς πολλοῖς δὲ ἡ ἀπάτη διὰ τὴν ἡδονὴν ἔοικε γίνεσθαι· οὐ γὰρ οὖσα ἀγαθὸν φαίνεται. αἱροῦνται οὖν τὸ ἡδὺ ὡς ἀγαθόν, τὴν δὲ λύπην ὡς κακὸν φεύγουσιν (*EN* 1113a31–b2).

Human Nature and the Social Basis for Communities   81

involve reasoning and choosing between alternatives that are value-laden;[71] in other words, humans, unlike other animals, are capable of moral judgment. We should notice that the capacity for *logos* belongs to the part of Aristotle's narrative on the political nature of human beings, and thus *logos* is clearly being treated as a capacity with political significance. Stephen Salkever comments that it is through argument, conjectures, or narratives that we might discover 'the kinds of goals in terms of which we can most sensibly organize our lives'.[72] Along similar lines, Trevor Saunders notes that 'the use of *logos* to "make clear" the just and the unjust implies deliberation and persuasion'.[73] *Logos*, then, takes human beings beyond the simple expression of pleasure and pain so that, by engaging in open dialogues and exchanges with others in the political community and through collective effort, humans can discriminate between the advantageous and the harmful, the just and the unjust, the good and the bad, which can only be reached through persuasion and reasoning.[74] What relevance does *logos* hold for the idea of *aidōs*? Unlike the Protagoras myth, Aristotle does not specifically mention *aidōs* as that which serves to unite human beings and gives them an advantage over other animals. *Aidōs* by Aristotle's definition signifies a fear of disrepute and is hence concerned with the adherence to certain values in society and the shunning of others. To live as a member of society, therefore, necessitates sharing certain values with others in that society and contributing towards upholding those values. In other words, *aidōs* and *aischunē* come into focus only in a social context, where notions of the advantageous and the harmful, the just and the unjust, the good and the bad and, we might say, the honourable and the disgraceful, are discussed and shared with others in a community, facilitated by human beings' possession of *logos*.

Turning now to Xunzi, we find that humans are distinguished from animals by their ability to form communities (*qun* 群),[75] make social divisions (*fen* 分),

---

71. *Cf.* Saunders 1995, 70: 'Aristotle may wish to imply that whereas animals merely act and react automatically, treating pleasurable as beneficial without reflection (cf. *Anim.* 414b4–6), men consider, debate, and choose alternatives, by *distinguishing* pleasurable and beneficial (neither is necessarily the other: *EN* 1113a33–b2).'

72. Salkever 2005, 40.

73. Saunders 1995, 70.

74. *Cf.* Trott 2014, 88: 'By associating *logos* with the political being of a human, Aristotle indicates how human beings are fundamentally together with others in the world and concerned for the good that characterizes human life.'

75. *Cf.* Sterckx's translation of 'a sense for social organization' for *qun* 群 (2002, 89). Worth noting is the fact that this character consists of the 'sheep' radical, conveying the idea of a 'flock', and is by convention used to describe the formation of groups or communities within the human as well as the animal kingdom (comparable to the sense of *agelaia* in Greek). Hence Xunzi is deliberately making a controversial claim by limiting its use to humans only, on the basis of a specific understanding of what *qun* involves.

82 *Aristotle and Xunzi on Shame*

and possess a sense of propriety. Having placed humans at the top of his scale of nature by virtue of their propensity for a sense of propriety, Xunzi explains why human beings are capable of using horses and oxen for their own purposes even though they are weaker in terms of physical prowess:

> In physical power they [human beings] are not so good as an ox, in swiftness they do not equal the horse, and yet the ox and horse can be put to their use. Why is that? I say it is because humans alone can form communities (*qun* 群) and they cannot. Why can humans form a community? I say it is due to making social divisions.[76] How can social divisions be translated into behaviour? I say it is because of humans' sense of propriety. Thus, if their sense of propriety is used to make social divisions, concord will result. If there is concord, unity will result; if there is unity, great physical power will result; if there is great physical power, real strength will result; if there is real strength, all objects can be overcome. For this reason, humans can acquire palaces and houses where they can dwell in safety. Thus, that they put the four seasons in their proper sequence, control the myriad of things, universally benefit all under heaven, is due to no other cause than that they are able to make social divisions and observe a sense of propriety. Accordingly, humans cannot live without forming communities.[77] If a society is formed without social divisions, strife results; if there is strife, disorder ensues; if there is disorder, fragmentation results; if there is fragmentation, weakness comes; if there is weakness, it is impossible to triumph over objects. For this reason, humans could not acquire palaces and houses in which to dwell with security. This is precisely why it is unacceptable to neglect ritual and a sense of propriety even for the briefest moment.[78]

---

76. Knoblock translates *fen* as 'division of society into classes' (1990, II, 104). This seems to capture one meaning of *fen* but *fen* in this context is not limited to the division of social classes, but could also imply the division of social roles. *Fen* in its etymology, of course, merely means the separation of things and so its semantic range far exceeds that of making social divisions. The term could take on a multiplicity of meanings depending on context. For example, in the *Xunzi* we find phrases such as 榮辱之大分—'the great distinctions between honour and disgrace' and 君子小人之分—'distinctions between the gentleman and the petty person', neither of which carries the sense of *social* division. In this particular instance, I adopt Hutton's translation of 'social divisions' for *fen* as I believe it to be the most appropriate in capturing the range of meaning.

77. Knoblock renders the phrase 人生不能無群 into 'from birth all men are capable of forming societies' (1990: II, 104). This is erroneous in my opinion, as it does not comply with the grammar of the Chinese and furthermore does not read well in relation to the rest of the text in this section. I have chosen to adopt 'humans cannot live without forming communities', which is in agreement with Hutton's version.

78. 29/9/70–74.

Human Nature and the Social Basis for Communities 83

The passage illustrates the necessity of social divisions for a harmonious society that is capable of providing for its people. Two contrasting situations are presented: in the first example, by virtue of a sense of propriety that allows for the making of social divisions, a set of positive outcomes is generated, so that human beings gain great strength as a collective group and are able to control a myriad of things (*wanwu* 萬物). Understandably, the making of appropriate social divisions brings these benefits because in their concerted efforts human beings are able to achieve things that an individual alone could not. That is what leads Xunzi to remark that human life cannot be without community. In the second example, a negative scenario is provided, in which a society without social divisions leads to a set of undesirable consequences including strife, disorder, fragmentation, weakness, and insecurity. In such a predicament, a society would not be able to provide for its people and the people would not have power over other beings.[79]

At a first reading we might wonder why, according to Xunzi, horses and oxen are unable to form communities (*qun*), particularly as these animals are known to live in herds. A closer reading of the passage reveals that Xunzi understands *qun* on the basis of the ability to *fen*, here understood as the making of social divisions. This implies the appropriate delegation of social roles so that each person fulfils his or her own role in society and does not transgress it.[80] We might argue, of course, that if we were to follow Aristotle's train of thought, certain animals such as ants and bees are also social in the sense that members of their communities have specific roles to play within their group. Nonetheless, on Xunzi's terms, even those animals cannot be said to form proper communities, and neither are they capable of making social divisions (*fen*) in any real sense, since at the root of *fen* lies a sense of propriety, which humans alone can possess through self-cultivation. Therefore, for Xunzi, a sense of propriety is that which ultimately sets human beings apart from animals, and the making of social distinctions is one way in which it finds its expression. In other words, in the animal world, even where one might find social divisions, such divisions do not arise out of a moral context, and animals do not lead truly moral lives.

---

79. We might understand this negative scenario that Xunzi is cautioning against to refer to the conflict and disorder during the Warring States period during which Xunzi lived.

80. Note the *Analects* passage that calls for the appropriate delegation of social roles: 'Duke Jing of Qi asked Confucius about government. Confucius answered, "Let the ruler be a ruler, the minister a minister, the father a father, the son a son"' (12.11/32/3; trans. my own).

84 Aristotle and Xunzi on Shame

In the chapter *Contra Physiognomy*, Xunzi gives another account that differentiates humans and animals by virtue of the former's ability to make distinctions, *bian* 辨:[81]

What is it that makes a person human? I say that it lies in his ability to make distinctions (*bian* 辨).[82] To desire food when hungry, to desire warmth when cold, to desire rest when tired, and to be fond of what is beneficial and to hate what is harmful—these are characteristics that a human being is born with, and he does not have to wait to develop them. They are identical in the case of a Yu and in the case of a Jie.[83] But even so, what makes a person really human lies not primarily in his being a featherless biped, but rather in his ability to make distinctions. For example, the ape resembles a human in form and is also a featherless biped, but the gentleman will nonetheless sip a broth and eat minced meat made from him.[84] Hence, what makes a person human lies not in his being a featherless biped but in his ability to make distinctions. Even though birds and beasts have parents and offspring, there is no natural affection between them as between father and son,[85] and though there are male and female of the species, there is no proper separation of sexes. Hence, the proper way of human beings lies in nothing other than their ability to make distinctions. Of such distinctions, none is greater than *fen*. Of [the instruments for distinguishing] *fen*, none are greater than rituals. Of the sources of rituals, none are more important than the sage kings.[86]

81. Xunzi is, of course, not the only philosopher to engage with the concept of *bian*. For a fuller treatment of the role of *bian* in early Chinese thought, see Fraser 2013a, for whom the notion of *bian* 'stands at the heart of early Chinese conceptions of many cognitive activities' (ibid., 2). The character *bian* 辨 is etymologically related to its homophone, *bian* 辯, which carries the meaning of engagement in argument/disputation.

82. Knoblock translates *bian* as 'draw boundaries' (1988, I, 206), while Hutton renders it 'have distinctions' (2014, 35). I agree with Hutton in reading *bian* in a more general sense, which I take to include the making of distinctions between honour and disgrace, right (*shi*) and wrong (*fei*), and even between the Ru and the Mohists etc., as employed in different chapters of the *Xunzi*.

83. Jie, being a legendary oppressive tyrant, is the counter example to Yu, the legendary sage king.

84. Knoblock (1988, I, 297n55) comments that the reasoning here is obscure. I believe the example of the ape resonates with a passage from the chapter *On the Regulations of a King*, in which it is said that 'in physical power they [humans] are not so good as an ox, in swiftness they do not equal the horse; yet the ox and horse can be put to their use' (29/9/70). Both passages bring out the idea that even though human beings can seem to resemble animals (in the case of the ape) or even appear inferior to them (in the case of the ox and the horse), ultimately these animals serve human needs because human beings are superior by virtue of their capacity to make distinctions.

85. Again, this is a case of Xunzi denying natural affection between parent and offspring in the animal kingdom even though elsewhere he does give examples of such cases.

86. 13/5/23–8.

Human Nature and the Social Basis for Communities 85

It appears, then, that *bian*, the making of distinctions, is very closely associated with *fen*, the making of social divisions, and according to Xunzi there is no greater distinction than the making of social divisions. Ritual, in particular that established by the sage kings, serves as the instrument for distinguishing social roles. It can be understood as the ultimate form of human expression that maintains order and stability, allowing for communities to survive and thrive. As Knoblock recognises, the idea of ritual as what distinguishes humans from animals can be found in other sources of early Chinese literature such as the *Book of Rites* where it is said that only birds and beasts lack ritual. In the *Mencius*, those who fail to exercise ritual propriety, humaneness, and loyalty are said to be mad and no different from birds and beasts.[87]

Let us now turn to examine the close relationship between the two types of *bian*. We might understand that it is first by making distinctions (*bian* 辨) and social divisions that one can engage in argument or discrimination through argument (*bian* 辯).[88] In a passage which directly contradicts Mencius on the idea of *bian*, Xunzi, in an act of disputation himself, calls for the gentleman to engage in *bian*:

> The gentleman must engage in *bian* (辯). Every person without exception is fond of discussing what he finds to be good, but this is especially so with the gentleman. For this reason, whereas the petty man engages in *bian* to discuss threats of danger, the gentleman engages in them to discuss humaneness. [. . .] Hence, advocating humaneness is of primary importance.[89]

For sure, this passage does not explicitly mention *bian* (argument) in relation to *bian* (the making of distinctions). Nonetheless, it is stated that every person is fond of discussing what he finds to be good, and that the gentleman engages in *bian* (argument) to discuss humaneness. Reaching an understanding of what is 'good' or 'humane' and in turn discussing it necessarily involves the making of distinctions, which, we are told elsewhere, is what distinguishes humans from

---

87. 8.28/43/32–8.38/44/8.

88. Knoblock translates *bian* 辯 as 'make discriminations'; therefore, he appears to take it as a synonym of *bian* 辨, which he translates as 'draw boundaries'. Hutton translates the line as 'the gentleman is sure to engage in argument', which rightly highlights the linguistic aspect of *bian* 辯. Fraser (2016, 313) claims that *bian* 辯 and *bian* 辨 are used interchangeably in the *Xunzi*, suggesting that 'Xunzi may have regarded them as alternate forms of a single word with two uses'. The two *bian* are clearly related, though the evidence suggests that they are sometimes but not always interchangeable. *Bian* 辯 is virtually always used in a verbal context, being frequently used in relation to *yan* 言, *ci* 辭 and *shuo/shui* 說. Passages concerning *bian* 辨, on the other hand, tend to emphasise the making of distinctions and are not restricted to speech.

89. 14/5/53–15/5/57. *Cf.* also 14/5/42.

86 *Aristotle and Xunzi on Shame*

animals. Therefore, there is sufficient textual evidence for us to establish the link between the making of distinctions and argument, and to understand that argument of the good sort is based upon a correct understanding of what constitutes propriety and humaneness. Chris Fraser notes that for Xunzi as well as for other classical Chinese dialecticians, 'the outcome of what we would call an argument, debate, or piece of reasoning was to draw a distinction one way rather than another'.[90] As has already been observed, Xunzi is not alone in recognising the importance of persuasion and discrimination as there are cases in other early Chinese texts where words are said to embellish a person's thoughts.[91] The positive approach that Xunzi adopts towards *bian* departs markedly from his immediate predecessor Mencius, who claims not to be fond of disputing but to be compelled to do it.[92] Nonetheless, as Fraser notes, Xunzi's view of disputation is not entirely positive—disputation is a necessary measure to prevent deviant teachings from causing disorder.[93] Those who 'dispute without use' (*bian er wu yong* 辯而無用), for example, are criticised in the chapter *Against the Twelve*.[94] For Xunzi, therefore, disputation is a reflection of the disputer's moral disposition, and the only kind that is to be commended is that in which the gentleman engages.

Xunzi does not explicitly say that *bian* (argument) is distinctive of humans; this marks a departure from Aristotle who distinguishes between voice and speech, the latter being a specifically human capacity. Yet there is no need for Xunzi to spell out the fact that animals cannot engage in argument—it goes without saying that they cannot do so. What is at stake is that *bian* (argument) relates to *bian* (the making of distinctions), just as *logos* (speech) relates to *logos* (the reasoning capacity), and it is by virtue of engaging in *logos* and *bian* in their multiplicity of senses that humans are distinguished from animals. An important commonality that Aristotle and Xunzi share is that both speak of human beings as having certain capacities that allow for community living; indeed, a community-oriented nature is an integral part of being human and distinguishes humans from animals. All humans are capable of speech (*logos*), just as all humans are capable of argument (*bian*), though that is not to say that all are capable of making the right kinds of speech or the right kinds of argument—only certain members of society are capable of doing so to further the good of the community.

90. Fraser 2016, 313.
91. *Cf.* Knoblock 1988, I, 201–02.
92. *Mencius* 6.9/34/15.
93. Fraser 2016, 313–14.
94. See Goldin (1999, 83ff.) for a discussion of Xunzi's reactions to the 'dialecticians' (*bianzhe* 辯者).

Both *logos* (speech) and *bian* (argument/disputation) can be situated in a heavily political context. In the Warring States, disputation often took place in the form of a public debate in the court, where advisors engaged in *shui* and *bian* in front of a political authority.[95] In the Greek case, public speech was very much a focal part of community life, taking place in assemblies and law courts and in other social institutions. What emerges from the comparisons earlier is that Xunzi's account of *bian* has strong resonances with Aristotle's conception of the role of *logos* in human political life. In both cases, human speech (*logos*) or engagement in argument (*bian*) provides a medium through which one is able to convey one's own values, reached through a process of deliberation or discrimination, to other members of society. Furthermore, in both cases, the making of speeches implies the making of value judgments, as reflected in the etymology of *bian* and *logos*. For Aristotle, *logos* allows one to make clear the advantageous and the harmful, and therefore the just and the unjust, and the good and bad. It equips humans well for community life, making them political in a different sense from other animals.[96] For Xunzi, *bian* involves arguing for what one finds to be good (*shan* 善), understood to have been reached through making distinctions (*bian* 辨); the gentleman must engage in *bian* so that *his* conception of the good, rather than that of the petty man, becomes a standard or norm for others to follow. *Bian* and *logos*, then, both involve discriminating between sets of opposite values so that society members can voice their values and make collective judgments that might further community life.

NATURE, EMOTIONS, AND MORALITY

In the early Chinese philosophical tradition, there is no direct equivalent to the Greek idea of *logos*, which has a very wide semantic range. Indeed, there is no one word that would correspond directly to 'rational' or 'rationality' in the Chinese corpus. But that is not to say that the idea of rationality does not figure in Chinese philosophy, or that the Chinese philosophers did not consider it important for humans to possess the capacity for rational decision-making.

Joseph Needham, in making a comparison between the *scala naturae* in Aristotle and Xunzi in volume 2 of *Science and Civilisation in China*, observes: 'It is typical of Chinese thought that what particularly characterised man should have been expressed as the sense of justice rather than the power of reasoning.'[97]

---

95. See Fraser 2016.

96. *Cf.* Saunders 1995, 69: 'Men are thus "fit for a state to a fuller extent": they are better *equipped*, in such a way as to be able to live in the complex association, *koinōnia*, which is the *state*.'

97. Needham 1956, 23.

88   *Aristotle and Xunzi on Shame*

Sterckx has—rightly in my opinion—expressed criticism of Needham's pitching morality against reason.[98] Indeed, Xunzi highlights humans' sense of propriety and Aristotle their reasoning capacity so that on the surface, they appear to be flagging up different qualities that they believe to be specific to humans. However, what we are confronted with is not a direct contrast—there is much that the two philosophers hold in common. For Xunzi, the correct functioning of the heart-mind allows the agent to act upon a certain degree of reflection and rational calculation rather than the primal responses and selfish tendencies that humans have by birth. In so doing, one exercises a sense of propriety which is against humans' inborn tendencies, indicating that rational thinking or reflection is involved. For Aristotle, by virtue of having the reasoning capacity, human beings are equipped with the ability to make moral choices, exercising both intellectual and practical virtues. Good purposive choice (*prohairesis spoudaia*) requires the reasoning to be true and the desire to be right (*EN* 1139a23–6), so that the two parts of the soul, the rational and the non-rational, are in harmony with each other. Animals, on the other hand, do not have purposive choice and cannot be virtuous in the strict sense—they, like children, only possess 'natural' virtue. As Aristotle says in the *Nicomachean Ethics*, 'the purpose of our examination is not to know what virtue is, but to become good, since otherwise the inquiry would be of no benefit to us' (*EN* 1103b27–9). Ultimately, for both Xunzi and Aristotle, the moral and the rational are closely intertwined: being moral would imply being rational, and humans, alone among the animals, are rational beings capable of leading moral lives, provided that they succeed in cultivating their ethical sense. However, the difference between the two is that for Xunzi, 'rationality' is couched in the terms of 'a sense of propriety' or 'morality', while for Aristotle, it is the other way around—humans are first and foremost defined by their reasoning capacity, which is the faculty that grants them the capacity to be moral. Difficult concepts such as 'rationality', then, translate differently into the philosophical language of different cultural traditions. Comparing the Chinese tradition with the Greek, and more specifically in this case Xunzi with Aristotle, alerts us to the fact that one often has to look beneath the surface of certain claims to uncover what is shared and what is distinctive about two philosophers, or philosophical traditions.

I have examined from a variety of perspectives the ways in which Aristotle and Xunzi construct their views of human nature, showing that both philosophers present us with a taxonomy whereby humans are distinguished from animals by having certain distinctive qualities, which involve, for Aristotle, the

---

98. Sterckx 2002, 89.

Human Nature and the Social Basis for Communities   89

reasoning capacity and for Xunzi, the sense of propriety. By way of discussing different kinds of courage, Aristotle and Xunzi distinguish humans' qualities from those of animals, including conveying (if only sometimes implicitly) the idea that a sense of shame is unique to humans. For Aristotle and Xunzi, animals do experience courage, but their kind of courage is on both accounts strongly contrasted with 'true' forms of courage. Animals in Aristotle's example are impelled to meet danger, while Xunzi's dog and boar do not try to avoid death or injury, both displaying a reckless kind of behaviour that does not arise out of a measured judgment of the situation, or proper knowledge about what is to be pursued or avoided; rather, they rely on an instinctive impulse that resembles an automatic response to external stimuli. The lack of a sense of shame in animals appears to be a crucial indicator of their lack of morality: it is by virtue of *aidōs* that one acts out of considerations for the fine, and by virtue of *lianchi* that Xunzi's gentleman correctly weighs the threat of death and the upholding of a sense of propriety. In other words, well-cultivated humans have a sense of shame as their moral compass, which distinguishes them from animals.

The summary I have given so far applies specifically to Aristotle and Xunzi; as has been pointed out by commentators, generalising about the ancient writers on the issue of animal morality can be problematic, when positions were heterogeneous. For sure, the Stoics were influential in their view that animals are irrational and cannot form judgments, including comprehending the impression of the disgraceful.[99] Yet, as Stephen Newmyer has shown, 'there is evidence that at least some ancient philosophers and naturists identified this emotion [a sense of shame] in certain non-human species', among them Pliny and Plutarch,[100] echoing discussions by contemporary ethologist Frans de Waal on the question of whether dogs can experience shame or at least exhibit shame-like behaviour.[101]

---

99. *Discourses* 3.27. The Stoics attribute animals' lack of rationality and their inability to form judgments to their absence of speech. Cf. Newmyer (2017, 54) on this point: 'While Aristotle only hints here at the ethical ramifications of a lack of a capacity for meaningful speech for non-human animals, the Stoics made the idea of the absence of speech in non-humans a cornerstone of their ethical system.' On the idea of *aidōs* in Epictetus, see Kamtekar 1998.

100. Newmyer 2017, 89.

101. De Waal 1996, 106–09. It is interesting to note that, for the ancient Greeks, the dog was frequently seen as the symbol for shamelessness, lacking in *aidōs*, which Franco (2014, 81) translates to a lack of restraint, 'the sense of shame that most effectively regulates social equilibrium'; see also ibid., 216n22. As Franco points out, 'dog-faced' is used as an insult for women who lack a sense of *aidōs* towards their husband and transgress social norms by breaking marital fidelity, an example being Aphrodite who is called a 'dog-faced girl' by Hephaestus after she is found to have committed adultery with Ares (*Od.* 8.319).

90 *Aristotle and Xunzi on Shame*

Certainly, there are commonalities in the questions posed in the ancient sources and in contemporary research: What marks out humans from other animals? What emotions can be ascribed to other animals and are these really emotions? More specifically, do animals experience shame, and what does that reveal about their emotional capacity and morality? At the same time, there are striking differences in the ancient and modern debates: we generally adhere to a robust evolutionary theory that tends to stress continuity, which can complicate the task of identifying differences. On the other hand, there is a recent tendency to ascribe to animals certain features that were previously commonly considered unique to the human species, the general shift in attempting to see the 'humane' in animal behaviour explained by two main developments in recent decades: firstly, the animal rights movement, a concept that was absent in the ancient world, and secondly, scientific advances in the areas of ethology, zoology, and neuroscience, which have revealed for the first time similarities between humans and certain species of animals in terms of brain structure and substance, so that the issues nowadays are not to be solved by introspection, but by experiment. The idea that morality is a distinctively human characteristic has been repeatedly challenged in recent discourse, marked by a general departure from the anthropocentric viewpoint or the 'man alone of animals' *topos*.[102] If morality is unique to human beings, is it inborn or acquired? And if it is not, to what degree do animals share in it? Indeed, can we legitimately analyse animal behaviour on the basis of human behaviour, inclinations, and thought processes? These are some of the questions that have sparked debate in recent decades. In answering the question whether animals can be moral, one important criterion has been their capacity to experience emotions (in particular 'secondary' or 'social' emotions as opposed to 'primary' emotions that are considered basic or reflex-like). The existing literature on human and nonhuman behaviour and cognition is vast and extends across a range of fields, though it is possible to highlight a small selection of literature to show how current concerns reflect debates which have been ongoing since antiquity. For example, while de Waal argues that human morality is on a continuum with animal sociality, he does not come to any definitive conclusions as to whether animals are moral beings. Marc Bekoff discusses the emotional lives of animals and animals' social play behaviour, making the stronger claim that 'some animals might be moral beings'.[103] Mark Rowlands argues from a philosophical perspective that Bekoff and Pierce are in fact not so different from their

102. For a helpful overview of this *topos*, see Newmyer 2017.
103. Bekoff 2007, 86.

predecessors Hume, Darwin, and de Waal in their position on animal behaviour. He stands by the even stronger claim that 'animals can be moral subjects in the sense that they can act on the basis of moral reasons, where these reasons take the form of emotions with identifiable moral content.'[104] Newmyer remarks that 'it seems likely that as the discipline advances, the findings of cognitive ethology will prove immensely useful in interpreting Greco-Roman attempts to delineate the emotional states of nonhuman animals.'[105] I believe that studying the ways that the ancients discussed the capacities of humans and animals and identified what was special about the human condition can in fact illuminate contemporary thought. The ancients may not have had the technological vantage point in examining and assessing animal behaviour; nonetheless, some of the issues that they grappled with on the topic of animal and human nature are still being debated today, including the important question of the role that the emotions play in a moral life, as well as the issue of whether morality is inborn or acquired.[106]

Going back to Aristotle and Xunzi, it is appropriate to highlight the important idea of habituation, which plays a crucial role in the fulfilment of human potential and the cultivation of the good life. Having identified *eudaimonia* as the human good and defined it as the activity of the soul in accordance with excellence, Aristotle speaks of the need to habituate oneself to performing the right kinds of actions and taking pleasure and pain in the right kinds of things. Thus our human nature in its habituation process needs *aidōs* in order that from an early stage we associate honour with pleasure and disgrace with pain to stop ourselves from making mistakes. Without this intermediate and auxiliary stage, the child finds himself being propelled merely by desires, just like the primal responses of animals, and is unable to 'activate' the capacity for reason which defines him as a human being. While Xunzi does not attribute a sense of shame to a particular stage in one's life, it is nevertheless something that is to be acquired, just like a sense of propriety, which will allow humans to flourish.

Yet the path to excellence may not be easy, as Aristotle cautions:

> Most people are not the sort to be guided by a sense of shame but by fear, and not to refrain from bad things on the grounds of their shamefulness but because of the punishments; living by emotion as they do, they pursue their own kinds of pleasures and the means to these, and shun the

---

104. Rowlands 2012, 35.

105. Newymer 2017, 96.

106. On the Veneer Theory, the idea that human morality is 'a cultural overlay, a thin veneer hiding an otherwise selfish and brutish nature', see de Waal 2009.

92   Aristotle and Xunzi on Shame

opposing pains, while not even having a conception of the fine and the truly pleasant, since they have had no taste of it.[107]

As has already been observed by some scholars, this passage elevates the status of *aidōs* somewhat so that it becomes associated with acting for the sake of what is fine and truly pleasant.[108] It points out that by nature most people are more likely to act through fear of punishment rather than through shame (even though *aidōs* is also associated with pain, it is a fear of disrepute rather than fear of punishment). Without education it would be difficult, if not impossible, to acquire a sense of what constitutes honourable and shameful behaviour and indeed even with education, some may still simply seek after pleasures rather than observe the standard of right and wrong that is defined by the honourable and the shameful. This acknowledgement of the natural tendencies of human beings that might stand in the way of moral education resonates with Xunzi's idea that everyone is born with a desire for personal benefit. With this thought, I now turn to the next chapter, to examine the role of shame on the path to moral goodness.

---

107. οὐ γὰρ πεφύκασιν αἰδοῖ πειθαρχεῖν ἀλλὰ φόβῳ, οὐδ᾽ ἀπέχεσθαι τῶν φαύλων διὰ τὸ αἰσχρὸν ἀλλὰ διὰ τὰς τιμωρίας· πάθει γὰρ ζῶντες τὰς οἰκείας ἡδονὰς διώκουσι καὶ δι᾽ ὧν αὗται ἔσονται, φεύγουσι δὲ τὰς ἀντικειμένας λύπας, τοῦ δὲ καλοῦ καὶ ὡς ἀληθῶς ἡδέος οὐδ᾽ ἔννοιαν ἔχουσιν, ἄγευστοι ὄντες (*EN* 1179b11–16).

108. *Cf.* Cairns 1993, 423–25.

4

Shame and the Path to Moral Goodness

Moral Education and the Ideal

The metaphor of the warped wood, strikingly employed by both Aristotle and Xunzi, provides a pertinent case for illustrating the relationship between human nature and the cultivation of morals in the two philosophers' accounts. Let us consider the following passages:

> We should consider the things that we ourselves, too, are more readily drawn towards, for different people have different natural inclinations; and this is something we shall be able to recognise from the pleasure and the pain that things bring about in us. We should drag ourselves away in the opposite direction; for by pulling far away from error we shall arrive at the intermediate point, in the way people do when they are straightening out warped pieces of wood.[1]
>
> — Aristotle

> Warped wood must await a straightening board, steaming and straightening before it will be straight.[2]

> Thus wood marked by the ink-line will become straight, and metal that is put to the whetstone will become sharp. The gentleman who studies widely and examines himself thrice each day will become clear in his knowledge and faultless in his conduct.[3]
>
> — Xunzi

What are we to make of these similes on moral self-cultivation, juxtaposed in this way? While both Aristotle and Xunzi recognise that a human being is endowed with the capacity to become a well cultivated person—a *phronimos* or a *junzi*—it is admittedly, because of humans' natural tendencies, a journey

---

1. σκοπεῖν δὲ δεῖ πρὸς ἃ καὶ αὐτοὶ εὐκατάφοροί ἐσμεν· ἄλλοι γὰρ πρὸς ἄλλα πεφύκαμεν· τοῦτο δ' ἔσται γνώριμον ἐκ τῆς ἡδονῆς καὶ τῆς λύπης τῆς γινομένης περὶ ἡμᾶς. εἰς τοὐναντίον δ' ἑαυτοὺς ἀφέλκειν δεῖ· πολὺ γὰρ ἀπάγοντες τοῦ ἁμαρτάνειν εἰς τὸ μέσον ἥξομεν, ὅπερ οἱ τὰ διεστραμμένα τῶν ξύλων ὀρθοῦντες ποιοῦσιν (*EN* 1109b1-7).

2. 故枸木必將待檃栝、烝、矯然後直 (87/23/5).

3. 故木受繩則直，金就礪則利，君子博學而日參省乎己，則智明而行無過矣 (1/1/2-3).

Aristotle and Xunzi on Shame, Moral Education, and the Good Life. Jingyi Jenny Zhao, Oxford University Press.
© Oxford University Press 2024. DOI: 10.1093/oso/9780197773161.003.0005

94   *Aristotle and Xunzi on Shame*

fraught with difficulties that must be overcome. A piece of wood that is naturally warped can be straightened; however, it is of utmost importance to recognise what might be effective in correcting the wood and straightening it. Xunzi chooses to pursue the line that 'human nature is bad' in order to convey the message that without education, one cannot realise one's potential to act in accordance with a sense of propriety and become the 'noblest under heaven'. His words counter with vehement rhetoric Mencius' claim that 'human nature is good' as well as Gaozi's claim, documented in the *Mencius*, that human nature is neither good nor bad. Yet, as I have already shown, Xunzi stresses, no less than Mencius, what is uniquely human and the necessity to realise that potential. For example, Xunzi compares humans who fight and have no sense of shame (*lianchi*) or propriety to animals that supposedly lack these qualities. Human beings are expected to have a sense of shame, and this extends to knowing where humans stand in relation to other animals. Unlike Mencius and Xunzi, Aristotle does not pursue the topic of human nature through the question of whether it is 'good' or 'bad'; rather, he says that 'the excellences develop in us neither by nature nor contrary to nature, but because we are naturally able to receive them and they are brought to completion by means of habituation'.[4] The teleological nature of his ethics comes to the fore through the expression *teleioumenois* in the passage; without habituation, the excellences would not be brought to completion.[5] In this way, for both philosophers, education and the accumulation of good practices are essential for one to develop into a human being in the fullest sense. As I shall attempt to show, both philosophers attribute a crucial role to 'shame' and related concepts in moral education and emphasise the internalisation of values within the agent himself (an idea which I shall come to explain), even though they differ in postulating exactly how such concepts can guide one to make the correct choices on the moral path.

Now, what does 'moral education' signify for the ancient philosophers? The phrase 'moral self-cultivation', which pervades much contemporary scholarship on Confucian ethics, helpfully draws attention to the idea that education is not a simple matter of the reception of an outside influence, but that it must also involve the active will and effort of the individual who accepts what is taught, gradually forms an understanding of why he should be taught those things, and tries to contribute to the success of that education himself by monitoring his own words and actions. In this way, education is not a one-way process of the educator

---

4. οὔτ' ἄρα φύσει οὔτε παρὰ φύσιν ἐγγίνονται αἱ ἀρεταί, ἀλλὰ πεφυκόσι μὲν ἡμῖν δέξασθαι αὐτάς, τελειουμένοις δὲ διὰ τοῦ ἔθους (*EN* 1103a23–26).

5. In *EN* 1179b20-31, Aristotle mentions nature and teaching as the other contributing factors to developing the excellences.

Shame and the Path to Moral Goodness 95

moulding an individual, but also involves recognition by the agent that he has the capacity to be cultivated and that it is a worthwhile activity to better himself through the cultivation process.[6] The concept in ancient Greek that is most commonly seen as the parallel to 'education' would be *paideia*, a word that has a broad meaning, extending from the acquisition of skills to notions of what is fine and what is disgraceful, both aspects of which are relevant to what one might mean in English by 'education', also a broad term. For Aristotle, moral education involves possessing intellectual as well as moral virtues so that one becomes habituated to performing the right kind of actions, doing them for the sake of the fine (*to kalon*) itself and leading a life of *eudaimonia*, which is the activity of the rational part of the soul in accordance with the virtues.[7] For Xunzi, learning (*xue* 學) is a prominent idea that pervades the corpus of the work, while *jiaohua* 教化 is commonly used to indicate personal transformation (usually in terms of moral disposition) as a result of teaching. The goal of moral education lies in the transformation of one's inborn character or natural tendencies through learning and self-cultivation (*xiushen* 修身) so as to act in accordance with what is prescribed by ritual and a sense of propriety (*liyi* 禮義). Although Aristotle's and Xunzi's conceptual frameworks of moral education differ, both consider it important to meet the goal or the ideal that is seen as the best state for a human being. As will become evident below, ideas of honour and shame are critical elements in an individual's moral development and in the achievement of the ideal.

Shame and the Pursuit of Goods

For Aristotle and Xunzi, notions of the fine and the honourable as well as their opposites have significant educative value for judging the place of the various goods in life such as pleasure, reputation, and personal benefit. Such notions guide one to pursue actions that are regarded as worthwhile by society and/ or by the individual, and to avoid others. This section examines in turn how Aristotle and Xunzi portray a priority of goods in life through shame-related discourse.

As is known, Aristotle paints an ambivalent picture of the relationship between *aidōs* and *aretē*, and between *aidōs* and *to kalon*. In some passages, *aidōs* bears a close relationship to virtue. In III.8, civic courage is said to come about

---

6. On 'self-cultivation' in early Chinese literature, see Weingarten 2015. For a critique of the psychological basis for 'moral self-cultivation' East and West, see Slote 2020, chapter 3.

7. Aristotle's conception of *eudaimonia* is associated with political activity in the earlier books and contemplation in Book X of the *EN*. There have been extended debates concerning ways to reconcile the contemplative and the practical life. Given the limitations of space, I will not treat this problem here but one may consult, for example, Ackrill 1980 and Cooper 1999 on this topic.

96 Aristotle and Xunzi on Shame

from virtue (*di' aretēn ginetai, EN* 1116a27–28), from *aidōs* and the desire of a noble object (i.e., honour). A distinction is made between civic courage, which is prompted by shame and the desire for honour,[8] and true courage, which is prompted by an aspiration towards the fine.[9] Even though civic courage is not identical with true courage, it is said to be most like it (*EN* 1116a17). Elsewhere, Aristotle remarks that there are modes of observing a mean in the sphere of and in relation to the *pathē*,[10] and *aidōs* and the *aidēmōn*—the modest person—are to be praised.[11] The description of the *aidēmōn* as a mean between the bashful (*kataplēx*) and the shameless (*anaischuntos*) recalls Aristotle's description of what a virtue is, which lies as a mean between the excessive and the deficient.[12] Similarly in the *EE, aidōs* is placed between two extremes, shamelessness (*anaischuntia*) and bashfulness (*kataplēxis*). The shameless person pays regard to nobody's opinion; the bashful person pays regard to everybody's opinion. The *aidēmōn* or the 'modest' person, on the other hand, regards the opinion of those that appear good;[13] he is properly disposed to feel shame since he is correct about whose opinion he should heed and where the source of social approval should lie. The praiseworthy nature of *aidōs* in the passages above makes it appear positive.

Sometimes, actions done out of a sense of honour or shame are closely assimilated to ideas of the fine itself. For example, in Aristotle's discussions of the magnanimous person (*megalopsuchos*), it is said that 'sometimes we praise the honour-loving person as someone who is manly and loves what is fine' (*EN* 1125b11–12) and that 'honour is a prize of excellence and is meted out to the good' (*EN* 1123b35–1124a1). Book X of the *EN* provides further evidence that having a sense of *aidōs* is to be praised, as we see Aristotle separating those who by nature are driven by a sense of shame and those—the many—who are moved only by fear (*EN* 1179b11–16). In making logical sense of the phrasing, it appears that Aristotle associates those who obey a sense of shame with abstaining from bad actions on account of their baseness, and those who obey fear with abstaining from bad actions through fear of punishment. Shunning bad actions because of their baseness suggests a genuine concern for the ethical character

---

8. δι' αἰδῶ γὰρ καὶ διὰ καλοῦ ὄρεξιν (τιμῆς γάρ) καὶ φυγὴν ὀνείδους, αἰσχροῦ ὄντος (*EN* 1116a28–29).

9. καλοῦ δὴ ἕνεκα ὁ ἀνδρεῖος ὑπομένει καὶ πράττει τὰ κατὰ τὴν ἀνδρείαν (*EN* 1115b23–24).

10. εἰσὶ δὲ καὶ ἐν τοῖς παθήμασι καὶ περὶ τὰ πάθη μεσότητες (*EN* 1108a30–31).

11. *EN* 1108a31–32. Note that this appears to conflict with some parts of the ethics, for example, *EN* II.5 and *EE* II.2, where Aristotle restricts praise and blame to capacities and dispositions only. See discussion in Jimenez 2020, 150–59.

12. *EN* 1108a33–34.

13. αἰδὼς δὲ μεσότης ἀναισχυντίας καὶ καταπλήξεως· ὁ μὲν γὰρ μηδεμιᾶς φροντίζων δόξης ἀναίσχυντος, ὁ δὲ πάσης ὁμοίως καταπλήξ, ὁ δὲ τῆς τῶν φαινομένων ἐπιεικῶν αἰδήμων (*EE* 1233b26–29).

of one's actions, hence this passage serves as further challenge to the idea that *aidōs* is solely concerned with conforming to social standards of what is noble.

Despite these assimilations to virtue and to the idea of the fine itself,[14] Aristotle explicitly denies that *aidōs* is a virtue in *EN* II.7 and IV.9. In Book IV, Aristotle gives a detailed treatment of *aidōs* and describes it as proper only to the young, but not to the older person (*EN* 1128b15–16). He then moves onto say that the decent person (*epieikēs*) simply should not experience shame regardless of whether the feeling is associated with past, present or future events because he should not find himself in a situation where shame would be appropriate. Shame is 'conditionally' or 'hypothetically' good in the sense that if he were to act disgracefully in a hypothetical situation, he would feel ashamed. Aristotle, it would seem, paints a rather unrealistic picture whereby the older person is expected to be morally perfect in his conduct so that shame would have no part to play in his life. One might find Aristotle's denial of shame to the decent person problematic—indeed, Aristotle himself is criticised for not attributing a prominent position to shame in his ethics.[15] Bryan Van Norden, for example, argues that Aristotle conflates 'the emotion of shame with a sense of shame',[16] believing Mencius and other early Confucians to be much clearer about the nature and significance of shame and related concepts than Aristotle and many other Western philosophers.[17] Along similar lines, though speaking in more general terms, Deonna et al. argue that one should distinguish between the 'moral aspects of dispositions associated with the sense of shame', that is, shame in its dispositional sense, and 'shame episodes', that is, shame in its occurrent sense. According to Deonna et al., focusing entirely on the latter sense leads one to think of this emotion in negative moral terms, when indeed a *sense* of shame, suggesting ideas of modesty, propriety and even honour, can have positive associations.[18] Indeed, one might say that Xunzi manages to avoid criticism of this kind since for him, *lianchi* carries the dispositional sense of 'a sense of shame', being something that the petty people are devoid of. Furthermore, Xunzi allows that one may feel a sense of shame on behalf of others' conduct, with *chi* in its verbal sense being often 'other-directed' and taking on the sense of

---

14. Note that *aidōs* is associated with *sōphrosunē* in *EE* 1234a32–33.

15. Cf. Taylor 2006, 235: 'Aristotle's insistence on that sensitivity (to what it would be fine or noble to do) as central to the motivation of the virtuous person ought to lead him to give a correspondingly prominent place to a sense of shame in that sensitivity.' On the issue of Aristotle's denial of shame as a virtue, see Raymond (2017, 159), who concludes that 'given that Aristotle acknowledges specific virtues concerned with honours great and small, there is no obvious reason why a sense of shame, properly circumscribed, should be denied the same status'.

16. Van Norden 2002, 52.

17. Ibid., 52n13.

18. Deonna et al. 2011, 11–12.

98   *Aristotle and Xunzi on Shame*

contempt. Thus in Xunzi's philosophy, one finds both the dispositional and occurrent senses of 'shame' at play, though they are not explicitly defined as such. Without defining *xiu* or *chi* as a virtue or a disposition, Xunzi avoids running into some of the difficulties that Aristotle does in defining *aidōs* and *aischunē* and categorising them as *pathē*.

Aidōs for Aristotle therefore belongs only to an intermediate stage in moral development, construed as of particular importance to the young who are on their path to excellence, who may be especially prone to experiencing the affection due to a number of factors. First, Aristotle attributes the appropriateness for the young to have *aidōs* to their living by affections and making many mistakes:

> But the affection in this case is not fitting for every time of life, only for youth; for we think that young people should have a sense of shame (*aidēmonas einai*) because they live by affection and so get many things wrong, but are held back by a sense of shame (*hupo tēs aidous de kōluesthai*); and we praise those young people who have it, whereas no one would praise an older person for being prone to feeling shame (*aischuntēlos*), since we think it necessary that he does nothing that gives rise to shame (*aischunē*). (*EN* 1128b15–21)

This statement, however, does not explain how living by affections might lead to inappropriate behaviour. To answer that question, we need to look to other parts of the *EN* where Aristotle discusses the particular characteristics of the young, and also to *Rhetoric* II.12 which features the various types of human character in relation to affections, states of character, age and fortune and starts with the youthful type of character.

First, the young are described as *epithumētikoi*, and changeable and fickle in their desires. They act by gratifying their desires, especially with regard to bodily ones. Furthermore, they live by affection, and more than anything pursue what is pleasant for them and what is immediately before them (*EN* 1156a32–3). Young people lack self-control (*akrateis*, *Rhet.* 1389a5), which, as we learn from Book III of the *EN*, means that actions are committed from appetitive desire (*epithumia*) but not purposive choice (*prohairesis*) (*EN* 1111b13–14). Purposive choice is deliberate desire (*orexis bouleutikē*), and good purposive choice (*prohairesis spoudaia*) requires the reasoning to be true and the desire to be right (*EN* 1139a23–5), so that the two parts of the soul, the rational and the non-rational, are in harmony with each other. It appears, then, that young people are prone to making mistakes because, when they act, they are driven by desire and have a tendency to pursue the pleasant at the expense of overriding rational judgment. That may explain also why their mistakes are in the direction of doing things excessively and vehemently (*Rhet.* 1389b2–3) and why their actions fail to arrive at the mean.

Apart from being prone to be swayed by affections and desires, young people are said to have a love of honour (*philotimia*) and cannot bear being slighted (*Rhet.* 1389a10–11). They are prone to shame (*aischunteloi*) and accept the rules of society in which they have been trained, but do not yet believe in any other standard of honour (*Rhet.* 1389a28–9). Those who experience shame, then, are aware of a social standard against which their actions and thoughts will be judged, and of the fact that they are members of a community with certain shared notions of right and wrong. We might imagine that someone who is indifferent to social standards of the 'fine' and the 'shameful' will live a lawless life resembling that of the Cyclopes who do not participate in community life but care only for themselves.[19] However, that idea is almost inconceivable since for us as well as for Aristotle, human beings live in societies (though of course the society that Aristotle envisages as a norm would be a *polis*) and are to a great extent dependent upon their communities for resources, interaction and personal development. A sense of shame, therefore, appears to be a prerequisite for a young person wishing to be integrated into the operations of the society in which he lives and not to be excluded as an outcast. Young people's honour-loving character may again be traced to their *epithumetikoi* nature, since for Aristotle *epithumiai* are not limited to bodily desires, but on occasion also extend to desire for wealth, victory and honour (*EN* 1148a25–6, *Rhet.* 1369a12–1, 1370b32–4).[20] As a result, the young strive towards anything that may gain them honour and they shun anything that may bring disgrace, so that love of honour motivates them to seek the honourable and reject the shameful.

Friendship plays an important role in young people's pursuit of excellence by helping them avoid mistakes (*EN* 1155a12–13); it can be seen as the third defining feature of young people's lives that encourages them to pursue honour and avoid shame. In the *Rhetoric*, we are told that people compete with their equals for honour (*Rhet.* 1384a31), that we find it shameful (*aischron*) if

---

19. In *Od.* 9.106–15, words such as '*athemiston*' and '*oute themistes*' are used to describe the Cyclopes, indicating that, unlike humans, they are not community-oriented. Aristotle uses *sporades* to describe the Cyclopes who live in scattered households (*Pol.* 1252b22–3). Cf. Lloyd 2009, 643: 'The Cyclopes, the Laestrygonians, the Lotus-Eaters, are just so many cases of social groups that deviate from the norm, helping to define that norm by their very deviations'.

20. For a detailed examination of *epithumia* and the scope of its objects, see Pearson 2012, 91–110. Pearson argues that the notion of *epithumia* 'is one which retains the link to pleasure, but extends the notion of pleasure in play to include other kinds of bodily pleasures and also non-bodily pleasures, such as pleasures of learning or victory. Aristotle thus appears to employ two different notions of *epithumia*, one narrow, one broad' (ibid., 110). One could say that Aristotle does not have two different notions of *epithumia* but two ranges of application.

100 *Aristotle and Xunzi on Shame*

we lack a share 'in the honourable things shared by everyone else, or by all or nearly all who are like ourselves' (*Rhet*. 1384a11–12), and that 'we feel most shame (*aischunontai*) before those who will always be with us and those who notice what we do, since in both cases their eyes are upon us' (*Rhet*. 1384a34–b1). Because young people spend much time in the company of friends whose judgments they greatly esteem and because they consider it shameful to lack a share in the honourable things shared by everyone else, for Aristotle, friends inadvertently act as monitors for one another by encouraging them to compete in the pursuit of honour. Friendships can be, of course, for interest, pleasure or for the good, according to Aristotle. Good friendships are those that exert positive peer pressure, helping the friends avoid mistakes and steering them onto the right path.[21]

Aristotle's discussion of different types of courage and assessment of the kinds of motivations behind them in *EN* III.7–8 shed light on his disinclination to attribute *aidōs* to an older and decent person. I have already mentioned the examples of courage in the previous chapter, focusing there on the distinctions between spirited courage and civic courage to highlight human beings' unique characteristics which distinguish them from animals. Let us now probe more deeply into the differences between the *truly* courageous person and the *civically* courageous, in terms of what they endure dangers for. This will help to explain how Aristotle distinguishes between internal and external factors in one's decision-making. The distinctions are drawn very clearly: the courageous person acts for the sake of the fine (*EN* 1115b23–24), while the civically courageous acts to avoid the penalties imposed by the laws and the reproaches he would otherwise incur, and on account of the honours that he could gain by undertaking such actions (*EN* 1116a18–19). The civically courageous person therefore acts not for the sake of 'the fine' *qua* fine, but out of concerns for external recognition, which should only come as a consequence or 'by-product' of fine actions and not as the motivator of the fine actions. Often enough, of course, what is prescribed by society and followed by the civically courageous person may just be what the truly virtuous person himself would choose to do. However, though the truly courageous and the civically courageous may both receive honour for their actions and accomplishments, they can be distinguished by their motivations.

In the existing literature, there is disagreement about what the difference between the civically courageous and the truly courageous person amounts to. Myles Burnyeat notes that shame, as a 'semi-virtue of the learner', allows one

---

21. For the idea that friends can help those in their prime towards fine action, see *EN* 1155a12–15.

to find pleasure in noble things and therefore make the right sorts of associations that are necessary for moral development.[22] Following this approach, Marta Jimenez terms shame a 'proto-virtue', that is, as a precursor to virtue.[23] Jimenez finds problems with the standard view of shame as predominantly a desire for reputation and instead argues that it is 'ultimately concerned with virtue and the noble'[24]. In her view, honours and reproaches 'are not only (or even mainly) goals and anti-goals for honor-lovers; they also function as guides and encouragements for character formation'.[25] She therefore sees a much closer resemblance between civic courage and true courage than is traditionally assumed.[26] Zena Hitz on the other hand has argued for a very different take on the role of shame in the acquisition of virtue. She believes that the one who acts for the sake of the fine and the one who acts out of a sense of shame do not reflect different *stages* in moral education, but different *kinds* of education altogether, so that different kinds of motivations are involved.[27] I am sympathetic to Hitz's views to a certain extent, particularly the idea that a method of education that relies too heavily on external incentives could be harmful to a person's moral development. Nonetheless, I am inclined to view the honour-driven young man and the morally mature man as belonging to different *stages* of moral development since Aristotle believes *aidōs* to be fitting for people of a particular age: it is a praiseworthy quality in youth, but not so in an older man who is not expected to rely on a fear of disrepute to check his actions (some older men, however, never reach that state of moral maturity).

My own position on the honour-driven person who is prompted by *aidōs* falls somewhere between Jimenez's and the traditional view, and is closer to how Cairns sees it. In my view, Cairns is right to say that shame '*can* give one a genuine desire to do what is *kalon* and avoid what is *aischron*' (emphasis added), and enable one to act, in some sense, 'for the sake of the noble'.[28] This softer formulation allows for the possibility that some instances of shame are concerned with the noble without committing to the stronger statement that shame is 'primarily' concerned with the noble (Jimenez). After all, *to kalon* implies that which is honourable, but what is honourable is not always done for the sake of *to kalon*; similarly, a fear of disrepute may or may not reflect a genuine desire to avoid what is *aischron*.

---

22. Burnyeat 1980.
23. Jimenez 2020, 2n4.
24. Ibid., 135.
25. Ibid., 133.
26. See especially Jimenez Chapter 4, 120–35.
27. Hitz 2012.
28. Cairns 1993, 425.

102 *Aristotle and Xunzi on Shame*

One notes that the definitions for both *aidōs* and *aischunē* feature the idea of *adoxia*—'disrepute', which reflects a concern with external judgments of what is improper and wrong. While Aristotle's own definitions do not always align with his actual usage of certain concepts, they should nonetheless be taken into account. Furthermore, despite their resemblance to each other, civic courage that arises out of *aidōs* and a desire for honour is explicitly contrasted with true courage that aims at *to kalon*. What makes this issue difficult is that Aristotle clearly attributes an ambivalent place to actions done out of *aidōs*, sometimes appearing to praise them unreservedly yet sometimes showing disapproval. The inherent contradictions and ambivalences within the ethics reflect the very complex nature of shame, which Aristotle himself must have recognised.[29] Individual morality is tied to social values in such a way that the two cannot often be easily separated, which is why it is not always possible to ascertain whether an action is done for the sake of honour, the fine itself, or contains elements of both.

Turning to the *Xunzi*, we notice that discussions of the role of shame in moral education are not centred on the youth who according to Aristotle live by affection and have particular tendencies to satisfy their strong and fickle desires.[30] Instead, Xunzi emphasises the idea that learning is a lifetime pursuit,[31] as is evident from the first chapter *An Exhortation to Learning*: 'learning ought not to stop' (1/1/1) and 'learning continues until death and only then does it stop' (2/1/27). He describes desires (*yu* 欲) as common to each and every person. Because human nature is bad in Xunzi's view and everyone is born a petty person, moral education plays a particularly significant role in transforming each person into a gentleman who is capable of moderating his desires and performing actions that are in accordance with ritual and a sense of propriety. In such a way, he will avoid detestable consequences and attain a life of true honour.

---

29. Jimenez (2020, 140) acknowledges that the alleged tensions between Aristotle's accounts of the status of shame reflects the very complexity of the idea in performing 'the mediating work' in moral development, whereby shame 'places learners in an intermediate position between those who merely follow their immediate affective tendencies and emotions and those who possess virtue'. On the relationship between shame and virtue, see Jimenez 2020, 160–84; Raymond 2017.

30. There is, however, one instance where Xunzi speaks of the 'bad youth' (*e shaozhe* 惡少者) and associates them with 'having no sense of shame' (5/2/42). While desires are common to all, the morally immature person is particularly prone to indulging in unseemly pleasures due to a lack of cultivation.

31. Cf. Van Norden 2000, 132n49: 'One of the major differences between Xunzi and Aristotle on self-cultivation is that Aristotle thinks one must have gone through the first stage by the onset of middle age, whereas Xunzi, in common with other Confucians, sees self-cultivation as a more long-term process.' Here I might add that even though Aristotle explicitly expresses in *EN* 4.9 that *aidōs* is only suitable to the young, assuming that the older man does nothing that gives rise to shame, in Book X of the *EN* he clearly portrays *aidōs* as a positive quality without specifying a particular age group for whom it would be appropriate.

Shame and the Path to Moral Goodness 103

A passage in *An Exhortation to Learning* makes causal connections between one's moral character and the outcome of one's actions—there is said to be a beginning for every type of phenomenon that occurs, and honour and disgrace are portrayed as necessarily reflections of (one's) *de* (1/1/13), virtue or virtuosity.[32] Honour (*rong* 榮) in the *Xunzi* is associated with things that are valued in a good life and promote survival, such as success (*tong* 通), peace/security (*an* 安), and benefit/profit (*li* 利), while disgrace (*ru*), on the other hand, is associated with all the things that endanger life, such as being in straits (*qiong* 窮), danger/crisis (*wei* 危), and harm (*hai* 害):

> The great distinctions between honour and disgrace and the invariable conditions of security and danger and of benefit and harm are thus: those who put a sense of propriety before benefit are honourable; those who place benefit before a sense of propriety are disgraceful. Those who are honourable always gain success; those who are disgraceful are always reduced to being in straits. The successful always exercise control over others; the poor are always controlled by others. Such is the great distinction between honour and disgrace (9/4/22–3).

This passage shows that the distinction between honour and disgrace ultimately depends upon how one chooses between personal benefit and a sense of propriety. Those who put a sense of propriety before benefit are honourable, often meet with success and have the ability to exercise control over others; by contrast, those who place benefit before a sense of propriety are disgraceful and find themselves in a state of poverty, being controlled by others. Honour and the good things that are associated with it are not bound in a one-way causal relationship in the sense that honour causes success, or success honour. Rather, honour belongs to a class of good things that constitute the results of praiseworthy action; the opposite can be said for disgrace and all the deplorable states associated with it.[33] In speaking about honour and disgrace and detailing the good and the bad things that follow upon one's choices, Xunzi is ultimately concerned with one's ethical choices themselves, which leads him to prescribe the right sorts of actions rather than making a point about obtaining honour and

---

32. 物類之起，必有所始。榮辱之來，必象其德 (1/1/13). For complexities surrounding the term *de*, conventionally though sometimes inadequately translated as 'virtue', see Gassmann (2011) who interprets the root meaning of *de* as 'to obligate' and Cheng (2012, 135–36), who discusses *de* in terms of 'kingly virtue', mediated as a form of power that is able to move other things without resorting to a form of external coercion. Just like terms such as *qing* and *xing*, *de* cannot be reduced to one meaning in our terminology and I adopt 'virtue' and/or 'virtuosity', depending on context.

33. 'Honour' and 'disgrace' in the *Xunzi*, then, resemble the contrast made in Aristotle between *to kalon* and *to aischron*.

104   *Aristotle and Xunzi on Shame*

shunning disgrace per se.[34] Likewise, by being 'apprehensive about avoiding disgrace' (6/2/45), Xunzi's gentleman is not simply afraid of the loss of reputation itself, but is all the more afraid of allowing himself to commit unworthy actions that he deems despicable. There is a sense that the gentleman is impervious to the capriciousness of external circumstances—being in a lowly position (*bei jian* 卑賤), which is typically regarded as disgraceful, is not for him a source of harm.[35]

Xunzi implies that even if the gentleman does not actively seek his own benefit, he will attain it, while the petty man will only obtain harm despite seeking benefit. *Li* (benefit), then, no longer stands in opposition to *yi* (propriety), but assumes the role of the antonym of *hai* (harm). In other words, *li* becomes a good in life that only the gentleman is able to obtain, paradoxically and precisely because he is able to put *yi* above the selfish drives that he is born with. What distinguishes the gentleman and the petty man is not what they are born with but the ethical choices that they make:

> In physical substance (*cai* 材),[36] nature (*xing* 性), awareness (*zhi* 知) and capability (*neng* 能), the gentleman and the petty man are one and the same. Liking honour and detesting disgrace, liking benefit and detesting harm, the gentleman and the petty man are the same. They differ, however, in the ways in which they seek these [i.e. honour and benefit]. (10/4/32–3)

The passage above suggests that obtaining personal benefit need not necessarily be associated with disgraceful behaviour. *How* one seeks benefit is of crucial importance, so the gentleman, by putting a sense of propriety before benefit, gains honour and other goods, while the petty man, by indulging in the desire for personal benefit, faces disgrace and other unwelcome consequences. In this way, Xunzi successfully links together private (*si* 私) and public (*gong* 公) interests and illustrates that they are far from being mutually exclusive.

Elsewhere, Xunzi goes to great lengths to distinguish between what lies within the agent himself and what is external and beyond his control. In the

34. I am therefore in agreement with Cua (2003, 180) that 'the emphasis in both Aristotle and Xunzi on the condition of moral agents paves the way toward a better appreciation of ethical shame, for what matters ultimately is not the feeling of pain or uneasiness, which is bound to be episodic anyway, but on the enduring state of moral character that is marked by the concern with intrinsic rather than extrinsic honor'.

35. 故富貴不足以益也，卑賤不足以損也：如此則可謂士矣 (106/31/12).

36. Knoblock and Hutton, in translating *cai* as 'natural talent' and 'endowment' respectively, appear to be taking *cai* 材 as the cognate 才, carrying the sense of aptitude. Since the ideas of *xing* and *neng* in the same line already suggest endowment and capability, I translate *cai* here as 'physical substance', believing it to convey the sense of 'natural material'.

Shame and the Path to Moral Goodness   105

distinctions that he makes between superficial and true honour, and superficial disgrace and true disgrace (69/18/104–8), Xunzi contrasts disgrace that derives from force of circumstances (*shiru* 勢辱), for example, corporal punishments, to disgrace that derives from inner disposition (*yiru* 義辱), that is, true disgrace that is a result of bad actions.[37] Xunzi makes a clear case that not all outward manifestations of honour are indications of a good moral disposition, nor all outward manifestations of disgrace indications of a bad moral character and consequent upon blameworthy action. Rather, one must be able to distinguish between ideas of true and false moral goodness. The importance of one's moral disposition, then, is placed far above the consequences of one's actions that may lead to honour or punishment. Rather than extolling high social positions for its own sake and the benefits that come with it, Xunzi praises the honour that reflects one's self-cultivation (69/18/105). In stating that disgrace may come about from forces outside of one's control, Xunzi here appears to be contradicting what is stated in *Exhortation to Learning* discussed above, namely that honour and disgrace are necessarily reflections of one's virtue or virtuosity (1/1/13). One may understand Xunzi here to be anticipating the problem of moral luck by providing a qualification to that statement and making distinctions between different types of honour and disgrace.

Just like Aristotle, Xunzi portrays good friendship as conducive to virtue, though he places no special emphasis on its impact on young people. Teachers (*shi* 師) and friends (*you* 友) are sometimes mentioned together as good forces setting examples for virtuous conduct; thus Xunzi highlights the importance of the social environment in shaping one's moral character. In the chapter *Human Nature is Bad*, Xunzi advises seeking wise teachers and befriending the good, while cautioning against associating with bad ones. Being with a good teacher allows one to hear about the ways of the sage kings of the past, while making friends with the right kinds of people will ensure that one is surrounded by acts of loyalty, trustworthiness, respect, and deference (*Zhong xin jing rang* 忠信敬讓), which propel one toward virtue without one's even being aware of it. By contrast, befriending the unworthy and being surrounded by base and reckless behaviour lead to greater risks of punishment and disgrace (*xing lu* 刑戮). In a different passage, Xunzi says that the gentleman esteems his teachers and has close relationships with his friends, both groups of people embodying the

---

37. Cua (2003) translates these terms as 'intrinsic shame' and 'extrinsic shame', while Van Norden (2002) renders them 'conventional shame' and 'ethical shame'. Hutton (2014) chooses to leave *yi* untranslated and offers 'honor in terms of *yi*' and 'honor in terms of one's circumstances'. My translation is based on that of Knoblock, though I modify it to 'honour/ disgrace that derives from inner disposition' and 'honour/ disgrace that derives from force of circumstances' to emphasise the differences in the causes of one's honour and disgrace.

106   *Aristotle and Xunzi on Shame*

good (*shan* 善), which the gentleman cherishes. In this instance, the roles of the teacher and the friend are contrasted: 'those who consider me to be in the wrong and are correct in doing so are my teachers, while those who consider me to be in the right and are correct in doing so are my friends'.[38] The responses of the teacher and the friend refer to different scenarios in which the former will assume a critical and admonitory role while the latter an approving and affirmative one. The praise and blame attached to these instances help the agent to reinforce certain values by making the right kinds of associations with what is good and bad.

PLEASURE, DESIRE, AND THE INTERNALISATION OF VALUES

I shall now investigate how shame relates to the idea of the 'internalisation' of values, an important aspect of moral education according to Aristotle and Xunzi. In contemporary discourse, 'guilt' has often been associated with the internalisation of values whereby the agent experiences remorse and a true understanding of the baseness of his conduct, while 'shame' has commonly been associated with an overwhelming concern for the opinions of others and thus with a sensitivity to external judgment. This dichotomy is often oversimplified, as Williams and Cairns have rightly shown, for 'shame' could certainly involve reflection upon one's behaviour that is not contingent upon other people's disapproval. As already mentioned, in the ancient Greek and early Chinese sources concerned, the 'guilt' vs. 'shame' conceptual pair is absent, and the distinctions between a genuine concern for one's moral integrity and a desire for mere social recognition are demarcated in specific ways. I address this question by analysing Aristotle's and Xunzi's discourses on pleasure and desire. Despite their differences in postulating how an agent might eventually come to act upon the right desires, Aristotle's and Xunzi's accounts of desire both recognise the importance of the internalisation of values, which is an important attribute of the morally mature individual. For both philosophers, good actions are not simply conducted on the grounds of securing honour, but are internally approved by the agent as being good in themselves, thereby reflecting the right kind of motivation for action.

Desire (*orexis*) is an important concept in Aristotle's ethics, being concerned with the pursuit of good things that the agent deems worthy, which in

---

38. 故非我而當者，吾師也；是我而當者，吾友也 (3/2/2).

Shame and the Path to Moral Goodness   107

turn serves as a reflection of the stage he has reached in moral development.[39] As mentioned above, Aristotle directly links appetitive desire (*epithumiai*) and the concept of shame by attributing young people's sense of shame to their being driven by desires (*epithumiai*) and hence making many mistakes. The older person is not expected to be making mistakes through excessive *epithumiai*, and so it should be unnecessary for him to check himself through experiencing *aidōs*. According to the *De Anima*, when the object is pleasant or painful, the soul makes a sort of affirmation (*kataphasa*) or negation (*apophasa*) and pursues or avoids the object (*De An.* 431a9–10). In Book II of the *EN*, Aristotle explains that, given the excellences have to do with actions and affections, and every affection and every action is accompanied by pleasure and pain, then excellence of character has to do with pleasures and pains. We need to be brought up in such a way as to delight in and be distressed by the things as appropriate (*EN* 1104b8–16). Although desiring something cannot be equated to taking pleasure in it on the grounds that the desire may only imply the *prospect* of taking pleasure,[40] it is clear that desires often anticipate pleasures that may or may not include those associated with excellence.

We might recall that *aidōs* and *aischunē* are defined respectively as a fear of disrepute and a kind of pain in respect of bad things that tend to lead to disrepute. The fact that young people have a particular tendency to pursue what is pleasant (*EN* 1156a31–3) and are driven by honour suggests that the pain associated with shame acts as a factor motivating the agent to avoid shameful behaviour. Aristotle distinguishes between different types of pleasure and claims that it is important to educate people to consider pleasant what is truly pleasant and not merely what is apparently pleasant. By following his sense of shame, a young person learns not to pursue what is immediately in front of him, which may be the apparently pleasant but not the truly pleasant. At an early stage in the education process, then, young people are to be habituated to pursuing honourable actions by associating them with pleasure, and to avoiding disgraceful ones by associating them with pain (cf. *EN* 1179b23–6, 1179b29–31). After they have acquired the correct habits ('the that'), it is then assumed that young people would

---

39. The scope of the current study does not allow for a close examination of all the roles of desire (including *epithumia*, *thumos*, *boulēsis*; rational and nonrational) in Aristotle's ethical and psychological works on a general level. See Pearson (2012), who studies desire to further understanding of Aristotle's accounts of 'for example, virtue, *akrasia*, choice (*prohairesis*), deliberation, voluntary action, moral education, and animal locomotion' (ibid., 2).

40. For a fuller discussion about the relationship between desire and pleasure, see Pearson (2012, 205) against Charles.

108 *Aristotle and Xunzi on Shame*

gradually come to understand the true reasons for acting in such a way ('the because').[41]

Someone who takes actions for the sake of avoiding disrepute can be contrasted with the morally mature person whose rational judgment and desire are in harmony and who acts in accordance with values of which he himself approves. Aristotle's discussions of the person who lacks self-control (*akratēs*) and the self-controlled person (*enkratēs*) are particularly enlightening as to what it means when desires conflict with rational thought. The person who lacks self-control acts in accordance with his desires (*epithumōn*) but does not make a correct purposive choice (*EN* 1111b13–14), thus giving in to temptation despite knowing it to be a vice, while the self-controlled person manages to carry out the correct actions but does so unwillingly because his desires encourage him to act otherwise. These less than ideal cases contrast with the morally mature person who arrives at a good purposive choice by aligning true reasoning with the correct desire (*EN* 1139a22–6).[42] Aristotle attaches great importance to having the appropriate affections for actions, for example feeling generous in bestowing gifts, which suggests internal approval for such actions. While young people act by following a social standard so as to achieve the pleasant (honour) and avoid pain (disrepute), the morally mature person acts out of an internalised standard of what is fine and what is shameful because his desire is in tune with true reasoning that allows him to carry out fine actions, and he exhibits the affections appropriate to the given situation. This is perhaps the reason why Aristotle is prepared to grant conditional shame to the morally mature person, in the sense that if he were to do something bad, he would feel ashamed, because he would know that it does not match his own criteria for fine action.

As for Xunzi, the moderation of desires is a central concept that involves the harmonisation of human nature and conscious exertion (*xing wei he* 性偽合), which brings about order in society and fulfilment[43] for the individual. The precise relationship between desire (*yu* 欲), nature (*xing* 性) and feelings (*qing* 情) can be difficult to gauge. In one part of the text, *yu* is construed as the response to *qing*: 'Nature is the consequence of heaven. *Qing* is the substance

---

41. There remains the thorny issue of how to bridge the gap between doing the right actions and acquiring virtue proper. Jimenez (2020, 19ff.) gives extensive treatment to this issue by reviewing the literature and arguing that shame provides such a bridge by turning the learners towards virtue.

42. Compare with Xunzi's description of the sage who follows his desires and embraces his dispositions (*qing*), and the things dependent on these simply turn out well-ordered. He carries out the Way without having to force himself (81/21/65–67).

43. Virág (2017, 186–87) notes the prevalence of terms in the *Xunzi* that relate to fulfilment, including *zhi* 至, *bei* 備, *ju* 俱, *jin* 盡, and *quan* 全, 'all of which convey ideas of perfection, realization, and completion'.

Shame and the Path to Moral Goodness 109

of nature. Desire is the response to *qing*.[44] Elsewhere, *yu* is included as an example of *qing*.[45] Xunzi, therefore, appears to represent these relationships in different ways at different junctures in the text. What we can surmise is that desires exist because of the make-up of human nature, and that they are a necessary part of human life. Xunzi criticises Song Xing's view that human desires are few (70/18/114–122) and instead argues that human beings are born with many desires, including the desire for food when hungry, for warmth when cold, for rest when tired, and being fond of what is beneficial and hating what is harmful (10/4/42–4, 13/5/24–5). Because these features are all part and parcel of the human condition, they are neither good nor bad in themselves, so Xunzi does not argue for the eradication of desires or even the limitation of the number of desires; he criticises those who advocate such views (85/22/55–7). For Xunzi, it is the *regulation* of desires (*jieyu* 節欲) that plays a crucial role in determining the correctness of one's conduct. Xunzi attributes this important task to the heart-mind (*xin* 心), which 'chooses' the desires that are to be fulfilled:

> *Qing* being so, the heart-mind's choosing between them is called 'deliberation' (*lü* 慮). Taking action upon the heart-mind's deliberation is called 'conscious exertion' (*wei* 偽). (83/22/3–4)

> Therefore, when the desires are excessive, action may not follow upon them because the heart-mind stops the desires [from being fulfilled]. If the dictates of the heart-mind are in accordance with the correct principles (*li* 理), then even if the desires are many, what harm do they do to order? When desires are deficient and yet action follows upon them, that is because the heart-mind directs them. If the dictates of the heart-mind are not in accordance with the correct principles, then even if the desires are few, the results could be far worse than disorder. Therefore order and disorder depend upon the dictates of the heart-mind, not upon the desires of *qing*. (85/22/60–2)

Xin, being 'the lord of the body and master of spiritual intelligence, issuing commands but not receiving commands',[46] plays a prominent role in human agency. An essential aspect of moral cultivation, then, consists in training *xin* so that it knows the Way (*zhidao* 知道) and directs the desires according to what is proper. So then, 'although desires cannot be got rid of, one seeks to moderate

---

44. 性者，天之就也；情者，性之質也；欲者，情之應也 (85/22/63). This passage is beset with textual problems, see Knoblock 1994, III, 344n101.

45. 11/4/60–62, 39/11/46–47, 70/18/115.

46. 心者，形之君也，而神明之主也，出令而無所受令 (80/21/44–5).

them' (85/22/65). There are two kinds of desires involved—the first being the unmoderated desires innate to all people, and the second being desires that have been approved by *xin*. In his analysis of *xin*, Antonio Cua contrasts 'natural' and 'reflective' desires, the former being 'a mere biological drive'.[47] In a similar vein, Kurtis Hagen speaks of 'basic desires' and 'specific desires', the former being the desires that cannot be altered and the latter the 'filtered' versions, that is, once *xin* has deliberated and moderated the initial desires.[48] The significance of *xin* lies in the fact that when functioning correctly, it allows the agent to act upon a certain degree of self-reflection and rational calculation rather than his primal innate responses.[49]

Like Aristotle, Xunzi suggests that the morally mature person gradually learns to have reflective desires that overcome his biological drive for immediate pleasures:

> The gentleman knows that which lacks completeness and purity does not deserve to be called fine. Therefore he recites and enumerates in order that he might perpetuate it, ponders in order that he will fully understand it, acts so as to be a person in such a disposition to deal with it, and eliminates what is harmful within him in order that he will nurture it. Thereby he causes his eye to be unwilling to see what is contrary to it, his ear unwilling to hear what is contrary to it, his mouth unwilling to speak anything contrary to it, and his heart-mind unwilling to contemplate anything contrary to it. (3/1/46–8)

In the passage above, it is not specified what it is that the *junzi* recites, enumerates and ponders, and so forth, and what he causes his eyes to be unwilling to see, ears to be unwilling to hear, mouth unwilling to speak and heart-mind unwilling to contemplate. I take the same approach as Hutton in interpreting it to refer to learning, so that only by perfecting his learning would the gentleman reach completeness and purity. There is a sense that the gentleman is forever seeking to better himself, knowing full well that learning never stops. A strong emphasis is placed on the importance of the accumulation of learning and the repetition of good practices so that whether one becomes the legendary sage kings Yao or Shun, or tyrant Jie or robber Zhi, workman or artisan, peasant or merchant, depends entirely on the accumulated effect of circumstances, on how one concentrates on laying plans, and on the influence of habits and customs

---

47. Cua 2005, 49–50n28.

48. Hagen 2011, 62.

49. Perkins 2014, 194: 'That we desire something [. . .] does not necessarily mean that we seek it. What we seek depends on the deliberations of the heart.'

Shame and the Path to Moral Goodness   111

(10/4/45–6).[50] Through a combination of teaching and the accumulation of good practices, one gradually forms an understanding of the good and comes to desire nothing that is contrary to *dao*. In other words, once the agent has acquired the appropriate knowledge from teachings and models (*shifa* 師法), he is capable of becoming master of his own learning process by internalising the things taught. One way in which the internalisation process manifests itself is through the individual's practice of self-reflection (*xing* 省 or *zixing* 自省, e.g., 1/1/2–3, 3/2/1–2), which is a sign that he no longer requires an external voice to issue prescriptions but relies on his inner self for the cultivation of morals.

Here it is worth going into some detail about just what self-reflection involves. It is interesting to note, although *xing* (reflection) is often attached to *zi* (self) to make *zixing* in compound form, the act of self-reflection is not restricted to evaluations about the self alone but often stems from a social context, based on one's interactions with *others* and observations of *others*:[51]

> When you observe goodness in others, then inspect yourself (*zicun*) so as to cultivate it. When you observe badness in others, then examine yourself (*zixing*), fearful of discovering it. If you find goodness in your person, then commend yourself (*zihao*) while holding firm to it. If you find badness in your person, then reproach yourself (*ziwu*) while regarding it as calamity.[52]

In this passage, then, we find different locutions involving *zi*, the self, this time not only *zixing* but also *zicun*, *zihao* and *ziwu*, all of which point to our responses to goodness and badness in other people. So then, Xunzi's exemplary person is acutely aware of the nature of his own actions and of those around him. Interpersonal relationships play a vital role: seeing the self against others leads one to make adjustments to one's own ethical conduct, rather like seeing oneself in a mirror. This idea can also be found in the *Analects*, for example the expression: 'When you see someone who is worthy, concentrate upon becoming their equal; when you see someone who is unworthy, use this as an opportunity to look within yourself (*zixing*)'.[53] For Xunzi (indeed the same can be said for

---

50. The notion of agency unites Xunzi's account with Aristotle's. For both, the individual has a big part to play in fashioning who he becomes. See Jimenez (2020, 189) on the notion of agency in Aristotle.

51. Tu (1989, 95) comments that for the Confucians, 'it is more difficult to imagine ourselves as isolable individuals than as centers of relationships constantly interacting with one another in a dynamic network of human related-ness'.

52. 見善，修然必以自存也；見不善，愀然必以自省也。善在身，介然必以自好也；不善在身，菑然必以自惡也 (3/2/1–2). I have followed Hutton's translation for this passage, in particular adopting 'calamity' rather than 'contamination' for *zi* 菑.

53. 見賢思齊焉，見不賢而內自省也 (4.17/8/13).

112   Aristotle and Xunzi on Shame

the *Analects*), merely being on the receiving end of moral teachings is not sufficient for one to become an exemplary person. Teachings and models instil an awareness of what constitutes appropriate and inappropriate conduct, what is to be pursued and what is to be avoided. Once the agent has acquired that knowledge, he is then equipped with the capacity to evaluate his own conduct and that of others. Motivating himself to put into practice what he has learnt by accumulating good conduct, the agent is then himself turned into a morally authoritative figure who can issue commands. In this way, despite humans' natural impulse to seek self-interest, it is nevertheless possible for humans to acquire a sense of propriety by internalising the values they have been taught.

The gentleman, then, constantly tries to improve his own ethical conduct, taking as a source of shame moral failings that fall within his own responsibilities, not those that lie beyond his powers:

> Because the gentleman reveres what lies within his power and does not long for what lies with heaven, he progresses day by day. Because the petty man lays aside what lies within his power and longs for what lies with heaven, he day by day retrogresses. (63/17/27–8)

> Thus the gentleman is ashamed of not practising self-cultivation but not ashamed of being vilified; he is ashamed of not being trustworthy but not ashamed of not being trusted; ashamed of not being an able person but not ashamed of being unrecognised. (17/6/40–1)

The structure of the sentence in the latter example allows the object towards whom *chi* 恥 is directed to be open-ended—it could be a sense of shame felt for himself and/or a sense of contempt for someone whose behaviour to him constitutes a source of shame. What these passages illustrate is that moral progress is made possible because the gentleman recognises the importance of the *self* in the cultivation process. He is capable of distinguishing between actions that are apparently shameful and those that are truly shameful; it is not the consequences that determine whether the actions are correct, but the motivations.[54] Unlike Aristotle's idea of the older person who should not feel shame at all, Xunzi's gentleman is forever examining himself to identify positive traits that ought to be preserved and negative traits that should be got rid of (even if he does not find any of the latter). While the heart-mind is frequently discussed in terms of checking or allowing certain actions to be carried out each time desire arises, *zixing* could be said to be an important mechanism for self-assessment

---

54. Cf. Confucius' distinctions between things that ought and ought not to generate shame, discussed in Chapter 1.

whereby the agent reflects upon what has already been practised, addresses any faults, and aspires to maintain excellence or make improvements. Such actions indicate that the agent has a sense of moral responsibility and is capable of assessing the character of his actions. Through the process of self-reflection, he is prompted to focus on what is important for the purpose of cultivation instead of letting himself get distracted by superficial honours. These activities point to a notion of the self that is not only aware of a standard or an ideal, but also strives to achieve it, internalising the values during the process.[55] Self-reflection is closely associated with a sense of shame, since anyone capable of assessing his own behaviour necessarily possesses an idea of what constitutes the honourable and the shameful. We might put it another way and say that the very capacity for feeling shame indicates one's ability to identify mistakes and thereby make progress in moral development. This can be contrasted with the petty person who is without a sense of shame (*wu lianchi*) and does not know right from wrong (*buzhi shifei*).

In his comparisons of Augustine and Xunzi, Stalnaker sets the two apart by claiming that 'Augustine exercises focus as much as possible on the mysterious source of our actions in our inward "heart of hearts." [. . .] Xunzi instead suggests that the most potent strategy for effecting lasting inward change is to focus on what we can control reasonably well—our outward movements, gestures, and speech—and by working to perfect those observable actions, slowly and *indirectly* reforming the impulses that move us spontaneously, until at last they lead just as surely to outwardly perfect action'.[56] I am in general agreement with Stalnaker's claim on the *Xunzi*. Instead of 'a careful sifting and interpretation of thoughts and desires to ferret out hidden sinfulness',[57] the way Xunzi conceives moral progress to be possible appears to be rather straightforward: that is, for one to take the initiative in examining one's own actions and carrying out appropriate measures to redress any potential faults. We have already come across the idea of self-reproach (*ziwu*) in the *Xunzi*; in the *Analects* this is expressed in terms of *zisong* 自訟, which, bearing associations with speech, plays the part of an 'inner voice'. We can say, therefore, that self-reflection provides a medium for bringing one close to one's values and moral conscience. The result of self-reflection need not involve any pain or sense of guilt: for example, in the *Analects*

---

55. Cf. discussion in Kamtekar (1998, 139) and Jimenez (2020, 129n22) of the difference between a) the distinction between having and lacking knowledge (or reliable beliefs) about the noble and the shameful, and b) the distinction between having and lacking a sincere desire to live according to nobility and virtue. The case of self-reflection in the *Xunzi* gives strong evidence that the gentleman satisfies both criteria.

56. Stalnaker 2006, 268.

57. Ibid., 268.

114   *Aristotle and Xunzi on Shame*

it is said that if upon self-reflection, one discovers nothing wrong, then there is nothing to be anxious about or to fear. Such characteristics are representative of the gentleman.[58] So if the agent approves of his actions and believes them to be consistent with the ethical ideal, self-reflection can be an affirmative process and far from the negative feelings of pain and remorse that are frequently associated with the 'pangs of conscience'. 'Conscience' is of course a loaded term that has strong associations with Christianity, and is related to the idea of 'sin' that is absent from both the Greek and Chinese sources. Nonetheless, it is useful to consider how the early Chinese sources represent the idea of an individual's judgment of his own wrongdoing. Paul Strohm in his book on conscience acknowledges that 'the West has no monopoly on ethical self-scrutiny',[59] though he goes on to claim that the origins of conscience (and to some extent, its sponsorship) are European and European-derived and that 'conscience deserves its reputation as one of the prouder western contributions to human dignity'.[60] If we regard conscience as 'a faculty that delivers *core moral judgments*, judgments that concern the reasons entailed by individual ideals',[61] then there is plenty of evidence for different expressions of it in the early Confucian texts, which directly counter Strohm's Eurocentric claims.

Alternative Ways of Conceptualising the 'Internal' and the 'External'

To summarise, through discourses on shame-related ideas, Aristotle and Xunzi make certain distinctions and establish models of behaviour that are to be followed, for a sense of shame calls for the overcoming of a 'falling short of something' and makes moral progress possible. In other words, notions of honour, shame, and disgrace intricately revolve around one's sense of self-worth and give one guidance as to which actions to adopt and which goods are to be prioritised over others. While Xunzi's discussions of honour and shame are framed by the correct ranking of a sense of propriety over personal benefit, Aristotle compares actions guided by a sense of shame (*aidōs*) with those guided by other motivations, so that actions stemming from a fear of punishment or a desire for honour are less noble, and those done for the sake of the fine itself are unreservedly good. Actions and thoughts are not to be judged primarily on their

---

58. 司馬牛問君子。子曰："君子不憂不懼。" 曰："不憂不懼，斯謂之君子已乎？" 子曰："內省不疚，夫何憂何懼？" (12.4/31/1-3).

59. Strohm 2013, 3.

60. Ibid., 4.

61. Swan and Vallier 2012, 3.

Shame and the Path to Moral Goodness 115

external effects, we learn from Aristotle and Xunzi, but more importantly through moral disposition, which indicates that motivation is an important criterion for judging actions.

Both philosophers recognise the fact that human beings in their natural state (that is, prior to receiving the kinds of moral education that Aristotle and Xunzi recommend) seek what is most pleasurable to them and avoid pain. We could say that their desires are for external goods that tend to generate immediate (and often physical) pleasure. Since they do not involve any moral considerations, such reactions are rather more 'instinctive' than 'reflective', involving a drive towards pleasures or desires that can lead to bad consequences. However, for Aristotle and Xunzi, the morally mature person is capable of fulfilling his unique human characteristics—the Aristotelian *phronimos* exercises purposive choice which involves the combination of rational calculation with the right kind of desire, while Xunzi's *junzi* has the capacity to reflect on his own thoughts and actions and a heart-mind that is so cultivated as to be able to 'choose' the right kinds of desires. Both philosophers, then, share the view that on the path to moral goodness, human beings must overcome their basic desires and learn to take action with a view to what constitutes the good. The exemplary person goes beyond mere public opinion and makes decisions based on a cultivated understanding of what is to be pursued. He not only conducts himself in the right way, but also desires to behave in such a way because he understands the goodness of his behaviour and has properly internalised the correct values.

5

Social Institutions and the Politics of Moral Education

THE POLITICAL NATURE OF MORAL EDUCATION

Having discussed in the previous chapter the role that shame plays in moral education and the training necessary to habituate oneself to act upon the right kinds of desires, I now turn to the social and political implications of moral education, in particular the social significance of shame.

Ryan Balot remarks, 'Perhaps the most notable difference between ancient Greek and modern politics and political thought is that ancient politics was intensely concerned with the ethical education of citizens.'[1] Xunzi and his predecessors Confucius and Mencius might be said to side with their Greek counterparts since concerns with the ethical education of the ruler and the ruled permeate their philosophy. Much has already been written about the interconnectedness of ethics and politics in Aristotle[2] and about moral education and government in Chinese philosophy,[3] yet little has been done to compare the ways in which ethics and politics are closely interwoven in the Aristotelian and Confucian traditions.[4] An exploration of 'shame' in Aristotle and Xunzi gives occasion to delve into the 'politics of morals', for while discourses on honour, shame, and disgrace concern the moral education of the individual, they are ultimately political in nature: given human beings' community-oriented nature, moral education, which encompasses the instillation of a sense of what constitutes the honourable and the shameful, has the dual purpose of improving the character of the individual and maintaining social stability and cohesion.

As mentioned in Chapter 1, the sociopolitical contexts in Aristotle's and Xunzi's societies were fundamentally different in several respects; in writing

---

1. Balot 2006, 4. By using the collective term 'ancient Greek', Balot implies that we are dealing with a homogeneous group even though different perspectives existed in the tradition.

2. Cf. Cashdollar 1973; Vander Waerdt 1985; Adkins 1991; Bodeüs 1993; Schofield 2006; Frede 2013.

3. Cf. Pines 2009; Cheng 2012; Harris 2013; Kim 2019. El Amine 2015 presents a radical departure from orthodox views by arguing for a divergence between Confucian ethics and politics. Her stance has been persuasively challenged by Hutton 2016, Harris 2019, and others.

4. See Kim 2019, 16.

Aristotle and Xunzi on Shame, Moral Education, and the Good Life. Jingyi Jenny Zhao, Oxford University Press.
© Oxford University Press 2024. DOI: 10.1093/oso/9780197773161.003.0006

about human nature, moral education, and government, each philosopher was responding to his own political situation. Nevertheless, as I have argued in the preceding chapter, in conceptualising the differences between human beings and other living things, and in situating humans within their social contexts, we can identify undeniable similarities between Aristotle and Xunzi: both believe human beings to be distinct from animals, for example, in their capacity to live in communities that actualise the potential for a good life, and their ability to make rational choices and to experience shame. For Aristotle, human beings are *zōa politika* (more so than other animals which are *politika*) and it is by virtue of living in a *polis* that they have the capacity to lead a life of *eudaimonia*. Xunzi attributes human beings' superiority to animals to their distinct ability to form communities (*qun* 群), which is made possible both by their possession of a sense of propriety (*yi* 義) and by their ability to make discriminations (*fen* 分). These points of similarity between Aristotle and Xunzi on the social and political nature of human beings show that both emphasise humans' participation in community life, which in turn implies the observation of certain socially approved codes of conduct that involve a capacity for 'shame' and the possibility of moral progress.

On this topic it is helpful to briefly consider the *Zhuangzi*, regarded as one of the foundational "Daoist" texts, as a counterexample to Xunzi, and indeed, to Aristotle. The *Zhuangzi* contains passages that mock Confucius' espousal of universal moral codes and social duty and argues instead for a life of seclusion free from political obligations. Where we find Aristotle and Xunzi emphasising the nature of human beings as members of communities leading social lives, Zhuangzi displays a lack of interest in state building and in a lifetime involved with political activity (though Zhuangzi's idea of seclusion implies a critique: the idea of political activity is still in the background against which he is reacting). As a result, Zhuangzi specifically argues against setting up distinctions between ideas related to humans' collective identity, such as honour and shame, instead seeing the very distinctions themselves as sources of *bing* 病, literally, 'illness'.[5] This accords with Zhuangzi's scepticism towards the making of distinctions in general, which marks a clear departure from Xunzi: 'The way I see it, the rules of humaneness and propriety and the paths of right and wrong all are hopelessly snarled and jumbled. How could I know anything about such discriminations?'[6] In this respect, Zhuangzi could not be more different from Xunzi, the contrast

---

5. 荣辱立然后睹所病 (*Zhuangzi* 25/75/9).

6. 自我觀之，仁義之端，是非之塗，樊然殽亂，吾惡能知其辯 (*Zhuangzi* 2/6/15, trans. based on Watson).

118 *Aristotle and Xunzi on Shame*

revealing itself in terms of the kind of human ideal that these philosophers hold. In the ideal life that Zhuangzi envisages, based on freedom and independence, where humans live without the need for social integration, there is no particular need to conform to prescribed social norms and to standards of what is 'honourable' and what is 'shameful'—the creation of a social bond and the regulation of social behaviour are superfluous.[7] The Zhuangzi example suggests that whether or not ideas of social distinction play a major role in a philosopher's ethical and political ideas depends crucially upon two factors: first, whether a strong emphasis is laid on ethical conduct, and more specifically ethical habituation, and second and more importantly, whether community life is regarded as an important part of being human. These two characteristics are absent from Zhuangzi but prominent in Aristotle and Xunzi, hence the latter two make a particularly apt pair for comparison.

In what ways, precisely, are Aristotle's and Xunzi's ideals of moral education political? Here I cite Bernard Yack, who defines the political nature of Aristotelian moral education thus:

> Aristotelian moral education is political in the broadest sense of the term in that it involves the exercise of authority by some individual or individuals to compel others to behave in a particular way. This will be the case no matter which social community—a family, a tribe, a club, or a state— provides moral training. In each, some individual or individuals will be determining how others should behave. Unlike many contemporary students of moral education, Aristotle does not sentimentalize 'private' as opposed to 'public' sources of moral education. But Aristotelian moral education is also political in the narrower, specifically Aristotelian sense [. . .], it requires, when best designed, active involvement by the political community.[8]

With reference to Yack's account, we might say that the broad sense in which moral education is political applies also to Xunzi, who calls for human behaviour to be regulated in a particular way. In specifying how moral education is political, for both Aristotle and Xunzi, I wish to go beyond Yack's account by drawing out the following parallels between the two philosophies:

---

7. Geaney notes in 2004, 139n42: 'it is surprising that, among the early philosophical texts, only the Confucian texts seem interested in shame'. While shame is rarely an object of discussion in the *Zhuangzi*, one can identify cases where Zhuangzi implicitly defends himself against the charge of lacking in shame, e.g., in the well-known case of the death of his wife, where he explains to Huizi the reasons for his drumming and singing.

8. Yack 1993, 248–49.

(1) The moral education of the ruler, who is the foremost figure in leading the state, affects the running of the state (although, as I shall illustrate, this idea is much more prominent in Xunzi than in Aristotle).

(2) The moral education of the ruled directly affects social stability and political order, hence it falls under the responsibility of the state and is not a private affair. In other words, it is within the interest of those in positions of power to establish social norms and to educate the people so that they learn to undertake good actions and avoid bad ones.

(3) Social institutions are in place to uphold social codes and to deal out punishments to individuals who fail to develop a moral character and thus transgress such norms.

The points highlight some of the areas common to Aristotle's and Xunzi's thought on the impact of moral education on the state, as well as on measures taken by the state to regulate behaviour. However, within those common areas, there are undeniably certain differences in how ethics and politics interact. Here examination of the sociopolitical backgrounds becomes useful in providing the context. I have already illustrated that an important difference which sets Xunzi apart from Aristotle is the context of persuasion. Xunzi's writings, much like those of contemporary 'itinerant scholars' (*youshi* 遊士), ultimately sought to win the attention of a ruler and his ministers who might promote the right kind of moral education and re-establish order and prosperity by adopting Xunzi's views. Hence one finds chapters in the *Xunzi* that are dedicated to prescribing codes of conduct to enable rulers to achieve a stable and successful rule, and which provide arguments linking the fate of the ruler to his treatment of the people and the fate of the state to the responsible actions of the ruler and the ministers, though the extent to which Xunzi and others are ambitious to achieve stability and good order may strike one as rather unrealistic. Aristotle also expresses concern for the moral character of the ruler, which is expected to surpass other people's, that is, *if* there happens to be someone who has such a capacity (*Pol.* 1325b12–14).[9] On this point, the difference between Aristotle and Xunzi is fairly clear: unlike Xunzi, Aristotle does not assume monarchical rule to be the

---

9. Cf. also the following passage: 'Hence the ruler ought to have excellence of character in perfection, for his function, taken absolutely, demands a master artificer, and reason is such an artificer; the subjects, on the other hand, require only that measure of excellence which is proper to each of them.' διὸ τὸν μὲν ἄρχοντα τελέαν ἔχειν δεῖ τὴν διανοητικὴν ἀρετήν (τὸ γὰρ ἔργον ἐστὶν ἁπλῶς τοῦ ἀρχιτέκτονος, ὁ δὲ λόγος ἀρχιτέκτων), τῶν δ' ἄλλων ἕκαστον ὅσον ἐπιβάλλει αὐτοῖς (*Pol.* 1260a17–20). Aristotle's discussion of the 'god-like ruler' has troubled some commentators, see e.g., Newell 1987, Mayhew 2009, and more recently, Buekenhout 2016. To what extent Aristotle's remarks on the 'god-like ruler' are a response to the ongoing changes in Greek political life that followed from the ascendency of Philip, if not also of Alexander in Macedon, is subject to debate.

120 *Aristotle and Xunzi on Shame*

norm—he presupposes a body of citizens who all participate to a greater or lesser degree in the political process, while the kingdoms of Warring States China with which Xunzi was familiar all had rulers who were the ultimate decision-takers and who were therefore the target of ambitious persuaders. Aristotle clearly envisioned his work having an impact upon legislators, writing with the legislator in mind in many places, especially in the *Ethics* and the *Politics*. For example, on the topic of voluntary and involuntary actions in Book III of the *EN*, Aristotle claims that distinctions between the natures of these actions would be useful for those framing laws and when it comes to fixing honours and methods of forcible correction.[10] To give another example, towards the beginning of Book VIII of the *Politics*, he writes that legislators should be particularly concerned with the education of the young, suggesting that the discussion that follows should be among the primary concerns of the legislator. Taking into account the number of times the topic of legislation is raised in the *EN* and the *Politics* as well as the level of detail with which Aristotle discusses the topic, I concur with Malcolm Schofield's claim that both works alike 'are best interpreted as writings that are addressed not to individuals in their private capacities, but to someone who is or aspires to be a politician—that is to say, a lawgiver'.[11] What Aristotle and Xunzi have in common is that both are addressing an elite audience of people who hold or have the potential to hold political power; as a result, any discourse on moral education in the texts is expected to impact individuals in their private capacity and in their public capacities in managing political affairs.[12]

How, then, might the moral education of the people (and in some cases the acquisition of a correct sense of honour and shame) contribute to community life? In the *Xunzi, wei* 偽, conscious exertion, is framed as the only way through which humans could learn to reform their inherent bad nature and dispel selfish motives. This opens up a discussion of the interconnectedness of individual and communal benefit, where Xunzi illustrates that it is only through moral training of the individual that conflict can be averted and community life sustained. By framing discussions of disgrace (*ru* 辱) in terms of the correct ranking of a sense of propriety (*yi* 義) over personal benefit (*li* 利), Xunzi highlights and in turn resolves the potential conflict of interest between actions that are propelled by selfishness and those driven by a regard for what is proper and for the public good. Two scenarios are offered: in the first one, humans act on their liking for

---

10. *EN* 1109b30ff.

11. Schofield 2006, 310. Bodéüs (1991, 247) makes the stronger claim that 'the entirety of Aristotle's reflections on human things (the study of ethical matters and of matters relating to the organization of cities) is addressed to legislators, whom he regards as responsible for education and thus as artisans of human happiness'. See also Bodéüs 1993, 118ff.

12. On holders of political power in the two societies, see Chapter 1.

profit (*haoli* 好利) and indulge their natural disposition (*zong qingxing* 纵情性); disregarding the practice of conscious exertion and giving in to their unbridled original nature lead to social disorder. In the second scenario, humans prioritise a sense of propriety that finds expression in the practice of ritual, in turn averting disorder and avoiding disgrace while at the same time having their personal desires fulfilled.

Ritual and propriety, standards imposed by the former kings, help to nurture desires and grant the people what they seek.[13] This appears counterintuitive, since ritual involves adherence to certain sets of rules that impose restrictions on one's actions. However, this apparent contradiction can be solved if we turn to Xunzi's idea that a sense of propriety (which leads one to adhere to ritual practice) and *li* 利, 'benefit' or more generally 'self-interest', are intricately connected. According to Xunzi, humans' basic desires are primal: they are born with a liking for profit, and even the sage kings cannot rid them of this liking. Furthermore, what they desire most is life or survival, and what they detest the most is death.[14] While it is simply within human nature to have various desires, the fact that humans live in communities with limited resources available necessitates that not all desires can be fulfilled. If everybody seeks to fulfil only his own desires, danger and disgrace for the profit-seeking individuals ensue. In a poverty-stricken society made unruly by widespread unbridled desires, human beings' basic desires cannot, on a general level, be satisfied.[15] If all people were to follow their natural instincts like Jie and Zhi and seek what they needed without a sense of concern for others, disaster would ensue:

> The nature of humans is such that one is born with a love for personal benefit. If one indulges in it, aggression and strife will thrive and courtesy and deference will disappear. Humans are born with envy and hatred; if one indulged in these, violence and crime would thrive and loyalty and trustworthiness would disappear. Humans are born with desires of the ears and the eyes, with a liking for beautiful sounds and sights; if one indulges in these, licentiousness and disorder will arise, while rituals, propriety and principles will disappear. Therefore, indulging in one's nature and following one's dispositions (*qing*) necessarily leads to aggression and

---

13. 先王惡其亂也，故制禮義以分之，以養人之欲，給人之求 (70/19/2). On the idea of 'nurture' (*yang* 養) in the *Xunzi*, particularly in relation to the notion of the good life, see Fraser 2013b.

14. 'There is nothing that humans desire more than life, and there is nothing that humans detest more than death.' 人之所欲，生甚矣，人之惡，死甚矣 (85/22/59).

15. Further discussion of the inseparability of individual and communal good can be found in Chapter 3 on human nature.

122 *Aristotle and Xunzi on Shame*

strife, together with the violation of social distinctions and forms of order, and ends in violence.[16]

On the other hand, if humans are collectively able to follow prescriptions of ritual and regulate their desires through the heart-mind, prizing a sense of propriety above all else, they will enjoy an ordered society and fulfil their own desires. The latter case does not entail that all desires can and should be fulfilled; after all, human desires are many and not all of them should be indulged at any given time. However, Xunzi stands by the view that humans are capable of doing good things that bring benefit to themselves without harming others; on that basis, he provides an account of how individuals' basic desires might be best accommodated in a society where ritual and a sense of propriety are followed.

Xunzi draws links between the fate of society and that of the individual by expressing the idea that whatever actions lead one to disgrace are likely to cause social disorder and instability, so that such actions have a negative impact on the community as well as on oneself and one's associates. At the same time, should society undergo chaos and disorder, one would not be able to satisfy one's own desires or gain honour, but would suffer disgrace alongside others. In fact, rather than portraying ritual and propriety as forces that place constraints on desires, Xunzi associates them with the idea of 'nurturing desires' (*yangyu* 養欲), thereby representing them as serving the function of furthering individual interests. Given that the *Xunzi* was written with the ambition of providing advice and counsel to a ruler and his ministers, the discussions on the consequences of disgraceful behaviour could be read as admonitions to those in positions of power: anyone indulging in his desires and disregarding learning and moral cultivation would come to a disgraceful end, causing people to suffer with him; should his state fail to be governed by ritual and propriety but fall into disorder and violence, the ruler himself would not derive any honour but would only be disgraced in such a situation. Xunzi's tactic is therefore to encourage those in positions of power to prioritise a sense of propriety over personal benefit by bringing their fate closer to that of the people, illustrating the practical benefits of ensuring peace and order in the state—for the people, as well as for the ruling powers themselves.[17] In Xunzi's discourse, then, disgraceful behaviour is frequently associated with disorder in society, and even the idea that human nature is bad is framed in terms of the negative impact of selfish behaviour on

---

16. 今人之性，生而有好利焉，順是，故爭奪生而辭讓亡焉；生而有疾惡焉，順是，故殘賊生而忠信亡焉；生而有耳目之欲，有好聲色焉，順是，故淫亂生而禮義文理亡焉。然則縱人之性，順人之情，必出於爭奪，合於犯分亂理而歸於暴 (86/23/1–86/23/3).

17. For a discussion of how ritual serves as an institution to support the pursuit of pleasure, see Nylan 2018, 193ff.

Social Institutions and the Politics of Moral Education 123

society, not in terms of any sense of 'original sin' such as that found in the Judeo-Christian tradition. Nonetheless, this does not make Xunzi a 'consequentialist', one who is solely concerned about the impact of moral education on society rather than its intrinsic goodness, as I have already illustrated in the previous chapter.[18] If we turn to the socio-historical background during Xunzi's time, it is not difficult to see why Xunzi might have repeatedly called for education and the proper practice of rituals. Among the interstate wars and infighting between powerful houses during the late Warring States period, restoring order and social distinctions were seen as deserving immediate attention.

The idea of *ru* or 'disgrace' in the *Xunzi* is frequently cited in the political context of serving and governing. Xunzi makes a strong case that the ruler's chances of bringing about a stable state rooted in honour are dependent upon choosing the right ministers:

> Those who are to maintain the state certainly cannot do so alone. Since this is the case, the strength, defensive security, honour and disgrace of a state lie in the selection of its prime minister.[19]

> If he [the ruler] establishes for his court exaltation of a standard of rectitude that is not suitable and if he hands over the multiple affairs of government to people who are not humane (*ren*), then he himself would toil away, the state would be in disorder, accomplishment would be frustrated, his reputation would be disgraced, and his state endangered. This is the pivotal force of being a ruler.[20]

In the first passage, it is the honour and disgrace of the state that is at stake while in the second passage, the ruler himself is disgraced through the employment of ministers who do not observe humane practice. In one sense, the ministers are an extension of the ruler himself since they stand in between him and the people and are expected to carry out the necessary work to sustain the ruler's governance and further a state's prosperity. The concept of *wuwei* 無為—spontaneity or effortless action—is only possible when the ruler himself sets a good example for those below, *and* when his closest associates prove themselves worthy of assisting with the running of the state. In making the honour and disgrace of the state and of the ruler to a certain extent synonymous, Xunzi ties together the

---

18. See Harris (2019, 115–16) for further discussions on this issue.

19. 彼持國者，必不可以獨也，然則彊固榮辱在於取相矣 (39/11/36). It has been suggested by Li Disheng (1979, 238) that *gu* 固 is to be read as *ruo* 弱 here to make better sense of the sentence and match the pattern of a set of antonyms—*rong* and *ru*—immediately following.

20. 立隆正本朝而不當，所使要百事者非仁人也，則身勞而國亂，功廢而名辱，社稷必危：是人君者之樞機也 (42/11/103–104).

124   Aristotle and Xunzi on Shame

fate of the state with that of the ruler and highlights the crucial importance of appointing the right ministers to government.

As for the ministers, Xunzi compares and contrasts several types. There are those who do not have regard for the ruler's honour and disgrace, are indifferent as to the condition of the state, form clandestine alliances and engage in unseemly indulgence for the sole purpose of retaining their emoluments and nurturing their companions. Xunzi calls such people *guozei* 國賊 or traitors.[21] Then there are those who are credited with assisting the ruler by way of loyal opposition, in an effort to save him and the state:

> To have the ability to obstruct the mandate of the ruler, to act without permission in matters of importance to the lord, and to overturn the undertakings of the ruler in order to secure the state against danger and to deliver the ruler from disgrace, resulting in accomplishments and military achievements sufficient to consummate the greatest benefits for the state, is called '(loyal) opposition'.[22]

In this case, the minister is commended for his actions despite his apparent opposition to the authority of the ruler because the ultimate aim of his opposition lies in achieving the greatest benefits for the state. He serves to deliver the ruler from disgrace by providing security for the state after a crisis, thereby granting the ruler security to exercise his powers. It would appear that certain expectations hold true for the ruler as well as for the minister: the minister has the duty to serve well by means of accruing honour and averting disgrace, for the ruler as well as for the state as a whole, while the ruler is expected to make the right decisions in appointing someone with such a capacity. *Ru*—disgrace—often does not appear on its own but is attached to a set of ideas associated with threats such as *wei* 危 (danger) and *luan* 亂 (disorder). Together, such stock phrases add to the admonitory tone of the text and convey the idea that the damage caused by a bad minister would extend to various aspects of the running of the state.

Let us now turn to Aristotle and observe the ways in which moral education, and more specifically ideas relating to shame, might relate to community life. Towards the beginning of the *EN*, politics is famously said to belong to the most sovereign, that is, the most 'architectonic' study, which renders ethics

---

21. 不卹君之榮辱，不卹國之臧否，偷合苟容,以之持祿養交而已耳，國賊也 (50/13/11–12).

22. 有能抗君之命，竊君之重，反君之事，以安國之危，除君之辱，功伐足以成國之大利，謂之拂 (50/13/15–16). The literal meaning of 拂 *fu* here is 'disobey'. I follow Knoblock in translating it as 'loyal opposition' to convey the idea that this kind of opposition reflects a minister's loyalty towards the ruler and the state.

Social Institutions and the Politics of Moral Education   125

subordinate to it. Aristotle remarks: 'Neither must we suppose that any one of the citizens belongs to himself, for they all belong to the state, and are each of them a part of the state, and the care of each part is inseparable from the care of the whole' (*Pol.* 1337a27–30). A direct link is made between education and politics at the beginning of Book VIII of the *Politics*, where it is said that education of the young requires the special attention of the lawgiver and that the neglect of education does harm to the constitution (*Pol.* 1337a11–14). Indeed, already in Book VII, Aristotle makes the remark that a city can be excellent only when the citizens who have a share in the government are excellent, and that even if we could suppose the citizen body to be excellent, without each citizen being so individually, it would still be better for the citizens to be excellent, since in the excellence of each the excellence of all is involved (*Pol.* 1332a36–38). Clearly, education relates not only to the achievement of *eudaimonia* on the part of the individual but is essential for the wellbeing of the state.[23]

For Aristotle, *aidōs* is important in maintaining social relations and allowing humans to engage in an active political life. It carries with it a sense of respect that is deemed appropriate for the young towards their seniors, understood as a sense of shame, modesty or humility in terms of acknowledging one's inferior position in the company of those deserving respect.[24] This sense of the word *aidōs* in such a situation can trace its influence from the Homeric epics, where it is generally a positive term used to mean awe, reverence and a sense of what is right (e.g., *Il.* 15.128–29, 24.44–45). An example from the *Odyssey* is particularly apt here, where the young man Telemachus addresses Athena, who is disguised as Mentor, and expresses his concern about speaking to Nestor who is far superior to him in age and experience: "Mentor, how shall I go, and how shall I greet him? I am as yet all unversed in subtle speech, and moreover a young man has shame (*aidōs*) to question an elder."[25] *Aidōs* here is closely woven into interpersonal relationships so that in his interaction with an elder, Telemachus is overcome by a sense of self-consciousness and is made to realise how Nestor's social status compares with his own.

---

23. Nonetheless, when compared with Xunzi, Aristotle does not discuss the impact of moral transgression on the wellbeing of the state at such length.

24. On the political relevance of Greek shame, in particular sexual shame, and its connections with ideas of awe and respect, see Ludwig (2002, 276). Taylor (2006, 235) points out that 'Aristotle's view that shame is a feeling appropriate only for young people reflects the fact that the term *aidōs* also connotes modesty, the attribute of someone who is restrained, and who does not flaunt him or herself (in particular, sexually) and who acknowledges the superior status of other, especially older, people'.

25. Μέντορ, πῶς τ' ἄρ' ἴω; πῶς τ' ἄρ προσπτύξομαι αὐτόν; οὐδέ τί πω μύθοισι πεπείρημαι πυκινοῖσιν· αἰδὼς δ' αὖ νέον ἄνδρα γεραίτερον ἐξερέεσθαι (*Od.* 3.22–24). For an extended treatment of *aidōs* in Homer, see Cairns 1993, chapter 2.

126 *Aristotle and Xunzi on Shame*

Aidōs also plays a role in the context of the family, where it is important for children to feel a sense of respect and humility towards their parents. Aristotle advises against youthful marriages for the reason that young parents do not inspire *aidōs* in their offspring: 'Nor ought they [the parents] be too nearly of an age [to their children]; to youthful marriages there are many objections—the children will be lacking in respect (*aidōs*) for the parents, who will seem to be their contemporaries, and disputes will arise in the management of the household' (*Pol.* 1335a1–4). There is a sense in which age in itself can be an instant marker for respect, and problems arise in the family when young parents fail to inspire *aidōs* in their children due to their age. Young people's sense of *aidōs* for their elders is not limited to the household, as shown by the *Odyssey* example above and also in Aristotle, where *aidōs* is associated with a sense of fear: 'Some of the magistrates should stay with the boys, while the grown-up men remain with the magistrates; for the presence of the magistrates is the best mode of inspiring true modesty (*aidōs*) and ingenuous fear' (*Pol.* 1331a39–b1). *Aidōs* towards their seniors in age and rank, then, enables young people to orient themselves correctly in their roles as daughter, son, or as a young citizen in the city-state, so that with respect and compliance they come under the influence of their superiors in doing the right kinds of things.[26] Here it is interesting to scrutinize certain cultural stereotypes with regard to 'shame metaphors'. Jane Geaney (2004), in writing about shame in early Confucianism, traces 'shame metaphors' in the classical texts and argues that Confucian shame metaphors are primarily concerned with the blurring of boundaries as opposed to the western sexual metaphors of seeing and hearing. In Geaney's view, such boundaries involve social status, with a more fundamental form of it being the boundary between humans and animals. This may be true in some instances; however, it is surely an overgeneralisation. Contrary to expectations, the Aristotelian examples show that the allegedly 'Confucian' idea of blurring the boundaries is at the same time evident here in the Greek materials, where the lack of shame or modesty entails the overstepping of one's social position. Even though not explicitly phrased in such a way, one might say that 'blurring of boundaries' is something that

---

26. The Roman equivalent of this aspect of *aidōs* would be *verecundia*. According to Kaster (2005, 26), most instances of *verecundia* have what might be called a 'vertical orientation', 'as the person who experiences the emotion signals, by experiencing it, that he knows where he stands on the social pyramid'. In addition, it 'animates the art of knowing your proper place in every social transaction and binds the free members of a civil community, exerting its force both vertically, across the different ranks of society, and horizontally, among members of comparable status' (ibid., 27).

Social Institutions and the Politics of Moral Education   127

would be a cause of concern to Aristotle if anyone failed to display respect for his or her parents and elders.[27]

WOMEN AND THE POLITICS OF 'SHAME'

At first sight a modern reader might be surprised at the relative lack of discussion of women's feelings of shame in either philosopher. But this speaks volumes about the nature of the texts they were composing and their preferred audiences—male members of the political elite. In that context issues to do with the shameful behaviour of women, or directed at women, were not an important part of their agenda. In the Greek tradition, the potentially destructive power of a woman's sexuality and shame is well documented in epic, tragedy and in prose writers such as in Herodotus's story of Gyges,[28] which show that sexual shame experienced by women can lead to drastic situations with heavy political repercussions. In the Herodotus example, king Candaules, obsessed with his wife's sexual allure, urges his guard Gyges to confirm his wife's beauty by seeing her naked. Gyges protests by saying 'When a woman takes off her clothes, she loses her respect/ shame (*aidōs*) at the same time' and asks the king not to make him do something that is lawless. Though Candaules arranges for Gyges to observe his wife in secret, the queen catches sight of Gyges and is ashamed (*aischuntheisa*), as a result of which she orders Gyges to choose between the alternatives of either killing the king and seizing both her and the kingdom, or himself be killed for seeing what he should not have seen. Gyges chooses the former option, killing king Candaules in the very bed chamber (*tou autou chōriou*) where the queen purportedly lost—and in the end regained—her *aidōs*.[29] There is a strong sense in the Greek tradition that a woman's loss

27. In Latin literature, one can also identify shame with the idea of 'blurring of boundaries'. An excellent example, cited by Kaster 2005, would be Livy 34. 2. 10, where the vocabulary of boundary ('finibus') itself is used: '*pudor* kept married women within the bounds of what was theirs by right' (*sui iuris finibus matronas contineret pudor*).

28. *Hist.* 1.8–12.

29. The rape of Lucretia that led to the overthrow of tyrannical rule would be another example of the potential political implications of sexual violation. Cicero describes how Lucretius, 'a modest (*pudens*) and noble woman', 'inflicted the death penalty upon herself on account of the wrong (*iniuria*) done to her', *Rep.* 2.46; see Kaster 2005, 36–7. On the topic of women's sexuality and power, Ludwig (2002, 279ff.) cites the contemporary example of women's head covering and veiling. Such acts are commonly (mis) understood in the West as 'solely an instrument of oppression', even though for indigenous peoples, they can be viewed as 'non-Western feminism', a symbol that the woman is aware of her erotic worth and demands interactions on a 'businesslike level'. This example shows how 'shame' can have close associations with ideas of respect and reverence, not simply in the ancient Greek context but in contemporary society. In the words of Ludwig, 'respect for the power of sexuality emerges as the central feature of traditional modesty' (ibid., 283).

128 *Aristotle and Xunzi on Shame*

of modesty involves disloyalty towards the household and can lead to disastrous political consequences, the case of Clytemnestra being a notorious example. In Euripides' *Hippolytus*, Phaedra's *aidōs* leads to her own death as well as Hippolytus', orchestrated by the goddesses Artemis and Athena.[30] Even though she is not involved in illicit sexual relations with her stepson, shame is clearly felt through the illegitimate *eros* itself, and her sense of honour lost through Hippolytus' rejection. In her first address to the women of Troezen (380ff.), she distinguishes between two types of shame (*aidōs*):

> Life has many pleasures: lengthy and idle chats, for example, and indolence, a pleasurable vice.
> And then there's shame, which has a double face: one, to be sure, is not a bad thing to possess; but there's the other shame, whose weight crushes whole households. And if good and bad shame were easy to distinguish, the word describing them would not be the same.[31]

Evident in this excerpt is Phaedra's clear awareness of the complexity of the idea of *aidōs*, which carries with it both the positive sense of respect and modesty as well as the implications of a dishonourable deed that causes misfortune for the entire household.

In the *History of Animals*, Aristotle compares the characteristics of male and female animals in general and claims that some of these characteristics are more manifest in humans than in other species. One characteristic of the female is that they are more shameless (*anaidesteron*).[32] No further explanation is given, but we may understand Aristotle's attribution of *anaidesteron* to females in relation to what he says about women's characteristics in general. In Book I of the *Politics* it is said that the woman has a deliberative faculty that is without authority (*Pol.* 1260a12–13), and the same can be said for women's excellence of character; furthermore, the temperance of women and men are not the same (*Pol.* 1260a20–24). By implication, women are by nature less capable of judging which actions are worthy of pursuit and which are shame-inducing. In *Rhetoric* II.6 where Aristotle outlines the situations that give rise to shame, the examples given are those of cowardice, withholding deposit, having sexual intercourse with the wrong people or at an inappropriate time or place, making profit in

---

30. For a fuller treatment of women's *aidōs*, see Cairns 1993, 120–26, 185–88, 305–40.

31. This passage is notoriously difficult to translate, see Cairns 1993, 321–40. I follow D'Angour's translation in his article 'Shame and guilt in ancient Greece'. For an extended discussion of shame and purity in the *Hippolytus*, see Segal 1970. Wray (2015, 208–11) gives a treatment of the idea of shame in Seneca's *Phaedra*.

32. *HA* 608a22–b18. For an extensive discussion of female animals in Aristotle, See Connell 2016.

Social Institutions and the Politics of Moral Education   129

disgraceful ways, and in money matters. We could say that these examples primarily concern the activities of men, with the exception of the case of sexual licentiousness, which is probably approached from the point of view of the male perpetrator, but could also be applicable to women.

In the Chinese tradition, there is no lack of examples of the 'femme fatale', beautiful women who seduce the ruler into a debauched lifestyle and cause dynastic collapse.[33] Philosophical accounts emphasise the dangers of the lack of distinction between men and women. Indeed, the *Guanzi* warns that if men and women are not separate, then the people will be without shame.[34] Female sexuality is usually mentioned in early philosophical works in the context of admonishing the male audience lest they succumb to female sexual allure, rather than offered as direct advice to the women themselves. In the *Xunzi*, 'shame' is generally discussed in a gender-neutral context, with no specific mention of the kinds of shame that are liable to be felt by women or men. Nonetheless, there is a passage in the chapter *Against Physiognomy* which suggests that women and men can have different reactions to scenarios that might be shame-inducing. In the passage, Xunzi cautions against the handsome and charming appearance of the disorderly lords and the wily rascals of the countryside, who wear exotic clothing and effeminate ornaments, and whose temperament (literally 'blood' and '*qi*') and bearing resemble those of a woman.[35] We are then told that these outwardly handsome but morally debauched men are regarded differently by women and men: while married women and unmarried girls desire them as husbands and suitors, crowding each other shoulder to shoulder and even deserting their families in order to elope with them, men consider it a source of shame to be associated with such figures:

> The average lord would be ashamed (*xiu*) to have them as ministers, the average father to have them as sons, the average elder brother to have them as younger brothers, and the average man to have them as friends.[36]

Xunzi here associates a man's effeminate form with moral failings, regarding gender transgression itself as a form of disgrace. Interestingly, in this episode, women are portrayed as being less inclined than men to feel a sense of shame for something that contravenes social norms. They are far too distracted by the physical appearance of these men to recognise their implied moral

---

33. See Zhou 2018 on a comparison between representations of Helen and the 'femme fatale' in the early Chinese tradition. See also Goldin 2001, in particular chapter 2, on women and sex roles.

34. 男女無別則民無廉恥 (*Guanzi, Quanxiu* 權修, 53).

35. See Geaney 2004, 124.

36. 然而中君羞以為臣，中父羞以為子，中兄羞以為弟，中人羞以為友 (13/5/17).

130 *Aristotle and Xunzi on Shame*

shortcomings, being willing even to do the dishonourable deed of eloping with them. The average man, on the other hand, is conscious of the moral threat that these men pose, considering it a source of shame to be associated with them. It is intriguing that in the only passage of the *Xunzi* where women are mentioned in association with the idea of shame (*xiu*, in this case), they should be portrayed in a negative light, as a group that fails to exercise a sense of shame in their dalliance with the good-looking but morally debauched men. Women are solely focused on these men as attractive partners, while it falls upon other men to regulate how a male member of society should fulfil his role as minister, son, brother, and friend. This has interesting implications for power dynamics: men are portrayed as having greater social responsibility, and therefore power, in ensuring that no person should pose a threat to the norms in family affairs as well as on the political stage, while women here are shown as lacking moral integrity in their dealings with members of the opposite sex.

Xunzi cannot be said, however, to be representative of a general trend in portraying women as being comparatively less inclined to experience shame than men.[37] The *Mencius* contains an episode where the opposite situation is presented, with a wife and a concubine feeling shame on behalf of their husband's behaviour. It is said that there is a man who would return home everyday satiated with spirits and meat. Upon being asked by his wife whom he ate and drank with, he would claim that it is the wealthy and the noble. His wife, suspicious of his activities on the account that no person of distinction ever visits them, follows his husband and finds out that the way he got himself satiated was by begging for food from those who are sacrificing at the tombs.[38] She shares her discovery with the concubine and the two mock their husband (*shan qi liangren* 訕其良人) and weep, before the husband comes back, carrying himself proudly. The author then comments that in the view of the *junzi*, there are few wives and concubines who would not feel ashamed (*xiu*) of how such men seek riches, noble status, profit and success.[39] This is an instance where the women in the household feel ashamed for their husband's detestable behaviour, while the husband exhibits no regret or remorse. There is a sense that the husband is failing the household: rather than upholding the honour of the house, he loses the respect of even his dependants—his wife and concubine, over whom he is expected to have a guiding role in morality. This passage draws out the social

37. On the applicability of 'gendered virtue' to Chinese classics, see Raphals 2002 and articles in Li ed. 2000, in particular contributions by Raphals and Goldin.

38. Cf. Aristotle *Rhet.* 1383b22–24 gives the example of making profit out of the weak (such as the dead) as something that is shame-inducing.

39. 由君子觀之，則人之所以求富貴利達者，其妻妾不羞也，而不相泣者，幾希矣 (*Mencius* 8.33/45/20).

Social Institutions and the Politics of Moral Education 131

aspect of *xiu*—one feels ashamed on account of what someone else has done, and the shame is even more acutely felt when that person is a family member, and worse, someone who is expected to set a moral example. Despite not feeling ashamed for his behaviour, the husband brings disgrace upon himself as well as upon the whole household.[40]

The relative neglect of women in discourses on shame, in Aristotle as well as in Xunzi, might be said to illustrate women's lack of political power and so their relative lack of relevance to the agenda that Aristotle and Xunzi set themselves. Women and their *aidōs*, in the two senses employed by Phaedra in her speech, feature as a prominent theme in tragedy, as has already been widely discussed in the literature. Women are expected to stay firmly in their social roles: to guard their chastity and not to be involved in politics. Tragedy shows the disastrous consequences caused when women transgress their roles as mothers and wives, commit *hubris* and lose their *aidōs*. Yet in normative discourses on virtue and politics, women occupy a peripheral presence: if the pursuit of honour and a fully virtuous life (becoming either a *junzi* or a *phronimos*) fall largely within the aspirations of elite males, who represent heads of households and wield political power, then it is not altogether surprising that discourses on honour and shame should be ultimately concerned with male conduct. Where women have limited rights and prerogatives and play a decidedly submissive role in the family and a cursory part on the social scene, their shame will only be relevant in a limited range of situations largely pertaining to their sexuality and domestic relationships.[41] Even where shame is mentioned in the context of female behaviour and in particular female sexuality, such episodes generally serve as guides for men in terms of how they should adopt behaviours and attitudes. The concentration on the key political agents to be persuaded is testimony in a way to the practical orientation of Aristotle's and Xunzi's discussion.

Social Institutions: *Nomos, Li, Fa*

What are the social institutions that play a role in maintaining norms? On this point Aristotle and Xunzi differ quite markedly, with Xunzi elevating the role

---

40. Compare with an example from a later text, the *Shiji* from the Han dynasty, where Chong'er, i.e., the later Lord Wen of Jin, is reprimanded by his wife for yielding to her sexual allure and failing to return to his state to conduct proper business. She says that she is ashamed of him (*wei zi xiu zhi* 為子羞之) (*Shiji* 39, 1698). See discussion of this passage in Goldin 2001, 62–63.

41. This phenomenon is not limited to the Greek and Chinese examples: writing on shame and the Romans, Kaster (1997, 9–10) comments that women's capacity for *pudor* 'was largely limited to a single frame of reference—the sexual: the *pudor* of women is, in effect, congruent with their *pudicitia*, or sexual respectability'.

132 *Aristotle and Xunzi on Shame*

of ritual, *li* 禮 and Aristotle, that of *nomos*, though as I shall set out below, it would be an oversimplification to juxtapose the two ideas and treat them as if they were the only kinds of social institution present in the respective societies when the picture is far more complex. In addition, although 'law' is one of the common translations for *nomos*, this Greek term in fact has a wide semantic range and overlaps the concept of *li* when carrying the sense of 'social custom'.

While Aristotle notes the importance of habituating oneself to recognise and practise actions that are fine and noble, highlighting the role of *aidōs* in inhibiting bad actions, he nevertheless acknowledges that most people are not the sort to be guided by a sense of shame (*aidōs*) but by fear, and not to refrain from bad things on the grounds of their shamefulness but because of the punishments (*EN* 1179b11-16). For such a reason, society cannot merely rely on individuals to develop a sense of shame but necessarily has to introduce certain measures to keep their actions in check. As I have suggested in the previous chapter, this passage is interesting because it complicates the idea of *aidōs*: in the earlier books, *aidōs* is construed as a something that is second best, as in the example of civic courage that is inferior to true courage due to its being prompted by *aidōs*. In the Book X example, however, being guided by *aidōs* is simply portrayed as the praiseworthy alternative to being constrained by fear. One might say that, even so, this passage does not present a fundamentally different view of *aidōs* as compared with earlier parts of the *EN*, since the contrast between actions that are motivated by shame and those motivated by fear is already set up in the case of civic courage versus spirited courage. Nonetheless, one might still see this passage as elevating the status of *aidōs* on the grounds that actions propelled by *aidōs* are portrayed here as unreservedly good, and not contrasted with any superior alternatives. Indeed, Aristotle, in saying that those who act out of a fear of punishment have no concept of what is fine and of what is truly pleasant, argues by extension that those who act on the basis of *aidōs* do have a concept of what is fine and of what is truly pleasant, which is praiseworthy in itself. So, how might we explain the fact that *aidōs* here is no longer portrayed as the lesser alternative to acting for the sake of the fine itself, as contrasted with the example of courage in Book III? The clue is that Aristotle here is addressing his students in their capacity as potential legislators, hence he is speaking about the tendencies of the hoi polloi and suggesting ways to regulate their behaviour. For the many, Aristotle does not entertain the expectation that they reach a state whereby they are acting out of a concern for the fine itself; instead, a concern for *aidōs* would be sufficient in propelling them towards acting in a way that accords with what is the fine. By contrast, in the earlier books of the *EN* where a concern for *aidōs* is discussed in contrast to the ultimate state of acting for the sake of the fine itself, Aristotle has the moral development of his students themselves in mind, students who would certainly not fall into the category of 'the many' and for whom Aristotle holds greater expectations. The context in which the idea of *aidōs* is mentioned, therefore, provides clarification as to why there might seem to be discrepancies in its usage in various parts of the *EN*.

A discussion about the incapacity of the many to be guided by *aidōs*, then, leads to an extended argument for the necessity for legislation, both in Book X of the *EN* and in the *Politics*,[42] providing further evidence that the ultimate concern in those parts lies not in the moral cultivation of the individual but in regulating the behaviour of the hoi polloi. Because it is the legislator who sets the standards for judging actions and dealing out rewards and punishments in accordance with what meets institutional approval, it is he who wields influence over popular morality and has a direct impact on ordinary people's values. For Aristotle, law embodies the golden and impartial standard against which people's actions are to be judged, since when humans govern, their appetite resembles a wild animal and *thumos* disrupts the rule even of the best, while law represents the ruling of god (*ton theon*) and reason (*ton noun*; *Pol.* 1287a28–32). A causal relationship is drawn between the habituation of citizens to the good and the good status of the constitution when Aristotle attributes to law the inculcation of good behaviour in the people: 'Lawgivers make the citizens good through habituation, and this is what every lawgiver *aims* at, but those who do it badly miss their mark; and this is what makes one constitution different from another, a good one from a bad one.'[43] Aristotle, then, was well aware of the importance of setting up a stringent legislative system that might serve a prohibitive and punitive function, especially designed with those who are not liable to be persuaded by reason or amenable to feelings of shame in mind. The system which oversees the dealing out of rewards and punishments must be a fair one if forms of party strife (*staseis*) are to be avoided, for we are told that gain and honour are objects about which forms of party strife are waged: 'The motives for waging strife are gain and honour, or their opposites; for men wage strife in cities to divert punishment or dishonour from themselves or their friends' (*Pol.* 1302a31–34).[44]

42. Compare with Plato's *Laws*, where *aidōs* is said to have acted as a kind of despot, making the Athenians live in willing subjection to the existing laws (*Leg.* 698b). Aristotle, then, is suggesting something along different lines, namely that because the many are not amenable to *aidōs*, legislation is necessary to restrain their behaviour.

43. οἱ γὰρ νομοθέται τοὺς πολίτας ἐθίζοντες ποιοῦσιν ἀγαθούς, καὶ τὸ μὲν βούλημα παντὸς νομοθέτου τοῦτ᾽ ἐστίν, ὅσοι δὲ μὴ εὖ αὐτὸ ποιοῦσιν ἁμαρτάνουσιν, καὶ διαφέρει τούτῳ πολιτεία πολιτείας ἀγαθὴ φαύλης (*EN* 1103b3–6).

44. Cf. *Pol.* 1302b10–14 for the idea that those who are dishonoured and who see others obtain honours rise in party strife. The honour or dishonour when undeserved is unjust; and just when awarded according to merit.

134   *Aristotle and Xunzi on Shame*

Before we turn to Xunzi's position on the kinds of social institutions necessary to regulate behaviour, let us first bring in a passage from the *Analects* that distinguishes between two ways to rule: one relies on inculcating a sense of shame, the other a sense of fear, reminiscent of the Aristotelian example in Book X of the *EN*. The following statement is famously attributed to Confucius:

> If you try to guide the common people with edicts (*zheng* 政) and keep them in line with punishments (*xing* 刑), the common people will stay out of trouble but have no sense of shame (*chi* 恥). If, however, you guide them with *de*, and keep them in line by means of ritual, the people will have a sense of shame and will rectify themselves.[45]

While the semantic range of *zheng* 政 is rather wide and encompasses the meanings of 'politics' and 'government', it could also take the narrower meanings of 'law', 'edict' or 'regulation', especially when used with *xing* 刑—'punishment', as is the case here.[46] In this passage, edicts and punishments are contrasted with *de*, virtue or virtuous capacity, and *li*, ritual. While all of them serve to discipline people and make them uniform (*qi* 齊), only *li* and *de* have the power to instil a sense of right and wrong in people so that they do not repudiate wrongful behaviour in order to avoid punishment. The point is that government through these different means might potentially guarantee the same outcome of conformity; however, only certain ways of ruling can instil good character in people at the same time as achieving conformity. For Confucius, it is important that people do not become disciplined through edicts and punishment, but through *de* and *li* that enable them to have a sense of shame (*youchi* 有恥). It could be understood that in this account, punishment does not prompt a sense of moral responsibility or lead to ways of self-improvement, but generates only fear of the punishment itself. Guiding people by *de* and *li*, on the other hand, allows for the gradual build-up of good character: while *de* connotes the capacity for the ruler to exert a positive moral influence, *li* suggests the observation of ritual propriety, both of which may *preclude* one from doing anything that might warrant punishment, since one has an idea of what constitutes good and bad behaviour. This provides us with a forceful reminder of Aristotle's account of 'shame' as the preferred deterrent over fear of punishment in the examples mentioned above.

---

45. 子曰：“道之以政，齊之以刑，民免而無恥；道之以德，齊之以禮，有恥且格” (*Analects* 2.3/2/29–30).

46. Cf. also: 'If, when good and wise men are in high office and able men are employed, a ruler takes advantage of times of peace to explain the *zheng* and *xing* to the people, then even larger states will certainly stand in awe of him.' 莫如貴德而尊士，賢者在位，能者在職。國家閒暇，及是時明其政刑。雖大國，必畏之矣 (*Mencius* 3.4/17/22–23).

Social Institutions and the Politics of Moral Education   135

In advocating the adherence to ritual and a sense of propriety rather than relying merely on the force of law, Xunzi can be said to be following in the footsteps of Confucius. Yet, unlike Confucius, in several places of the text Xunzi does spell out the importance of *zheng* and *fa*, law, standard, or rule.[47] Furthermore, Xunzi employs the vocabulary of *lü* 律 (statutes) and *ling* 令 (ordinances), which can be said to fall into the cluster of terms concerned with social institutions and the enforcement of rules.[48] Consider the following passages:

> From the position of *shi* upwards, all must be moderated through ritual and music. The ordinary masses, the Hundred Clans, must be controlled by laws and measures (*fashu* 法數).[49]

> He [the exemplary ruler] will surely cultivate ritual in order to set straight the court, rectify the standards (*fa* 法) in order to set straight the officials, and make his government (*zheng* 政) evenhanded in order to set straight the common people.[50]

Statements such as the above mark a clear departure from Confucius' stance in the *Analects*: *fa* and *zheng* are no longer seen as entirely unattractive alternatives to 'rule by virtuosity', but as necessary measures to maintain social control, especially when it comes to the ordinary masses.[51] It is interesting to note that *fa* in the *Xunzi* has a close association with *li*, ritual, and the combined term *lifa* 禮法 is not found in the *Analects*, the *Mencius* or pre-Qin texts generally, but is distinctive of the *Xunzi*. Ritual is said to contain the model for the primary social distinctions and the categories for the guiding rules (*fa*), and for ordering norms

---

47. *Fa* can prove problematic when translated into English. Goldin (2011, 91) draws attention to the fact that while '*fa* can surely include law, it covers a much larger semantic range, and it is precisely in this larger range that the word usually has to be located'. He notes that the two basic meanings of *fa* are 'method' and 'standard'. In the case of Xunzi, a phrase such as *shifa jiaohua* 師法教化 would mean cultivation through teaching and discipline, where 'fa' does not specifically refer to law but rather to a standard that is to be observed. For a fuller survey of the usages of *fa* in classical Chinese philosophy, see Hansen 1994, Pines 2023 and Pines ed. (forthcoming).

48. Archaeological excavations from recent years have revealed details of a range of legal codes and social sanctions that prescribe 'normative behaviour' in Xunzi's time; interestingly, in those materials norms and laws are rarely spoken of as *fa*. For a study and translation of the Zhangjiashan 張家山 legal texts see Barbieri-Low & Yates eds. 2015.

49. 由士以上則必以禮樂節之，眾庶百姓則必以法數制之 (32/10/18–19). Knoblock translates the term *fashu* as 'law and norms of behavior', Hutton renders it 'legal arrangements'.

50. 必將修禮以齊朝，正法以齊官，平政以齊民；然後節奏齊於朝，百事齊於官，眾庶齊於下 (37/10/122–123). I adopt Hutton's translation for this passage, with modification. Knoblock translates *fa* in this passage as 'laws', while Hutton offers 'models for conduct'. I thank Avital Rom for suggesting 'standards'.

51. Cf. Harris (2013, 98ff.) for a discussion on the significance of law in Xunzi's political philosophy, especially on the relationship between law and the ruler.

136 *Aristotle and Xunzi on Shame*

of behaviour.[52] In answering the question of how rituals and a sense of propriety might come about if human nature is indeed bad, Xunzi states that both *li* and *fa* are products of the sage. Laws and standards are said to be founded upon ritual and a sense of propriety; as such they could be understood as an extension of ritual principles and a way to ensure that a sense of propriety is followed in day-to-day conduct:

> Thus, the sage practises conscious exertion by transforming his nature. From conscious exertion, he creates ritual principles and a sense of propriety. Having established them, he institutes the regulations of laws and standards (*fadu* 法度). This being so, ritual principles, a sense of propriety, laws and standards are all products of the sage.[53]

I have already discussed above Xunzi's explanations for the origins of ritual, which serves to regulate people's desires so as to avert disorder. We might also understand laws and standards to serve a similar purpose. Despite the close associations between *li* and *fa*, these two concepts can be distinguished in certain ways. Scott Cook comments thus on the differences between ritual and laws: 'The central role of ritual institutions and practices may be said to be to promote the internalization of the hierarchical structure of society and the inherent duties and obligations for each of its stations. These differ from laws in that they do not so much coerce each individual into obedience as they guide or lead him into a gradual familiarity with and acceptance of his role in society.'[54] Speaking of early Chinese philosophy in the Confucian tradition, Tongdong Bai remarks that laws can and need to be used as '"fallback mechanisms" that regulate the common people as the last resort.'[55] This is not altogether different from the contrasts made by Eirik Lang Harris (2013) between Xunzi's conceptions of ideal and non-ideal societies, whereby conditions present in a non-ideal society are said to call especially for the power of law.[56] According to Xunzi, learning comes to its end when it has been perfected in rituals (2/1/29). On that basis,

---

52. 禮者、法之大分、類之綱紀也 (2/1/28–29).

53. 故聖人化性而起偽，偽起而生禮義，禮義生而制法度。然則禮義法度者，是聖人之所生也 (87/23/28).

54. Cook 1997, 16.

55. Bai 2014, 352.

56. More recently, Hutton 2021 has examined the relationship between ritual and legislation by drawing up a set of similarities and differences between great lawgivers and the sages. Hutton, in line with the interpretations cited above, argues that in the Confucian tradition, enforcement mechanisms and use of force rank second in value at best. However, he alerts readers to the fact that sometimes similarities between ritual and legislation can be overlooked as a result of apparent differences, as 'good legislation may play an equally crucial role in achieving the sorts of goods at which the sages' rituals aim', for example, guarding things that we take to be of fundamental in value (ibid., 61).

Social Institutions and the Politics of Moral Education   137

we can see that there are two dimensions to ritual in terms of its ends, one of which is personal, the other social. On the level of the individual, adhering to ritual allows one to nurture one's desires and reform one's original nature so as to become morally cultivated. As one fulfils one's potential of becoming an individual with the right kind of moral disposition, one contributes to order and social cohesion, which constitute the other dimension to ritual.

Analysing the functions of social institutions in Aristotle and Xunzi leads us to notice certain similarities and differences. Concepts such as *nomos*, *li*, and *fa* all mark social institutions that uphold values and approved codes of conduct in Aristotle's and Xunzi's respective societies; yet complications emerge when we realise that these terms have a wide semantic range, which often proves problematic when we try to render them into English. Furthermore, it is not appropriate to restrict comparisons to 'legislation' in Aristotle and 'ritual' in Xunzi as if they were the only social institutions available, since Xunzi does speak of the power of *fa*, and, as for Aristotle, customs and unwritten laws constitute other forms of social authority that have significant value. To carry out an extended comparison of the roles of the social institutions in the two philosophers' political ideals would fall beyond the remits of this study.[57] However, certain observations can be made on the basis of what has been sketched above: Aristotle's and Xunzi's indebtedness to their predecessors and their responses to the social contexts are made clear—both operate within a framework that has already been established. Despite the fact that Aristotle in Book X of the *EN* is forthright in denying credit to Plato by claiming that his predecessors had left the subject of legislation unexamined, the influence of Plato's *Laws* on Aristotle's thought cannot be overlooked. As for Xunzi, even though he departs from Confucius in attributing importance to laws and standards, he in fact never steers far from the original picture of the ideal community where people are guided by the good moral disposition of the ruler and by the positive impact of ritual rather than simply by coercive measures that threaten punishment. Despite the tremendous differences in the actual political set-up and the political involvement of the people in the two cases, where Aristotle's students were expected to be active in political debates in ways that were not exactly paralleled in Xunzi, one point of similarity is clear: both philosophers distinguish between what can be relied on in some members of the elite, namely, moral cultivation and a sense of shame or

---

57. As one Oxford University Press reader suggested, scholars such as Arthur Adkins and Kenneth Dover had much to say on individual morality and social institutions in ancient Greece. Given the focus of the present work on Aristotle and Xunzi, space does not permit me to discuss the ancient Greek context from a general perspective.

138   *Aristotle and Xunzi on Shame*

restraint, and what is needed for the common people—external sanctions that serve a disciplining function.

In both bodies of texts, then, we find the individual implicated in the values of society, and where individuals cannot be relied on to practise good actions and cultivate themselves so as to become morally upright, social institutions such as law and ritual are introduced to ensure that all uphold a certain set of social values and moral codes. In that sense, both Aristotle and Xunzi recognise that practising the right kinds of actions is not only crucial for personal development into a moral individual, but also has heavy political implications for social order and cohesion. For Xunzi, it is only when everybody learns to reform his or her nature by prioritising a sense of propriety over personal benefit that they can live peacefully with others, allow their own desires to be fulfilled and avoid disgrace. Furthermore, the topic of shame and disgrace is frequently discussed in the context of governing, so that the moral disposition of the ruler and the ministers has a direct impact on social stability. For Aristotle, good constitutions are dependent upon the success of the legislators in getting people accustomed to practising the right kinds of actions, and in setting the standards for people, especially the young, to follow. For both, human life is organised in such a way that discussion of the moral education of the individual inevitably involves discussion of the political ideal.

Epilogue

This comparative study experimented with ways to bring together two philosophers from two distant societies—distant in the sense that ancient Greece and early China represented two geographically and culturally distant traditions, and distant, too, in that both societies are far removed from the contemporary world. Its aims were threefold: (1) to further understanding of the ancient texts on the important topic of shame and moral education by identifying the distinctive features of Aristotle and Xunzi, (2) to illustrate areas where the ancient philosophers' discourses on emotions and on moral psychology in general might have relevance for contemporary discussion, and finally (3) to contribute to developing methodologies for cross-cultural comparison, in particular where ancient Greece and early China are concerned, thus combining 'a comparison of philosophies' with 'the philosophy of comparison'. I hope to have shown that not only are 'individual' emotions such as 'shame' worth comparing, but the philosophers' approaches to what we might term the 'emotions' in general also revealed interesting differences. Let me conclude first of all by pinpointing the methodological features of the present study and their implications for future studies, next by reviewing the distinctive features of Xunzi's and Aristotle's ideas that this study has revealed, taking into account the variety of factors that influenced their thought, and finally by revisiting the important question of contemporary relevance.

In the preceding chapters, I identified three main challenges in comparing emotions and values across cultures. The first difficulty, and the most apparent one, concerns the fact that Greek and Chinese terms do not map onto one another exactly, nor on to our own generally preferred—and often disputed—vocabulary. Throughout the work I have drawn attention to important Greek and Chinese terms that needed to be understood in their own cultural milieu, in particular the notions of 'human nature' (*phusis*/*xing*) and 'feelings/emotions'

140 *Epilogue*

(*pathos/qing*). On the topic of 'shame' in particular, I have shown that *aidōs* and *aischunē* on the Greek side and *xiu*, *chi*, *ru*, and their binomes on the Chinese side all have their own semantic fields and connotations, which suggests differences in how shame-related ideas are conceptualised. What has become clear is that in making cross-cultural comparisons of 'shame' and indeed of any such concept, one needs to engage with *clusters* of concepts rather than single terms, for related concepts are quite often entangled in a way that makes separation impossible and undesirable. In the absence of a common language and a neutral vocabulary, using a 'third' language—in this case, English—to engage with ancient materials in fact had its advantages: English does not inherit its shame-related clusters from the ancient Greeks or the Chinese, and so is relatively neutral; furthermore, differences in shame-related conceptual clusters between the Greeks, Chinese, and the contemporary Anglophone world challenged me to engage deeply with what is at stake in the comparisons and to reflect on what it is that can be usefully compared. Going beyond philological analysis, I used shame-related concepts as a way into examining ideals of moral education and the good life in Aristotle and Xunzi, which involved an investigation into the *values* that were present in the ancient philosophers and in the societies to which they belonged. In each case, behind simple terms and concepts lies an ethical system that must be explored before any sense can be made of particular clusters of terms. Any kind of cross-cultural comparative study on ethical ideas, then, goes beyond comparing concepts to comparing ethical schemes before coming back to re-examine the concepts *within* the larger ethical concerns. For this reason, the fact that vocabularies across cultures do not map onto one another exactly presents no insurmountable obstacle to the comparative enterprise, but serves as a window through which we might see how ideas about 'honour', 'shame' and 'disgrace', and so forth are construed by different authors and how they operate within a complex network of ideas. 'Placeholder' terms such as 'shame' are useful, provided that they are explained and reinterpreted as one engages deeper with the ancient materials.

The second difficulty lies in the fact that the subject-matter has been confounded by stereotypes of the 'shame culture' versus 'guilt culture' debate and by the problematic 'shame' and 'guilt' divide. In talking about ancient traditions that do not share similar conceptual clusters, it makes little sense to assume that 'shame' and 'guilt' represent the 'external' and 'internal' aspects respectively of an agent's motivations, especially when the vocabulary of 'guilt' and 'conscience' have strong Christian overtones and are therefore often unsuited to the ancient Greek and early Chinese contexts. The polarisation of 'shame' and 'guilt' mistakenly implies that these feelings are mutually exclusive and can always be clearly distinguished, while the idea that an entity as large as a 'cultural tradition'

Epilogue 141

can be easily classified as either a 'guilt culture' or a 'shame culture' is unfounded and creates 'an imaginary opposition of China and the West'.[1] Focusing on Aristotle and Xunzi, this study has contributed additional evidence in support of the work carried out by Williams, Cairns, and others, who have successfully argued against the 'shame culture' and 'guilt culture' dichotomy. It is clear from the preceding chapter that Aristotle and Xunzi in their own ways emphasise the internalisation of values within the agent himself over concerns about external recognition, and the moral disposition and motivations of the individual far outweigh the concern to be seen to be 'acting well'. It is therefore a gross generalisation to associate both societies with a 'shame culture' that purportedly relies on the idea of a 'loss of face' or public disgrace to inculcate good behaviour. Even though I have attempted to steer clear of the 'guilt'/'shame' polarisation in my discussions of the ancient Greek and Chinese materials, traditional ways of distinguishing between the two concepts prompted me to think harder about what was at issue. This led me to formulate, on the basis of the classical texts, alternative ways of discussing the topic of moral responsibility by distinguishing between actions that are motivated by external recognition (as manifested in honours, awards, and social rank, etc.) or disapproval (as manifested in blame, loss of reputation and punishment, etc.), and those that are motivated by an agent's inner moral disposition on the basis of a correct understanding of what the right course of action should be. In this way, I was able to avoid adopting the 'shame'/'guilt' model, which is fraught with problems and could instead concentrate on the ways in which Xunzi and Aristotle themselves differentiate between internal and external motivations. As I have shown, both Aristotle and Xunzi believe that the attainment of honour befits a virtuous person, though both stress, albeit in different ways, the importance of having the right kind of moral disposition and motivations that go beyond the mere attainment of honours. For sure, the philosophers in question certainly do not represent the views of common people. But that does not mean they cannot serve as evidence to show the flaws in the application of the notion of 'shame culture' to Greek or to Chinese societies.

The third difficulty concerns the universalism versus relativism debate which was briefly mentioned in the introductory chapter. To ask whether there is a set of emotions that is universal to humankind may not be as fruitful as we hope, at least in this kind of study, for we will probably never get to the bottom of whether 'shame' as such is universal. For one thing, each culture expresses the emotions differently, employing its own vocabulary and ways of description

---

1. Zhang 1998, 17.

142 *Epilogue*

so that English emotion terms cannot be applied universally. Given the focus of this study on Aristotle and Xunzi, commenting upon the universality or relativity of the emotions themselves falls outside the remit of the current investigation. However, what *can* be said with a degree of certainty is that using 'shame' as a placeholder gives us access to complexes of ideas relating to the self and the need to take responsibility in an undesirable situation, ideas that are evident in the writings of both philosophers under study. We might say that while the inquiries carried out into shame and moral education are far from the same in the Greek and Chinese traditions, discourses on the emotions do very often reflect values and ideals about the good life. Sidestepping the universalism versus relativism question, the study has shown that a more fruitful way of carrying out Sino-Hellenic comparisons of shame-related ideas involves examining how discourses on such emotions reflect the values of prominent Greek and Chinese philosophers and how such philosophers chose to respond to their predecessors and to the social and political background of their times. By focusing on two philosophers or 'bodies of texts', I aimed to do justice to the complex philosophical systems concerned and avoid superficial comparisons and oversimplifications.

While both philosophers are in the business of offering advice and focus on clusters of concepts, including shame-related notions, in developing ideas about morality and education, various differences in their backgrounds can help to explain the directions their discourses have taken. Examining what influenced philosophical enquiry in each case, both in terms of content and form, has allowed me to avoid buying into merely apparent similarities and differences. By exploring just to what extent Aristotle and Xunzi launched polemics against their predecessors and contemporaries on certain fundamental questions, I have illustrated that the plurality and diversity of thought within the two ancient cultural traditions should not be underestimated. As we would expect, it is by criticising others that Chinese and Greek philosophers constructed their own theories and created for themselves an identity as figures of authority. But however much these philosophers sought to distance themselves from their predecessors, they were nonetheless greatly influenced by them and inherited certain fundamental convictions, often in more ways than they cared to acknowledge. Chapter 3 illustrated this by showing that Aristotle and Xunzi approached the question of human nature and set about constructing their scales of nature as a response to what had been proposed by their respective predecessors Plato and Mencius. Chapter 5 has shown that Aristotle adopted ideas about legislation from Plato's *Laws* and developed them, while Xunzi elaborated upon ideas of *li* (ritual) and *yi* (propriety), familiar notions in the *Analects* and in the *Mencius*, in discussing moral cultivation and forms of social control.

Epilogue 143

Even though the primary focus of this work has been on Aristotle and Xunzi, the broader background to the debates has been relevant to an understanding of Aristotle's and Xunzi's novel contributions and the techniques of persuasion that they employed.

Aristotle's and Xunzi's own civic status together with that of their audiences played a big part in influencing the content and style of their discourse on shame and moral education in general. Xunzi, like many other itinerant scholars of the time, operated within the courts of the political rulers and sought to offer advice on government. Aristotle lived as a metic in Athens and had knowledge of the constitutions of many Greek city-states. Though he was famously known to have served as tutor to the young Alexander the Great, his primary audience consisted of students and associates of the Lyceum, some of whom later became important political figures in their own city-states. It is worth noting that the usual situation that Greek politicians faced in the classical Greek city-state—the assemblies, councils, law courts—had no parallel in China before, let alone after, the unification by the state of Qin.

What Aristotle and Xunzi had in common was that both were addressing an elite audience who had a certain degree of power in the politics of their respective societies; they were figures that the philosophers had hoped would provide a moral example. When Aristotle mentions in Book X of the *EN* that 'most people are not the sort to be guided by a sense of shame (*aidōs*) but by fear, and not to refrain from bad things on the grounds of their shamefulness but because of the punishments', he is of course not addressing his audience as if they were the hoi polloi; rather, his students are expected to play the role of legislators who would draft laws most suitable for the constitution and for checking the actions of the masses. The fact that Aristotle requires his audience to have already been habituated to pursuing the right kinds of pleasures is a sign that they are expected to have come from a good social environment. Similarly, when Xunzi says that the gentleman and the petty man have the same nature and potential and yet only the former is capable of observing a sense of propriety in his conduct that is distinctively human, he is expecting *his* audience to aspire to become moral exemplars and to follow the path of the sages of the past. There is a point of difference here between Aristotle, for whom legislators play an important role in determining the direction of the city-state, and Xunzi, who emphasises the need to follow ritual and propriety that have already been established by the sage kings of the past. Nonetheless, rulers and ministers in Xunzi's society do hold a great degree of power in guiding the common people to obtain the right kind of education and to follow social norms.

What we might glean from observations about the audience of Aristotle's and Xunzi's works is that persuasion took different forms depending on who

144 *Epilogue*

the targets of persuasion were and what was assumed of them. It is only fitting that Aristotle discusses *aischunē* as one of the *pathē* in the *Rhetoric*, since having good knowledge of how the emotions function was thought to be essential for people giving speeches and debates in the assembly and the law courts. Xunzi, on the other hand, does not discuss the emotions systematically nor analyse them one by one; rather, he looks more to the negative effects of disgraceful behaviour and highlights the need to have a sense of shame. He aimed at persuading rulers and ministers to take actions that are in accordance with ritual and propriety; hence there are plenty of examples of *xiu*, *chi*, and *ru* in the context of ruling and serving which reflect political concerns. Xunzi's preoccupation with restoring order in society prompted him to adopt an altogether more protreptic tone in his writings, as illustrated for example in the repeated use of the term *wu lianchi* to warn against shameless behaviour, in his drawing attention to the negative tendencies of human nature, and in the recurring theme that learning is a lifelong project.

What have shame-related discourses revealed about Aristotle's and Xunzi's ideas on human nature and on one's relationship with the social environment? In both philosophers the key is the way humans are characterized in relation to other animals: for example, Aristotle's definition of humans stresses their rational capacity and their ability to have *logos*, while Xunzi attributes a sense of propriety and the ability to form communities on the basis of making social distinctions to humans alone. At the same time, we can surmise that Aristotle and Xunzi agree that humans, alone among the animals, have the capacity to morally assess their situations in a way that allows them to make reasoned judgments on what is to be pursued or avoided, instead of taking actions instinctively on the basis of pursuing what is immediately pleasurable or avoiding what is painful. As the examples of 'courage' (*andreia/yong*) show, in each case, humans alone are capable of experiencing a sense of shame that involves an evaluation of what constitutes good or bad conduct. While human beings are often discussed as a collective group and are said to share certain traits and capacities,[2] fulfilment of human potential and achievement of the moral ideals are certainly subject to a variety of factors and are *not* universal across the population. Indeed, both Xunzi and Aristotle show an awareness that certain members of their society are beyond the reach of persuasion—such people are often used as a foil to highlight the qualities of the *junzi* and the *phronimos*. In their distinctive ways, Aristotle and Xunzi show that the 'ethical' and the 'political' are intertwined; the same

---

2. There is certainly a greater degree of emphasis in the *Xunzi* that all humans have one and the same nature, while for Aristotle women and slaves are excluded from having the full human function though they, too, are *anthrōpoi*.

Epilogue 145

may be said for individual and community good. This explains the importance of moral education in each case, as well as the necessity for certain social institutions to control people's behaviour which involve, for Aristotle, *nomos* and for Xunzi, *li* and *fa*, the complexities surrounding which terms I have explained. Shame-related ideas in particular are powerful tools in linking the individual and society so that in being aware of what constitutes the honourable and the disgraceful, one abides by what is to be socially approved and disapproved, thereby becoming an integrated member of a community that promotes certain values. Investigating the topic of shame and moral education, therefore, allows us to probe into the question of the relationship in all its complexity between the individual and the society. As for the question of whose benefit moral education is for, we might say that ultimately, it is for the individual *and* for society, and the line between the two becomes ever harder to draw as we come to speak about the 'internalisation' of values—values that are initially imparted to us by society.

At first glance, Aristotle and Xunzi appear to fit certain stereotypes, on the one hand of the Greek philosopher who calls for individualism and on the other, the Chinese philosopher who prioritises the good of the community at the expense of individual welfare. If one focuses on the parts where Xunzi speaks, in line with his predecessors, of 'all under heaven' and heavily concerns himself with social and political stability, calling for adherence to ritual practices, the idea of a conformist society might spring to mind. Those parts could be compared with Aristotle where he elaborates on the attainment of *eudaimonia* by the individual, and in discussions of *aischunē*, focuses on its effects on the individual rather than on society as a whole. However, that is only a part of the picture. A detailed examination, looking below the surface, shows the inadequacy of that account, for one can equally zoom in on features of 'individualism' in the *Xunzi* and of 'collectivism' in Aristotle. For Xunzi, social stability and order for 'all under heaven' is only achieved when individual members are educated, therefore there is a strong emphasis on the moral education and self-cultivation of the individual. Community life benefits individual human beings, for it grants them strength over animals so that they can gain wealth and material goods. Even ritual, which serves a regulating function, could help individuals to channel their *qing* and fulfil their desires. Indeed, prioritising a sense of propriety and relegating the inborn drive for self-interest to second place contributes to social order, and it is on this basis that individual happiness becomes possible. As for Aristotle, ethics and politics are closely intertwined and the *Politics* presents a powerful case for how human beings can flourish in a social and political context. The community-oriented nature of human beings is evident in Aristotle's discussions of *aischunē*, which is a fear of disapproval from 'significant others', a feeling that is especially applicable to young people

146 *Epilogue*

who are liable to form friendships. In this sense, the young person for whom *aidōs* acts as an inhibitory force is fully aware of his being a member of society and of being liable to be judged by others. Even though Aristotle, unlike Xunzi, does not repeatedly warn against the repercussions of shameful behaviour on society as a whole, it is clear that for him, moral education of the individual makes a great impact on the wellbeing of the state, since the neglect of education is understood to harm the constitution. In comparing cultural traditions, there is often a tendency to view the Chinese and the Greeks as opposites and to ascribe emotional or behavioural tendencies to particular cultures; this study has shown how simplistic that account is.

In some ways, we in the twenty-first century are navigating similar sets of problems concerning the human condition as did the ancients: the answers to some questions still remain unclear, for example, the moral education of the young, where there is tension between encouraging freedom of expression and the need for social integration, and the relationship between humans and other animals, where despite scientific breakthroughs in the areas of ethology and neuroscience, the emotional lives and the morality of animals remain topics that are contentious and divisive. On the other hand, some questions relating to emotions and morality are new, having come into view only in the past few decades or so against the background of rapid developments in technology, in the field of artificial intelligence (AI) in particular. One pressing issue concerns the differences between humans and 'other minds', namely machines that have the capacity to perform human tasks where the rules for judging success or failure are fully determinate, for example, the games of chess and go, though how far the claims that the same applies or will apply across the board where other manifestations of intelligence, including those that demand moral judgement, are involved, is far from clear. This vast topic is one of urgency and already the subject of numerous studies; however, let me outline just a few ethical questions relating to shame and the emotions that are particularly relevant: How far does it seem possible to create 'moral', reliable and inclusive AI systems? What contributions might ancient 'virtue ethics'—'Confucian' and 'Aristotelian'—make in instilling a moral character in machines?[3] What are the implications of 'affective computing' that can interpret and simulate human affects)?[4] Can machines ever succeed in correctly identifying human facial expressions and emotions (bearing in mind that facial expressions can be faked and are not always a reliable reflection of inner states), in particular with regard to 'shame' and 'guilt'

3. Wallach & Allen 2008; Song ed. 2021.
4. DeLancey 2002; Picard 2003; Minsky 2006.

Epilogue   147

that do not have obvious readouts? In situations where shame and social stigma might arise, particularly in the context of human-to-human interactions, what roles might machines play in mitigating damage to the agent's self-esteem and encouraging social inclusion?[5] These questions point to the extraordinary potential that AI systems have in complementing human 'intelligence', creating new possibilities and benefitting society; at the same time, they foreshadow some of the risks involved in living with human-like (or in some cases, God-like) machines that will lead to fresh sets of ethical dilemmas. At what point, one might ask, do the capabilities of AI systems transcend the input of those—humans— who have created them? Aside from the question of similarities and differences between humans and other animals, therefore, we must now reconfigure our taxonomies to accommodate AI systems that have an ambivalent existence and reconsider the question of 'what makes us human'. However, unlike the worlds of ancient Greece and China that were isolated from each other, the current age sees AI presenting problems—and opportunities—of a global nature. This universal challenge provides all the more reason for us to explore the potential contributions of different philosophical traditions to current ethical issues. In investigating Aristotle and Xunzi, two paradigmatic philosophers from ancient Greece and early China from a comparative perspective, I hope that this book has provoked fresh ways for thinking about the relevance of 'shame' in moral education and social cohesion, and about the potential contributions of a cross-cultural engagement with philosophical ideas.

5. Holthöwer & Doorn 2022.

Bibliography

EDITIONS OF GRECO-ROMAN SOURCES

Anonymous. (1892). *Ethica Nicomachea Commentaria*. Edited by G. Heylbut. Commentaria in Aristotelem Graeca 20. Berlin: Reimer.

Antiphon and Andocides. (1941). *Minor Attic Orators, Vol I*. Edited and translated by K. J. Maidment. Cambridge, MA: Harvard University Press.

Aristotle. (1884). *Ethica Eudemia*. Edited by Franz Susemihl. Lipsiae: B.G. Teubneri, 1884.

Aristotle. (1935). *Ethica Nicomachea*. Edited by I. Bywater. Oxford: Clarendon Press.

Aristotle. (1957). *Politica*. Edited by W. D. Ross. Oxford: Clarendon Press.

Aristotle. (1959). *Ars Rhetorica*. Edited by W. D. Ross. Oxford: Clarendon Press.

Aristotle. (1963). *De Anima*. Edited by W. D. Ross. Oxford: Clarendon Press.

Aristotle. (1963). *Metaphysica*. Edited by Werner Jaeger. Oxford: Clarendon Press.

Aristotle. (1963). *Physica*. Edited by W. D. Ross. Oxford: Clarendon Press.

Aristotle. (2002). *Historia Animalium*. Edited by D. M. Balme and A. Gotthelf. Cambridge Classical Texts and Commentaries 38. Cambridge: Cambridge University Press.

von Arnim, J. (ed.) [1905] (1964). *Stoicorum Veterum Fragmenta*. Stuttgart: Teubner.

Cicero. (1928). *On the Republic. On the Laws*. Edited and translated by C. W. Keyes. Cambridge, MA: Harvard University Press.

Diehls, H., & W. Kranz. (1952). *Die Fragmente der Vorsokratiker*. Berlin: Weidmann.

Diogenes Laertius. (2013). *Lives of Eminent Philosophers*. Edited by Tiziano Dorandi. Cambridge: Cambridge University Press.

Euripides. (1995). *Children of Heracles, Hippolytus, Andromache, Hecuba*. Edited and translated by David Kovacs. Cambridge: Harvard University Press.

Herodotus. (1922). *The Persian Wars*. Edited and translated by A. D. Godley. 4 vols. Cambridge, MA: Harvard University Press.

Hesiod. (2007). *Theogony, Works and Days, Testimonia*. Edited and translated by Glenn W. Most. Cambridge, MA: Harvard University Press.

Homer. (1919). *The Odyssey*. Edited and translated by A. T. Murray. 2 vols. Cambridge, MA: Harvard University Press.

Homer. (1924). *The Iliad*. Edited and translated by A. T. Murray. 2 vols. London: Heinemann.

Livy. (2017). *History of Rome, Vol. IX: Books 31--34*. Edited and translated by J. C. Yardley. Cambridge, MA: Harvard University Press.

Nemesius. (1987). *De Natura Hominis*. Edited by Moreno Morani. Leipzig: Teubner.

150   *Bibliography*

Plato. (1900). *Opera*. Edited by John Burnet. 5 vols. Oxford: Clarendon Press.

Schenkl, H. (ed.). (1916). *Epicteti Dissertationes ab Arriano Digestae*. 2nd edition. Leipzig: Teubner.

Theognis. (1961). *Theognis*. Edited by Ernst Diehl and Douglas Young. Lipsiae: B. G. Teubner.

Thucydides. (1919). *History of the Peloponnesian War*. Translated by C. F. Smith. 4 vols. Cambridge: Harvard University Press.

EDITIONS OF CHINESE SOURCES

Chen, G. 陳鼓應. (1983). *Zhuangzi jinzhu jinyi* 莊子今註今譯. 2 vols. Beijing: Zhong hua shu ju 北京：中華書局.

Duan, Yu. 段玉裁. [Xu, Shen 許慎]. (1981). *Shuowen jiezi zhu*. 說文解字註. Shanghai: Shang hai gu ji chu ban she 上海：上海古籍出版社.

Hung, W. 洪業. (ed.). (1966). *Concordance to* Hsün Tzu. Harvard-Yenching Institute Sinological Index Series. Supplement no. 22. Taipei: Chinese Materials and Research Aids Service Center.

Jingmen shi bo wu guan 荊門市博物館. (ed.). (1998). *Guo dian chu mu zhu jian* 郭店楚墓竹簡. Beijing: Wen wu chu ban she 北京：文物出版社.

Lau, D. C., He, C. W., & Chen, F. C. 何志華，劉殿爵，陳方正. (eds.). (1995a). *A Concordance to the Lunyu* 論語逐字索引. ICS Series. Hong Kong: Commercial Press 香港：商務印書館.

Lau, D. C., He, C. W., & Chen, F. C. 何志華，劉殿爵，陳方正. (eds.). (1995b). *A Concordance to the Mengzi* 孟子逐字索引. ICS Series. Hong Kong: Commercial Press 香港：商務印書館.

Lau, D. C., He, C. W., & Chen, F. C. 何志華，劉殿爵，陳方正. (eds.). (2000). *A Concordance to the Zhuangzi* 莊子逐字索引. ICS Series. Hong Kong: Commercial Press 香港：商務印書館.

Li, D. 李滌生. (1979). *Xunzi jishi* 荀子集釋. Taibei: Taiwan xuesheng shuju 台北：台湾学生書局.

Li, X. 黎翔鳳. (2004). *Guanzi jiaozhu* 管子校注. 3 vols. Beijing: Zhong hua shu ju. 北京：中華書局.

Liang, Q. 梁啟雄. (1983). *Xunzi jianshi* 荀子簡釋. Beijing: Zhong hua shu ju. 北京：中華書局.

Sima Z., & Zhang S. 司馬貞，張守節. (1982). *Sima Qian:* Shiji 司马迁：史記. 10 vols. Beijing: Zhong hua shu ju 北京：中華書局.

Wang, X. 王先謙. (1988). *Xunzi jijie* 荀子集解. 2 vols. Beijing: Zhong hua shu ju. 北京：中華書局.

Yang, B. 楊伯峻. (1960). *Mengzi yizhu* 孟子譯註. Beijing: Zhong hua shu ju. 北京：中華書局.

Yang, B. 楊伯峻. (1958). *Lunyu yizhu* 論語譯註. Beijing: Zhong hua shu ju. 北京：中華書局.

Yang, L. 楊柳橋. (1985). *Xunzi guyi* 荀子詁譯. Jinan: Qi lu shu she 濟南：齊魯書社.

Yang, T. 楊天宇. (2004). *Liji yizhu* 禮記譯註. 2 vols. Shanghai: Shang hai gu ji chu ban she 上海：上海古籍出版社.

Ying, S. 應劭. (1922). *Fengsu tongyi* 風俗通義. 10 vols. Shanghai: Shang wu yin shu guan 上海：商務印書館.

Bibliography 151

SECONDARY LITERATURE

Ackrill, J. L. (1980). "Aristotle on *Eudaimonia*," in A. O. Rorty (ed.), *Essays on Aristotle's Ethics*. Berkeley: University of California Press, 15–33.

Adkins, A. W. H. (1970). *From the Many to the One: A Study of Personality and Views of Human Nature in the Context of Ancient Greek Society, Values and Beliefs*. London: Constable.

Adkins, A. W. H. (1972). *Moral Values and Political Behaviour in Ancient Greece: From Homer to the End of the Fifth Century*. New York: W. W. Norton & Company.

Adkins, A. W. H. (1991). "The Connection Between Aristotle's Ethics and Politics," in Keyt, D., & Miller, F. D. (eds.), *A Companion to Aristotle's Politics*. Oxford: Blackwell Publishing, 75–93.

Aygün, Ö. (2018). "Human *Logos* in Aristotle," in Kirkland, S. D., & Sanday, E. (eds.), *A Companion to Ancient Philosophy*. Evanston: Northwestern University Press, 177–90.

Ahmed, S. (2007). *The Cultural Politics of Emotion*. New York: Routledge.

Ames, R. T. (1994). *The Art of Rulership: A Study of Ancient Chinese Political Thought*. Albany: State University of New York Press.

Angier, T., & Raphals, L. (eds.). (2021). *Skill in Ancient Ethics: The Legacy of China, Greece and Rome*. London: Bloomsbury.

Angle, S. C., and Slote, M. (eds.). (2013). *Virtue Ethics and Confucianism*. New York: Routledge.

Annas, J. (1996). "Aristotle's 'Politics': A Symposium: Aristotle on Human Nature and Political Virtue." *Review of Metaphysics* 49, no. 4: 731–53.

Appiah, A. (2010). *The Honor Code: How Moral Revolutions Happen*. New York: W. W. Norton & Company.

Bai, T. (2012). *China: The Political Philosophy of the Middle Kingdom*. London: Zed Books.

Bai, T. (2014). "Early Confucian Political Philosophy and Its Contemporary Relevance," in Shen, V. (ed.) *Dao Companion to Classical Confucian Philosophy*. Dordrecht: Springer Netherlands, 335–61.

Balot, R. K. (2006). *Greek Political Thought*. Malden, MA: Blackwell Publishing.

Baracchi, C. (2012). "Aristotle on Becoming Human." *Topicos* 43: 93–121.

Barbieri-Low, A. J., & Yates, R. D. S. (eds.). (2015). *Law, State and Society in Early Imperial China: A Study with Critical Edition and Translation of the Legal Texts from Zhangjiashan Tomb no. 247*. Leiden: Brill.

Barclay, K, Crozier-de Rosa, S., & Stearns, P. N. (eds.). (2021). *Sources for the History of Emotions: A Guide*. London: Routledge.

Barnes, J. (1979). *The Presocratic Philosophers*. 2 vols. London: Routledge & Kegan Paul Ltd.

Barnes, J. (ed.). (1984). *Complete Works of Aristotle: The Revised Oxford Translation*. 2 vols. Princeton, NJ: Princeton University Press.

Barnes, J. (ed.). (1995). *The Cambridge Companion to Aristotle*. Cambridge: Cambridge University Press.

Barrett, L. F. (2017). *How Emotions are Made: The Secret Life of the Brain*. London: Pan Macmillan.

Beck, H, & Vankeerberghen, G. (eds.). (2021). *Rulers and Ruled in Ancient Greece, Rome, and China*. Cambridge: Cambridge University Press.

Beecroft, A. (2010). *Authorship and Cultural Identity in Early Greece and China: Patterns of Literary Circulation*. Cambridge: Cambridge University Press.

Bekoff, M. (2007). *The Emotional Lives of Animals: A Leading Scientist Explores Animal Joy, Sorrow, and Empathy—and Why They Matter*. Novato, CA: New World Library.

152 Bibliography

Bekoff, M., & Pierce, J. (2009). *Wild Justice: The Moral Lives of Animals*. Chicago: Chicago University Press.

Benedict, R. (1946). *The Chrysanthemum and the Sword: Patterns of Japanese Culture*. Boston: Houghton Mifflin.

Besser-Jones, L., & Slote, M. (eds.). (2015). *The Routledge Companion to Virtue Ethics*. London: Routledge.

Bodéüs, R. (1991). "Law and the Regime in Aristotle," in Lord, C., O'Connor, D. K., & Bodéüs, R. (eds.), *Essays on the Foundations of Aristotelian Political Science*. Berkeley: University of California Press, 234–48.

Bodéüs, R. (1993). *The Political Dimensions of Aristotle's Ethics*. Albany: State University of New York Press. (Originally published as *Le philosophie et la cite: Recherches sur les rapports entre morale et politique dans la pensée d'Aristote*. Bibliothèque de la faculté de philosophie et lettres de l'université de Liège. Paris: Les Belles Lettres, 1982)

Boddice, R. (2018). *The History of Emotions*. Manchester: Manchester University Press.

Boltz, W. G. (2008). "The Composite Nature of Early Chinese Texts," in Kern, M. (ed.), *Text and Ritual in Early China*. Seattle: University of Washington Press, 50–78.

Bonitz, H. (1955). *Index Aristotelicus*. Darmstadt: Wissenschaftliche Buchgesellschaft.

Bostock, D. (2000). *Aristotle's Ethics*. Oxford: Oxford University Press.

Braund, S. & Most, G. W. (eds.) (2004). *Ancient Anger: Perspectives from Homer to Galen*. Cambridge: Cambridge University Press.

Brindley, E. (2010). *Individualism in Early China: Human Agency and the Self in Thought and Politics*. Honolulu: University of Hawai'i Press.

Broadie, S. (1991). *Ethics with Aristotle*. New York: Oxford University Press.

Broadie, S. & Rowe, C. (2002). *Aristotle: Nicomachean Ethics*. Translation, Introduction and Commentary. Oxford: Oxford University Press.

Buekenhout, B. (2016). "Kingly versus Political Rule in Aristotle's Politics." *Apeiron* 49, no. 4: 515–37.

Burger, R. (2008). *Aristotle's Dialogue with Socrates: On the Nicomachean Ethics*. Chicago: University of Chicago Press.

Burik, S. (2009). *The End of Comparative Philosophy and the Task of Comparative Thinking: Heidegger, Derrida, and Daoism*. Albany: State University of New York Press.

Burnet, J. (1903). *Aristotle on Education: Being Extracts from the Ethics and Politics, Translated and Edited by John Burnet*. Cambridge: Cambridge University Press.

Burnyeat, M. F. (1980). "Aristotle on Learning to Be Good," in Rorty, A. O. (ed.), *Essays on Aristotle's Ethics*. Berkeley: University of California Press, 69–92.

Cairns, D. L. (1993). *Aidos: The Psychology and Ethics of Honour and Shame in Ancient Greek Literature*. Oxford: Clarendon Press.

Cairns, D. L. (2011). "Honour and Shame: Modern Controversies and Ancient Values." *Critical Quarterly*, 53, no. 1: 23–41.

Cairns, D. L. (ed.). (2019). *A Cultural History of the Emotions in Antiquity*, vol. 1. London: Bloomsbury.

Cairns, D. L. (2019). "Introduction: Emotion History and the Classics," in Cairns, D. (ed.), *A Cultural History of the Emotions in Antiquity*, vol. 1. London: Bloomsbury, 1–16.

Cairns, D. L. (2022). "Introduction A: Emotions Through Time?" in Cairns, D., Hinterberger, M., Pizzone, A., Zaccarini, M. (eds.), *Emotions through Time: From Antiquity to Byzantium*. Tübingen: Mohr Siebeck, 3–34.

Cairns, D. L., & Fulkerson, L. (eds.). (2015). *Emotions between Greece and Rome. BICS supplement, 125*. London: Institute of Classical Studies, School of Advanced Study, University of London.

Bibliography 153

Cairns, D., Nelis, D. (eds.) (2017). *Emotions in the Classical World: Methods, Approaches, and Directions*. Heidelberg: Franz Steiner.

Cairns, D., Hinterberger, M., Pizzone, A., & Zaccarini, M. (eds.). (2022). *Emotions through Time: From Antiquity to Byzantium*. Tübingen: Mohr Siebeck.

Cairns, D. L., & Virág, C. (eds.) (forthcoming). *In the Mind, in the Body and in the World: Emotions in Early China and Ancient Greece*. New York: Oxford University Press.

Campbell, G. L. (ed.). (2014). *The Oxford Handbook of Animals in Classical Thought and Life*. Oxford: Oxford University Press.

Candiotto, L., & Renaut, O. (eds.). (2020). *Emotions in Plato*. Brill's Plato Studies Series, vol. 4. Leiden: Brill.

Candiotto, L., & Renaut, O. (2020). "Introduction Why Plato Comes First," in Candiotto, L., & Renaut, O. (eds.), *Emotions in Plato*. Leiden: Brill, 1–14.

Carr, E. H. (1961). *What Is History?* London: Penguin.

Cashdollar, S. (1973). "Aristotle's Politics of Morals." *Journal of the History of Philosophy* 11, no. 2: 145–160.

Caston, R. R. & Kaster, R. A. (eds.) (2016). *Hope, Joy, and Affection in the Classical World*. New York: Oxford University Press.

Chakrabarti, A., & Weber, R. (eds.). (2016). *Comparative Philosophy Without Borders*. London: Bloomsbury.

Chamberlain, C. (1984). "The Meaning of *Prohairesis* in Aristotle's Ethics." *Transactions of the American Philological Association* 114: 147–57.

Chan, S. (2009). "Human Nature and Moral Cultivation in the Guodian 郭店 Text of the *Xing Zi Ming Chu* 性自命出 (Nature Derives from Mandate)." *Dao: A Journal of Comparative Philosophy* 8, no. 4: 361–82.

Chaniotis, A. (ed.) (2012). *Unveiling Emotions: Sources and Methods for the Study of Emotions in the Greek World*. Stuttgart: Franz Steiner Verlag.

Chaniotis, A. (ed.) (2021). *Unveiling Emotions III: Arousal, Display, and Performance of Emotions in the Greek World*. Stuttgart: Franz Steiner Verlag.

Chaniotis, A., & Ducrey, P. (eds.) (2013). *Unveiling Emotions II: Emotions in Greece and Rome: Texts, Images, Material Culture*. Stuttgart: Franz Steiner Verlag.

Charles, D. (2006). 'Aristotle's Desire,' in Hirvonen, V., Holopainen, T. J., & Tuominen, M. (eds.), *Mind and Modality: Studies in the History of Philosophy in Honour of Simo Knuuttila*. Leiden: Brill, 19–40.

Chemla, K, (ed.). (2012). *The History of Mathematical Proof in Ancient Traditions*. Cambridge: Cambridge University Press.

Chen, L. (2010a). "The Guodian Bamboo Slips and Confucian Theories of Human Nature." *Journal of Chinese Philosophy* 37: 33–50.

Chen, L. (2010b). "Virtue Ethics and Confucian Ethics." *Dao: A Journal of Comparative Philosophy* 9, no. 3: 275–87.

Chen, S. (2017). "A Phenomenological Analysis of Shame." *Contemporary Chinese Thought*, 48: 2: 55–67.

Cheng, A. (ed.). (2005). *Y A-t-il Une Philosophie Chinoise? Un État De La Question. Extrême-Orient, Extrême-Occident* 27. Saint-Denis: Presses Univ. de Vincennes.

Cheng, A. (2013). *Can China Think? Inaugural lecture delivered on Thursday 11 December 2008* [online]. Paris: Collège de France. https://doi.org/10.4000/books.cdf.2207. Accessed 3 March 2019.

Cheng, A. (ed.). (2012). "Virtue and Politics: Some Conceptions of Sovereignty in Ancient China." *Journal of Chinese Philosophy* 38, supplement 1: 133–45.

154 Bibliography

Chong, K-c. (2003). "Xunzi's Systematic Critique of Mencius." *Philosophy East & West* 53, no. 2: 215–33.

Chong, K-c. (2008). "Xunzi and the Essentialist Mode of Thinking on Human Nature." *Journal of Chinese Philosophy* 35, no. 1: 63–78.

Chong, K-c, & Tan, S-h. (eds.). (2003). *The Moral Circle and the Self: Chinese and Western Approaches*. La Salle, IL: Open Court.

Chroust, A-H. (1967). "Aristotle Leaves the Academy." *Greece & Rome (Second Series)* 14, no. 1: 39–43.

Cline, E. M. (2013). *Confucius, Rawls, and the Sense of Justice*. New York: Fordham University Press.

Cohen, D. (1995). *Law, Violence, and Community in Classical Athens*. Key Themes in Ancient History. Cambridge: Cambridge University Press.

Connell, S. M. (2016). *Aristotle on Female Animals: A Study of the Generation of Animals*. Cambridge: Cambridge University Press.

Connolly, T. (2015). *Doing Philosophy Comparatively*. London: Bloomsbury.

Cook, S. (1997). "Xunzi on Ritual and Music." *Monumenta Serica* 45: 1–38.

Cook, S. (2012). *The Bamboo Texts of Guodian: A Study and Complete Translation*. 2 vols. Ithaca: Cornell University East Asia Program.

Cooper, J. M. (1986). *Reason and Human Good in Aristotle*. Indianapolis: Hackett Publishing.

Cooper, J. M. (1999). *Reason and Emotion: Essays on Ancient Moral Psychology and Ethical Theory*. Princeton, NJ: Princeton University Press.

Cope, E. M., & Sandys, J. E. [1877]. (2010). *Aristotle: Rhetoric*. 3 vols. Cambridge: Cambridge University Press.

Creighton, M. R. (1990). "Revisiting Shame and Guilt Cultures: A Forty-Year Pilgrimage." *Ethos* 18, no. 3: 279–307.

Crone, T. (2020) *Between Disaster, Punishment, and Blame: The Semantic Field of Guilt in Early Chinese Texts*. Wiesbaden: Harrassowitz Verlag.

Csikszentmihalyi, M. (2004). *Material Virtue: Ethics and the Body in Early China*. Leiden: Brill.

Csikszentmihalyi, M., & Nylan, M. (2003). "Constructing Lineages and Inventing Traditions through Exemplary Figures in Early China." *T'oung Pao*, Second Series, 89, no. 1/3: 59–99.

Cua, A. S. (1985). *Ethical Argumentation: A Study in Hsün Tzu's Moral Epistemology*. Honolulu: University of Hawai'i Press.

Cua, A. S. (2003). "The Ethical Significance of Shame: Insights of Aristotle and Xunzi." *Philosophy East & West* 53, no. 2: 147–202.

Cua, A. S. (2005). *Human Nature, Ritual, and History Studies in Xunzi and Chinese Philosophy*. Washington, DC: Catholic University of America Press.

Curzer, H. J. (2002). "Aristotle's Painful Path to Virtue." *Journal of the History of Philosophy* 40, no. 2: 141–62.

D'Angour, A. "Shame and Guilt in Ancient Greece." https://www.armand-dangour.com/2017/03/shame-and-guilt-in-ancient-greece/.

Darwin, C. [1872] (1998). *The Expression of the Emotions in Man and Animals*. 3rd edition. New York: Oxford University Press.

Davidson, D. (1973). "Radical Interpretation." *Dialectica* 27, no. 3–4: 313–28.

Defoort, C. (2001). "Is There Such a Thing as Chinese Philosophy? Arguments of an Implicit Debate." *Philosophy East and West* 51, no. 3: 393–413.

Defoort, C. (2008). "The Profit that Does Not Profit: Paradoxes with *Li* in Early Chinese Texts." *Asia Major*, vol. 21, no. 1: 153–181.

Deigh, J. (2008). *Emotions, Values, and the Law*. New York: Oxford University Press.

Bibliography 155

DeLancey, C. (2002). *Passionate Engines: What Emotions Reveal about the Mind and Artificial Intelligence*. Oxford: Oxford University Press.

Denecke, W. (2011). *The Dynamics of Masters Literature: Early Chinese Thought from Confucius to Han Feizi*. Harvard-Yenching Monographs 74. Cambridge, MA: Harvard University Asia Center.

Denecke, W. (2014). *Classical World Literatures: Sino-Japanese and Greco-Roman Comparisons*. Oxford: Oxford University Press.

Denyer, N. (2008). *Plato: Protagoras*. Cambridge: Cambridge University Press.

Deonna, J. A., Rodogno, R., & Teroni, F. (2011). *In Defense of Shame: The Faces of an Emotion*. Oxford: Oxford University Press.

Depew, D. J. (1995). "Humans and Other Political Animals in Aristotle's 'History of Animals.'" *Phronesis* 40, no. 2: 156–81.

Deslauriers, M., & Destrée, P. (eds.). (2013). *The Cambridge Companion to Aristotle's Politics*. Cambridge: Cambridge University Press.

Detienne, M. (2008). *Comparing the Incomparable*. Translated by Janet Lloyd. Stanford, CA: Stanford University Press.

Deutsch, E. (ed.). (1991). *Culture and Modernity: East-West Philosophic Perspectives*. Honolulu: University of Hawai'i Press.

Depew, D. (1995). "Humans and Other Political Animals in Aristotle's *History of Animals*." *Phronesis* 40, no. 2: 156–181.

De Waal, F. (1996). *Good Natured: The Origins of Right and Wrong in Humans and Other Animals*. Cambridge, MA: Harvard University Press.

De Waal, F. (2009). "Veneer Theory," in Macedo, S., & Ober, J. (eds.), *Primates and Philosophers: How Morality Evolved*. Princeton, NJ: Princeton University Press, 3–58.

Dodds, E. R. (1951). *The Greeks and the Irrational*. Berkeley: University of California Press.

Dover, K. J. (1994). *Greek Popular Morality in the Time of Plato and Aristotle*. Indianapolis: Hackett Publishing.

Dow, Jamie. (2011). "Aristotle's Theory of the Emotions: Emotions as Pleasures and Pains," in Pakaluk, M., & Pearson, G. (eds.). *Moral Psychology and Human Action in Aristotle*. Oxford: Oxford University Press, 47–74.

Dow, Jamie. (2015). *Passions and Persuasion in Aristotle's Rhetoric*. Oxford: Oxford University Press.

Dubs, H. (1927). *Hsüntze, the Moulder of Ancient Confucianism*. London: Arthur Probsthain.

Dubs, H. (1928). *The Works of Hsüntze*. Translated from the Chinese, with notes. London: Arthur Probsthain.

Eberhard, W. (1967). *Guilt and Sin in Traditional China*. Berkeley: University of California Press.

Eifring, H. (ed.). (2004). *Love and Emotions in Traditional Chinese Literature*. Leiden: Brill.

Ekman, P. & Friesen, W. V. (1971). "Constants across Cultures in the Face and Emotion." *Journal of Personality and Social Psychology* 17: 124–9.

Ekman, P. & Cordaro, D. (2011). "What is Meant by Calling Emotions Basic?" *Emotion Review* 3: 364–70.

El Amine, L. (2015). *Classical Confucian Political Thought: A New Interpretation*. Princeton, NJ: Princeton University Press.

Eno, R. (1990). *The Confucian Creation of Heaven Philosophy and the Defense of Ritual Mastery*. Albany: State University of New York Press.

Farrar, C. (1988). *The Origins of Democratic Thinking: The Invention of Politics in Classical Athens*. Cambridge: Cambridge University Press.

156   Bibliography

Fisher, N. R. E. (1992). *Hybris: A Study in the Values of Honour and Shame in Ancient Greece*. Warminster: Aris & Phillips.

Flanagan, O. (2021). *How to Do Things with Emotions: The Morality of Anger and Shame across Cultures*. Princeton, NJ: Princeton University Press.

Fleming, J. (2003). "Comparative Philosophy: Its Aims and Methods." *Journal of Chinese Philosophy* 30, no. 2: 259–70.

Fortenbaugh, W. W. (1975). *Aristotle on Emotion: A Contribution to Philosophical Psychology, Rhetoric, Poetics, Politics, and Ethics*. London: Duckworth.

Franco, C. (2014). *The Canine and the Feminine in Ancient Greece*. Berkeley: University of California Press.

Fraser, C. (2013a). "Distinctions, Judgement, and Reasoning in Classical Chinese Thought", *History and Philosophy of Logic*, 34, no. 1: 1–24.

Fraser, C. (2013b). "Happiness in Classical Confucianism: Xúnzǐ." *Philosophical Topics* 41, no. 1: 53–79.

Fraser, C. (2016). "Language and Logic in the Xunzi," in Hutton, E. L. (ed.), *Dao Companion to the Philosophy of Xunzi*, Dordrecht: Springer, 291–321.

Fraser, C. (2020). "School of Names." *The Stanford Encyclopedia of Philosophy*. https://plato.stanford.edu/entries/school-names/.

Frede, D. (2013). "The Political Character of Aristotle's Ethics," in Deslauriers, M., & Destrée, P. (eds.), *The Cambridge Companion to Aristotle's* Politics. Cambridge: Cambridge University Press, 14–37.

Frede, M., & Striker, G. (eds.). (1996). *Rationality in Greek Thought*. Oxford: Clarendon Press.

Frevert, U. (2016). "The History of Emotions," in Barrett, L. F., Lewis, M., & Haviland-Jones, J. M. (eds.), *The Handbook of Emotions*. 4th edition. London: The Guilford Press, 49–65.

Frevert, U. (2020). *The Politics of Humiliation*. Oxford: Oxford University Press.

Fung, H. (1999). "Becoming a Moral Child: The Socialization of Shame among Young Chinese Children." *Ethos* 27: 180–209.

Fulkerson, L. (2013). *No Regrets: Remorse in Classical Antiquity*. Oxford: Oxford University Press.

Fung, Y-l. [1952]. (1983). *A History of Chinese Philosophy*. 2nd edition in English, translated by Derk Bodde. 2 vols. London: George Allen & Unwin Ltd.

Fung Y-m. (2012). "Two Senses of 'Wei 偽': A New Interpretation of Xunzi's Theory of Human Nature." *Dao: A Journal of Comparative Philosophy* 11: 187–200.

Furley, D. J., & Nehamas, A. (1994). *Aristotle's "Rhetoric": Philosophical Essays*. Princeton, NJ: Princeton University Press.

Fussi, A. (2015). "Aristotle on Shame." *Ancient Philosophy* 35, vol. 1: 113–135.

Gagné, R., Goldhill, S., & Lloyd, G. E. R. (eds.). (2019). *Regimes of Comparatism: Frameworks of Comparison in History*, Religion and Anthropology. Leiden: Brill.

Gao, Z. 高正. (2010). *Xun zi ban ben yuan liu kao* 荀子版本源流考. Beijing: Zhong hua shu ju 北京：中華書局.

Garver, E. (2011). *Aristotle's Politics: Living Well and Living Together*. Chicago: University of Chicago Press.

Gassmann, R. (2011). "Coming to Terms with *Dé*: the Deconstruction of 'Virtue' and an Exercise in Scientific Morality," in King, R. A. H., & Schilling, D. R. (eds.), *How Should One Live? Comparing Ethics in Ancient China and Greco-Roman Antiquity*. Berlin: de Gruyter, 92–125.

Gauthier, R. A., & Jolif, J. Y. (1958). *L'Ethique À Nicomaque; Aristote. Introduction, Traduction et Commentaire*. 2 vols. Paris: Publications Universitaires de Louvain.

Bibliography 157

Geaney, J. (2004). "Guarding Moral Boundaries: Shame in Early Confucianism." *Philosophy East & West* 54, vol. 2: 113–142.

Geertz, C. (1973). *The Interpretation of Cultures: Selected Essays*. New York: Basic Books.

Gera, D. L. (2003). *Ancient Greek Ideas on Speech, Language, and Civilization*. Oxford: Oxford University Press.

Gilbert, P. (2003). "Evolution, Social Roles, and the Differences in Shame and Guilt." *Social Research: An International Quarterly*, 70, 1205–30.

Goldin, P. R. (1999). *Rituals of the Way: The Philosophy of Xunzi*. La Salle, IL: Open Court.

Goldin, P. R. (2000a). "Xunzi in the Light of the Guodian Manuscripts." *Early China* 25: 113–146.

Goldin, P. R. (2000b). "The View of Women in Early Confucianism," in Li, C. (ed.), *The Sage and the Second Sex: Confucianism, Ethics, and Gender*. La Salle, IL: Open Court, 133–61.

Goldin, P. R. (2001). *The Culture of Sex in Ancient China*. Honolulu: University of Hawai'i Press.

Goldin, P. R. (2005). *After Confucius: Studies in Early Chinese Philosophy*. Honolulu: University of Hawai'i Press.

Goldin, P. R. (2008). "The Myth that China Has No Creation Myth." *Monumenta Serica* 56, no. 1: 1–22.

Goldin, P. R. (2011). "Persistent Misconceptions about Chinese 'Legalism.'" *Journal of Chinese Philosophy* 38: 88–104.

Goldin, P. R. (2021). Review of *Honor and Shame in Early China* by Lewis, M. E. *T'oung Pao* 107: 481–507.

Goldin, P. R. (2022). *Ancient Chinese Civilization: Bibliography of Materials in Western Languages*. https://www.academia.edu/37490636/Ancient_Chinese_Civilization_Bibliography_of_ Materials_in_Western_Languages. Accessed 4 March 2022.

Goodman, L. E., & Talisse, R. B. (eds.). (2007). *Aristotle's Politics Today*. Albany: State University of New York Press.

Gottlieb, P. (2021). *Aristotle on Thought and Feeling*. Cambridge: Cambridge University Press.

Graham, A. C. (1990). *Studies in Chinese Philosophy and Philosophical Literature*. Albany, NY: State University of New York Press, 7–66. Originally published in 1967 as "The Background of the Mencian Theory of Human Nature." *Tsing Hua Journal of Chinese Studies* 6: 215–71.

Graver, M. (2007). *Stoicism and Emotion*. Chicago: University of Chicago Press.

Graziosi, B., Vasunia, P., & Boys-Stones, G. (eds.). (2009). *The Oxford Handbook of Hellenic Studies*. Oxford: Oxford University Press.

Griffiths, P. (1997). *What Emotions Really Are: The Problem of Psychological Categories*. Chicago: University of Chicago Press.

Grimaldi, W. M. A. (1980, 1988). *Aristotle, Rhetoric: A Commentary I & II*. 2 vols. New York: Fordham University Press.

Hagen, K. (2011). "Xunzi and the Prudence of Dao: Desire as the Motive to Become Good." *Dao: A Journal of Comparative Philosophy* 10, no. 1: 53–70.

Hall, D. L., & Ames, R. T. (1987). *Thinking Through Confucius*. Albany: State University of New York Press.

Halperin, D. M., & Traub, V. (eds.). (2009). *Gay Shame*. Chicago: University of Chicago Press.

Hamburger, M. (1959). "Aristotle and Confucius: A Comparison." *Journal of the History of Ideas* 20, no. 2: 236–49.

Hamlyn, D. W. (1993). *Aristotle: De Anima, Books II and III (with Passages from Book I)*. Translated with introduction and notes. With a report of recent work and a revised bibliography by Christopher Shields. Oxford: Clarendon Press.

158 Bibliography

Hansen, C. (1994). "*Fa* (Standards: Laws) and Meaning Changes in Chinese Philosophy." *Philosophy East and West* 44, no. 3: 435–88.

Hansen, C. (1995). "Qing (Emotions) 情 in Pre-Buddhist Chinese Thought," in Marks, J., & Ames, R. T. (eds.), *Emotions in Asian Thought: A Dialogue in Comparative Philosophy.* Albany: State University of New York Press, 181–212.

Hansen, M. H. (1991). *The Athenian Democracy in the Age of Demosthenes: Structure, Principles, and Ideology.* Translated by J. A. Crook. Oxford: Blackwell.

Harbsmeier, C. (1998). *Science and Civilisation in China: Volume 7, The Social Background, Part 1, Language and Logic in Traditional China.* Cambridge: Cambridge University Press.

Harbsmeier, C. (2004). "The Semantics of *Qing* in Pre-Buddhist Chinese," in Eifring, H. (ed.), *Love and Emotions in Traditional Chinese Literature.* Leiden: Brill, 69–148.

Harré, R. (1986). *The Social Construction of Emotions.* New York: Blackwell.

Harris, E. L. (2013). "The Role of Virtue in Xunzi's 荀子 Political Philosophy." *Dao: A Journal of Comparative Philosophy* 12: 93–110.

Harris, E. L. (2019). "Relating the Political to the Ethical: Thoughts on Early Confucian Political Theory." *Dao: A Journal of Comparative Philosophy* 18: 277–83.

Harte, V., & Lane, M. (eds.). (2013). *Politeia in Greek and Roman Philosophy.* New York: Cambridge University Press.

Hatton, R. (1987). "Chinese Philosophy or Chinese 'Philosophy'? Linguistic Analysis and the Chinese Philosophical Tradition, Again." *Journal of Chinese Philosophy* 14, no. 4: 445–73.

Heath, J. (2005). *The Talking Greeks: Speech, Animals, and the Other in Homer, Aeschylus, and Plato.* Cambridge: Cambridge University Press.

Hegel, G. W. F. (1995). *Lectures on the History of Philosophy.* Translated by E. S. Haldane and F. C. Beiser. Lincoln: University of Nebraska Press.

Hitz, Z. (2012). "Aristotle on Law and Moral Education." *Oxford Studies in Ancient Philosophy* 42: 263–306.

Holthöwer, J., & van Doorn, J. (2022). "Robots Do Not Judge: Service Robots Can Alleviate Embarrassment in Service Encounters." *Journal of the Academy of Marketing Science.* https://doi.org/10.1007/s11747-022-00862-x (online first article)

Hu, H. C. (1944). "The Chinese Concepts of 'Face.'" *American Anthropologist* 46, no. 1, pt. 1: 45–64.

Hu, J. I. (2022). "Shame, Vulnerability, and Change." *Journal of the American Philosophical Association* 8, no. 2: 373–90.

Hübner, J. (2011). "Aristotle: Ethics without Morality?" In King, R. A. H., & Schilling, D. R. (eds.) *How Should One Live? Comparing Ethics in Ancient China and Greco-Roman Antiquity.* Berlin: de Gruyter, 191–207.

Hughes, E. R. (ed.), (1937). *The Individual in East and West.* Oxford: Oxford University Press.

Hutchinson, D., & Johnson, M. (2014). "Protreptic Aspects of Aristotle's *Nicomachean Ethics,*" in Polansky, R. (ed.), *The Cambridge Companion to Aristotle's Nicomachean Ethics.* Cambridge: Cambridge University Press, 383–409.

Hutton, E. L. (2000). "Does Xunzi Have a Consistent Theory of Human Nature?" in Kline III, T. C., & Ivanhoe, P. J. (eds.), *Virtue, Nature, and Moral Agency in the Xunzi.* Indianapolis: Hackett Publishing, 220–236.

Hutton, E. L. (2002). "Moral Reasoning in Aristotle and Xunzi." *Journal of Chinese Philosophy* 29, no. 3: 355–84.

Hutton, E. L. (2014). *Xunzi: The Complete Text.* Translated and with an Introduction. Princeton, NJ: Princeton University Press.

Hutton, E. L. (2015). "On the "Virtue Turn" and the Problem of Categorizing Chinese Thought." *Dao* 14: 331–53.

Hutton, E. L. (ed.). (2016). *Dao Companion to the Philosophy of Xunzi*. Dordrecht: Springer.

Hutton, E. L. (2016). Review of the book *Classical Confucian Political Thought: A New Interpretation*, by El Amine, L. Notre Dame Philosophical Reviews, https://ndpr.nd.edu/reviews/classical-confucian-political-thought-a-new-interpretation/

Hutton, E. L. (2021). "On Ritual and Legislation." *European Journal for Philosophy of Religion* 13, no. 2: 45–64.

Hwang, K-k. (1987). "Face and Favor: The Chinese Power Game." *American Journal of Sociology* 92, no. 4: 944–74.

Irwin, T. (1999). Aristotle: *Nicomachean Ethics*. Translated, with introduction, notes and glossary. 2nd edition. Indianapolis: Hackett Publishing.

Isenberg, A. (1980). "Natural Pride and Natural Shame," in Rorty, A. O. (ed.), *Explaining Emotions*. Berkeley: University of California Press, 355–84.

Ivanhoe, P. J. (1994). "Human Nature and Moral Understanding in Xunzi," *International Philosophical Quarterly* 34, no. 2: 163–75.

Ivanhoe, P. J., & Nivison, D. S. (eds.). (1996). *Chinese Language, Thought, and Culture: Nivison and His Critics*. La Salle, IL: Open Court.

Jacquet, J. (2015). *Is Shame Necessary? New Uses for an Old Tool*. London: Penguin.

Jaeger, W. (1939). *Paideia: The Ideals of Greek Culture*. Translated by Gilbert Highet. 2 vols. Oxford: Basil Blackwell.

James, W. (1884) "What Is an Emotion?" *Mind* 9, no. 34: 188–205.

Jaspers, K. (1953). *The Origin and Goal of History. Translated from the German by Michael Bullock*. London: Routledge & Keegan Paul. Originally published in 1949 as *Vom Ursprung und Ziel der Geschichte. München: Piper*.

Jiang, T. (2021). *Origins of Moral-Political Philosophy in Early China*. New York: Oxford University Press.

Jiang, X. (2012). "Confucius's View of Courage." *Journal of Chinese Philosophy* 39, no. 1: 44–59.

Jimenez, M. (2011). *The Virtues of Shame: Aristotle on the Positive Role of Shame in Moral Development*. PhD dissertation. University of Toronto.

Jimenez, M. (2020). *Aristotle on Shame and Learning to be Good*. New York: Oxford University Press.

Kalimtzis, K. (2012). *Taming Anger: The Hellenic Approach to the Limitations of Reason*. London: Bristol Classical Press.

Kamtekar, P. (1998). "*Aidōs* in Epictetus." *Classical Philology* 93: 136–60.

Kamtekar, P. (2014). "The Relationship between Aristotle's Ethical and Political Discourses (*NE* x 9)," in Polansky, R. (ed.), *The Cambridge Companion to Aristotle's Nicomachean Ethics*. Cambridge: Cambridge University Press, 370–82.

Kaster, R. A. (1997). "The Shame of the Romans." *Transactions of the American Philological Association* 127: 1–19.

Kaster, R. A. (2005). *Emotion, Restraint, and Community in Ancient Rome*. Oxford; New York: Oxford University Press.

Kekes, J. (1988). "Shame and Moral Progress." *Midwest Studies in Philosophy* 13, no. 1: 282–96.

Kenny, A. (2000). *Essays on the Aristotelian Tradition*. New York: Oxford University Press.

Kern, M. (2008). *Text and Ritual in Early China*. Seattle: University of Washington Press.

Kern, M. 柯馬丁. (2012). "Xun zi de shi xing feng ge." "《荀子》的詩性風格." *Han dan xue yuan xue bao* 邯鄲學院學報 2, no. 4: 107–119.

Keyt, D., & Miller, F. D. (eds.). (1991). *A Companion to Aristotle's Politics*. Oxford: Blackwell Publishing.

Keyt, D., & Miller, F. D. (eds.). (2007). *Freedom, Reason, and the Polis: Essays in Ancient Greek Political Philosophy*. Cambridge: Cambridge University Press.

Bibliography

Kim, H. J. (2009). *Ethnicity and Foreigners in Ancient Greece and China*. London: Duckworth.

Kim, S. (2011). "From Desire to Civility: Is Xunzi a Hobbesian?" *Dao: A Journal of Comparative Philosophy* 10: 291–309.

Kim, S. (2019). *Theorizing Confucian Virtue Politics: The Political Philosophy of Mencius and Xunzi*. Cambridge: Cambridge University Press.

King, R. A. H. (2011). "Rudimentary Remarks on Comparing Ancient Chinese and Graeco-Roman Ethics," in King, R. A. H., & Schilling, D. R. (eds.), *How Should One Live? Comparing Ethics in Ancient China and Greco-Roman Antiquity*. Berlin: de Gruyter, 3–17.

King, R. A. H. "*Ren* in the Analects: Skeptical Prolegomena." *Journal of Chinese Philosophy* 39, no. 1 (2012): 89–105.

King, R. A. H. (ed.). (2015). *The Good Life and Conceptions of Life in Early China and Graeco-Roman Antiquity*. Berlin: de Gruyter.

King, R. A. H, & Schilling, D. R. (eds.). (2011). *How Should One Live? Comparing Ethics in Ancient China and Greco-Roman Antiquity*. Berlin: de Gruyter.

Kirkland, S. D., & Sanday, E. (eds.). (2018). *A Companion to Ancient Philosophy*. Evanston, IL: Northwestern University Press.

Kleczkowska, K. (2014). "Those Who Cannot Speak. Animals as Others in Ancient Greek Thought." *Maska* 24: 97–108.

Kline III, T. C., & Ivanhoe, P. J. (eds.). (2000). *Virtue, Nature, and Moral Agency in the* Xunzi. Indianapolis: Hackett Publishing.

Knoblock, J. (1988, 1990, 1994). *Xunzi: A Translation and Study of the Complete Works*. 3 vols. Stanford, CA: Stanford University Press.

Knuuttila, S. (2004). *Emotions in Ancient and Medieval Philosophy*. Oxford: Oxford University Press.

Konstan, D. (2001). *Pity Transformed: Classical Inter/faces*. London: Duckworth.

Konstan, D. (2003). "Shame in Ancient Greece." *Social Research* 70, no. 4, Shame, 1031–60.

Konstan, D. (2006). *The Emotions of the Ancient Greeks*. Toronto: University of Toronto Press.

Konstan, D. (2010) *Before Forgiveness: The Origins of a Moral Idea*. Cambridge: Cambridge University Press.

Konstan, D. (2020). "Afterword: The Invention of Emotion?" in Candiotto, L., & Renaut, O. (eds.), *Emotions in Plato*. Leiden: Brill, 372–81.

Konstan, D. (ed.) (2022). *Emotions across Cultures: Ancient China and Greece*. Berlin: de Gruyter.

Konstan, D. (2022). "Introduction: Comparing Emotions Historically," in Konstan, D. (ed.), *Emotions across Cultures: Ancient China and Greece*. Berlin: de Gruyter, 1–18.

Koziak, B. (2000). *Retrieving Political Emotion: Thumos, Aristotle, and Gender*. University Park: Pennsylvania State University Press.

Kraut, R. (1997). *Aristotle: Politics. Books VII and VIII*. Translated with a commentary. Oxford: Oxford University Press.

Kraut, R. (ed.). (2006). *The Blackwell Guide to Aristotle's Nicomachean Ethics*. Oxford: Blackwell Publishing.

Kraut, R. (2007). "Nature in Aristotle's Ethics and Politics," in Keyt, D., & Miller, F. B. (eds.), *Freedom, Reason, and the Polis: Essays in Ancient Greek Political Philosophy*. Cambridge: Cambridge University Press, 199–219.

Kraut, R., and Skultety, S. (eds.). (2005). *Aristotle's Politics: Critical Essays*. Lanham: Rowman & Littlefield Publishers.

Kristjánsson, K. (2007). *Aristotle, Emotions, and Education*. Aldershot: Ashgate Publishing.

Kuhn, T. (1970). *The Structure of Scientific Revolutions*. 2nd edition. Chicago: University of Chicago Press.

Kupperman, J. J. (2000). "Xunzi: Morality as Psychological Constraint," in Kline III, T. C., & Ivanhoe, P. J. (eds.), *Virtue, Nature, and Moral Agency in the Xunzi*. Indianapolis: Hackett Publishing, 89–102.

Kupperman, J. J. (2010) *Theories of Human Nature*. Indianapolis: Hackett Publishing.

Lai, K., R. Benitez, & Kim, H. J. (eds.). (2019). *Cultivating a Good Life in Early Chinese and Ancient Greek Philosophy: Perspectives and Reverberations*. London: Bloomsbury.

Lane, M. (2009). "Comparing Greek and Chinese Political Thought: The Case of Plato's Republic." *Journal of Chinese Philosophy* 36, no. 4: 585–601.

Larson, G. J., & Deutsch, E. (eds.). (1988). *Interpreting across Boundaries: New Essays in Comparative Philosophy*. Princeton: Princeton University Press.

Lateiner, D., & Spatharas, D. (eds.). (2016). *The Ancient Emotion of Disgust*. New York: Oxford University Press.

Lau, D. C. [1970] (2003) *Mencius*. Translated with an introduction and notes. London: Penguin.

Lear, J. (1988). *Aristotle: The Desire to Understand*. New York: Cambridge University Press.

Lear, G. R. (2006). *Happy Lives and the Highest Good: An Essay on Aristotle's* Nicomachean Ethics. Princeton, NJ: Princeton University Press.

Lebron, C. (2013). *The Color of Our Shame: Race and Justice in Our Time*. New York: Oxford University Press.

Leighton, S. R. (1988). "Aristotle's Courageous Passions." *Phronesis* 33, no. 1: 76–99.

Lennox, J. G., & Bolton, R. (eds.). (2010). *Being, Nature, and Life in Aristotle: Essays in Honor of Allan Gotthelf*. Cambridge: Cambridge University Press.

Lewis, H. B. (1971). *Shame and Guilt in Neurosis*. New York: International Universities Press.

Lewis, J. (2020). "Emotional Rescue: The Emotional Turn in the Study of History." *Journal of Interdisciplinary History* 51, no. 1: 121–29.

Lewis, M. (1995). *Shame: The Exposed Self*. New York: Free Press.

Lewis, M. (2016). "Self-conscious Emotions: Embarrassment, Pride, Shame, and Guilt," in Lewis, M., Haviland-Jones, J. M., & Barrett, L. F. (eds.), *Handbook of Emotions*. 4th edition. New York: Guilford Press, 742–56.

Lewis, M., Haviland-Jones, J. M., & L. F. Barrett (eds.). (2016). *The Handbook of Emotions*. 4th edition. London: The Guilford Press.

Lewis, M. E. (1999). *Writing and Authority in Early China*. Albany: State University of New York Press.

Lewis, M. E. (2021). *Honor and Shame in Early China*. Cambridge: Cambridge University Press.

Li, C. (ed.). (2000). *The Sage and the Second Sex: Confucianism, Ethics, and Gender*. Chicago: Open Court.

Li, C. (2011). "Xunzi on the Origin of Goodness: A New Interpretation." *Journal of Chinese Philosophy* 38: 46–63.

Li, J., Wang, L., & Fischer, K. (2004). "The Organisation of Chinese Shame Concepts?" *Cognition and Emotion* 18, no. 6: 767–97.

Liang, Q. 梁啓超. (2003). *Xian qin zheng zhi si xiang shi* 先秦政治思想史. Tianjin: Tian jin gu ji chu ban she 天津：天津古籍出版社.

Libbrecht, U. (2007). *Within the Four Seas*. Leuven: Peeters.

Liddell, H. G., Scott, R., Jones, H. S., McKenzie, R., & Glare, P. G. W. (1996). *A Greek-English Lexicon*. Ninth edition with revised supplement. Oxford: Clarendon Press.

Lin, L. (2022). *Die Helfer der Vernunft: Scham und verwandte Emotionen bei Platon*. Berlin: de Gruyter.

Liu, Q. (2011). "Emotionales in Confucianism and Daoism: A New Interpretation." *Journal of Chinese Philosophy* 38, no. 1: 118–33.

162 Bibliography

Lloyd, G. E. R. (1966). *Polarity and Analogy: Two Types of Argumentation in Early Greek Thought*. Cambridge: Cambridge University Press.

Lloyd, G. E. R. (1990). *Demystifying Mentalities*. Cambridge: Cambridge University Press.

Lloyd, G. E. R. (1991). *Methods and Problems in Greek Science*. Cambridge: Cambridge University Press.

Lloyd, G. E. R. (1996). *Adversaries and Authorities: Investigations into Ancient Greek and Chinese Science*. Cambridge: Cambridge University Press.

Lloyd, G. E. R. (2005). "'Philosophy': What Did the Greeks Invent and Is It Relevant to China?" In Cheng, A. (ed.), *Y A-t-il Une Philosophie Chinoise? Un État De La Question. Extrême-Orient, Extrême-Occident* 27. Saint-Denis: Presses Univ. de Vincennes, 149–59.

Lloyd, G. E. R. (2007). *Cognitive Variations: Reflections on the Unity and Diversity of the Human Mind*. Oxford: Clarendon Press.

Lloyd, G. E. R. (2009). "Comparative Approaches to the Study of Culture," in Graziosi, B., Vasunia, P., & Boys-Stones, G. (eds.), *The Oxford Handbook of Hellenic Studies*. Oxford: Oxford University Press, 643–52.

Lloyd, G. E. R. (2010). "History and Human Nature: Cross-Cultural Universals and Cultural Relativities." *Interdisciplinary Science Reviews* 35, no. 3–4: 201–14.

Lloyd, G. E. R. (2011). "Comparative Ethics: Some Methodological Considerations," in King, R. A. H., & Schilling, D. R. (eds.), *How Should One Live? Comparing Ethics in Ancient China and Greco-Roman Antiquity*. Berlin: de Gruyter, 18–21.

Lloyd, G. E. R. (2012). *Being, Humanity, and Understanding: Studies in Ancient and Modern Societies*. Oxford: Oxford University Press.

Lloyd, G. E. R. (2017). *The Ambivalences of Rationality*. Cambridge: Cambridge University Press.

Lloyd, G. E. R. (2020). *Intelligence and Intelligibility: Cross-Cultural Studies of Human Cognitive Experience*. Oxford: Oxford University Press.

Lloyd, Geoffrey., & Sivin, N. (2002). *The Way and the Word: Science and Medicine in Early China and Greece*. New Haven; London: Yale University Press.

Lloyd, G. E. R., & Zhao, J. J. (eds.). (2018). *Ancient Greece and China Compared*. In collaboration with Qiaosheng Dong. Cambridge: Cambridge University Press.

Loewe, M. (ed.). (1993). "Hsün Tzu 荀子," in Loewe, M. (ed.), *Early Chinese Texts: At Bibliographical Guide*. Berkeley: The Society for the Study of Early China and the Institute of East Asian Studies, University of California, Berkeley, 178–88.

Loewe, M., & Shaughnessy, E. L. (eds.). (1999). *The Cambridge History of Ancient China: From the Origins of Civilization to 221 BC*. New York: Cambridge University Press.

Long, A. A. (1992). "Finding Oneself in Greek Philosophy." *Tijdschrift Voor Filosofie* 54: 257–79.

Long, A. A. (2001). "Ancient Philosophy's Hardest Question: What to Make of Oneself?" *Representations* 74: 19–36.

Lord, C., O'Connor, K., & Bodéüs, R. (eds.). (1991). *Essays on the Foundations of Aristotelian Political Science*. Berkeley: University of California Press.

Lu, J. 陸建華. (2004). *Xun zi li xue yan jiu* 荀子禮學研究. Anhui: An hui da xue chu ban she 安徽：安徽大學出版社.

Ludwig, P. W. (2002). *Eros & Polis: Desire and Community in Greek Political Theory*. Cambridge: Cambridge University Press.

Lutz, C. (1988). *Unnatural Emotions: Everyday Sentiments on a Micronesian Atoll and Their Challenge to Western Theory*. Chicago: University of Chicago Press.

Lynd, H. M. (1958). *On Shame and the Search for Identity*. New York: Harcourt, Brace and Company.

Ma, L., & van Brakel, J. (2016). *Fundamentals of Comparative and Intercultural Philosophy*. Albany: State University of New York Press.

Machle, E. J. (1993). *Nature and Heaven in the* Xunzi: *A Study of the Tian Lun*. Albany: State University of New York Press.

MacIntyre, A. (1984). *After Virtue: A Study in Moral Theory*. 2nd edition. Notre Dame, IN: University of Notre Dame Press.

MacIntyre, A. (1991). "Incommensurability, Truth, and the Conversation Between Confucians and Aristotelians about the Virtues," in Deutsch, E. (ed.), *Culture and Modernity: East-West Philosophic Perspectives*. Honolulu: University of Hawai'i Press, 104–123.

Marks, J., & Ames, R. T. (eds.). (1995). *Emotions in Asian Thought: A Dialogue in Comparative Philosophy*. Albany: State University of New York Press.

Marks, J. (1995). "Emotions in Western Thought: Some Background for a Comparative Dialogue," in Marks, J., & Ames, R. T. (eds.), *Emotions in Asian Thought: A Dialogue in Comparative Philosophy*. Albany: State University of New York Press, 1–37.

Mayhew, R. (2009) "Rulers and Ruled," in Anagnostopoulos, G. (ed.), *A Companion to Aristotle*. Oxford: Blackwell, 526–39.

McCready-Flora, I. C. (2019) "Speech and the Rational Soul," in Keil, G., & Kreft, N. (eds.), *Aristotle's Anthropology*. Cambridge: Cambridge University Press, 44–59.

Merlan, P. (1954). "Isocrates, Aristotle and Alexander the Great." *Historia: Zeitschrift Für Alte Geschichte* 3, no. 1: 60–81.

Meyer, D. (2011). *Philosophy on Bamboo: Text and the Production of Meaning in Early China*. Leiden: Brill.

Meyer, S. S. (2011). *Aristotle on Moral Responsibility, Character and Cause*. Oxford: Oxford University Press.

Militello, C. (2020). "Αἰσχύνη and the Λογιστικόν in Plato's Republic," in Candiotto, L., & Renaut, O. (eds.). *Emotions in Plato*. Leiden: Brill, 238–51.

Miller, F. D. (1995). *Nature, Justice, and Rights in Aristotle's* Politics. Oxford: Clarendon Press.

Minsky, M. (2006). *The Emotion Machine*. Simon & Schuster.

Mokyr, J. (2018). *A Culture of Growth: The Origins of the Modern Economy*. Princeton, NJ: Princeton University Press.

Molina, J. M., Swearer, D. K., & McGarry, S. L. (eds.). (2010). *Rethinking the Human*. Cambridge, MA: Harvard University Press.

Moss, J. (2014). "Right Reason in Plato and Aristotle: On the Meaning of *Logos*," *Phronesis* 59, no.3: 181–230.

Morrison, A. P. (1989). *Shame: The Underside of Narcissism*. Hillsdale, NJ: Analytic Press.

Most, G. W., & Puett, M. (eds.). (2023). *After Wisdom: Sapiential Traditions and Ancient Scholarship in Comparative Perspective. Philological Encounters Monographs*. Leiden: Brill.

Mou, B. (ed.). (2001). *Two Roads to Wisdom? Chinese and Analytic Philosophical Traditions*. La Salle, IL: Open Court.

Mou, B. (ed.), (2003). *Comparative Approaches to Chinese Philosophy*. Aldershot: Ashgate.

Munro, D. J. (1996). "A Villain in the *Xunzi*," in Ivanhoe, P. J., & Nivison, D. S. (eds.), *Chinese Language, Thought, and Culture: Nivison and His Critics*. La Salle, IL: Open Court, 193–201.

Munt, S. R. (2009). *Queer Attachments: The Cultural Politics of Shame*. London: Routledge.

Mutschler, F-H. (ed.). (2018). *The Homeric Epics and the Chinese Book of Songs*. Newcastle: Cambridge Scholars Publishing.

Nagy, P. & Bouquet, D. (2011). "Historical Emotions, Historians' Emotion," 15, trans. G. Robinson, https://emma.hypotheses.org/1213. Originally published as "Emotions historiques, emotions historiennes," *Ecrire l'historie*, 2, 15–26.

164   Bibliography

Natali, C. (2013). *Aristotle: His Life and School*. Princeton, NJ: Princeton University Press.

Needham, J. (1956). *Science and Civilisation in China: Volume 2, History of Scientific Thought*. Cambridge: Cambridge University Press.

Neville, R. C. (2001). "Two Forms of Comparative Philosophy." *Dao: A Journal of Comparative Philosophy* 1, no. 1: 1–13.

Newell, W. R. (1987). "Superlative Virtue: The Problem of Monarchy in Aristotle's 'Politics.'" *The Western Political Quarterly* 40: 159–78.

Newmyer, S. T. (2012). "Ancient and Modern Views of the Expression of Shame in Animals." *Journal of Animal Ethics* 2, no. 1: 87–97.

Newmyer, S. T. (2014). "Being the One and Becoming the Other: Animals in Ancient Philosophical Schools," in Campbell, G. L. (ed.), *The Oxford Handbook of Animals in Classical Thought and Life*. Oxford: Oxford University Press, 507–34.

Newmyer, S. T. (2017). *The Animal and the Human in Ancient and Modern Thought: The 'Man Alone of Animals' Concept*. Abingdon: Routledge.

Ng, M. N. (1981). "Internal Shame as a Moral Sanction." *Journal of Chinese Philosophy* 8, no. 1: 75–86.

Nisbett, R. E. (2003). *The Geography of Thought: How Asians and Westerners Think Differently—and Why*. New York: The Free Press.

Nivison, D. S. (1996). "Xunzi on Human Nature," in Nivison, D. S., *The Ways of Confucianism: Investigations in Chinese Philosophy*, edited with an introduction by B. W. Van Norden. La Salle, IL: Open Court, 203–14.

Nussbaum, M. C. (1980). "Shame, Separateness, and Political Unity: Aristotle's Criticism of Plato," in *Essays on Aristotle's Ethics*, edited by A. O. Rorty. Berkeley: University of California Press, 395–435.

Nussbaum, M. C. (1990). *Upheavals of Thought: The Intelligence of Emotions*. New York: Cambridge University Press.

Nussbaum, M. C. (2004). *Hiding from Humanity: Disgust, Shame, and the Law*. Princeton, NJ: Princeton University Press.

Nylan, M. (2001). "On the Politics of Pleasure." *Asia Major* 14, no. 1: 73–124.

Nylan, M. (2012). "'Living Without Sin': Reflections on the Pre-Buddhist World of Early China," in Granoff, Phyllis & Shinohara, Koichi (eds), *Sins and Sinners: Perspectives from Asian Religions*. Leiden: Brill, 57–72.

Nylan, M. (2016). "Xunzi: An Early Reception History, Han through Tang," in Hutton, E. L. (ed.), *Dao Companion to the Philosophy of Xunzi*. Dordrecht: Springer, 395–433.

Nylan, M. (2018). *The Chinese Pleasure Book*. New York: Zone Books.

Oele, M. (2007). *Aristotle on Pathos*. PhD dissertation. University of San Francisco.

Oele, M. (2018) "Aristotle on *Physis*: Analyzing the Inner Ambiguities and Transgression of Nature," in Kirkland, S. D., & Sanday, E. (eds.), *A Companion to Ancient Philosophy*. Evanston, IL: Northwestern University Press, 161–75.

Osborne, C. (2007). *Dumb Beasts and Dead Philosophers: Humanity and the Humane in Ancient Philosophy and Literature*. Oxford: Clarendon Press.

Osborne, R. (2010). *Athens and Athenian Democracy*. Cambridge: Cambridge University Press.

Oxford English Dictionary. (June 2022). 'Shame, n.' *OED* Online, https://doi.org/10.1093/OED/1015780933. Oxford: Oxford University Press.

Pakaluk, M., & Pearson, G. (eds.). (2011). *Moral Psychology and Human Action in Aristotle*. Oxford: Oxford University Press.

Panikkar, R. (1988). "What Is Comparative Philosophy Comparing?", in Larson, G. J., & Deutsch, E. (eds.), *Interpreting across Boundaries: New Essays in Comparative Philosophy*. Princeton, NJ: Princeton University Press, 116–36.

Bibliography   165

Pearson, G. (2012). *Aristotle on Desire*. Cambridge: Cambridge University Press.

Perkins, F. (2010). "Recontextualizing Xing: Self-Cultivation and Human Nature in the Guodian Texts." *Journal of Chinese Philosophy* 37, supplement 1: 16–32.

Perkins, F. (2014). *Heaven and Earth Are Not Humane: The Problem of Evil in Classical Chinese Philosophy*. Bloomington, IN: Indiana University Press.

Pfefferkorn, J. (2020). "Shame and Virtue in Plato's *Laws*: Two Kinds of Fear and the Drunken Puppet," in Candiotto, L., & Renaut, O. (eds.). *Emotions in Plato*. Leiden: Brill, 252–69.

Picard, R. (2003). "Affective Computing: Challenges." *International Journal of Human-Computer Studies*, 59, no.1–2: 55–64.

Piers, G., & Singer, M. B. (1953). *Shame and Guilt: A Psychoanalytic and a Cultural Study*. Springfield, IL: Charles C. Thomas.

Pines, Y. (2009). *Envisioning Eternal Empire: Chinese Political Thought of the Warring States Era*. Honolulu: University of Hawai'i Press.

Pines, Y. (2023). "Legalism in Chinese Philosophy," in Edward N. Zalta & Uri Nodelman (eds.), *The Stanford Encyclopedia of Philosophy*. https://plato.stanford.edu/archives/sum2 023/entries/chinese-legalism/.

Pines, Y. ed. (forthcoming) *Dao Companion to China's* fa *Tradition: The Philosophy of Governance by Impartial Standards*. Dordrecht: Springer.

Plamper, J. (2015). *The History of Emotions: An Introduction*. Oxford: Oxford University Press.

Polansky, R. (ed.). (2014). *The Cambridge Companion to Aristotle's* Nicomachean Ethics. Cambridge: Cambridge University Press.

Puett, M. J. (2001). *The Ambivalence of Creation: Debates Concerning Innovation and Artifice in Early China*. Stanford, CA: Stanford University Press.

Puett, M. J. (2004). "The Ethics of Responding Properly: The Notion of *Qing* 情 in Early Chinese Thought," in Eifring, H. (ed.), *Love and Emotions in Traditional Chinese Literature*. Leiden: Brill, 37–68.

Puett, M. J. (2010). "The Haunted World of Humanity: Ritual Theory from Early China," in Molina, M. J., Swearer, D. K., & McGarry, S. L. (eds.), *Rethinking the Human*. Cambridge, MA: Harvard University Press, 95–111.

Puett, M. J. (2018). "Genealogies of Gods, Ghosts and Humans: The Capriciousness of the Divine in Early Greece and Early China," in Lloyd, G. E. R., & Zhao, J. J. (eds.), *Ancient Greece and China Compared*. Cambridge: Cambridge University Press, 160–85.

Quine, W. V. O. [1960] (2001). *Word and Object*. 24th printing. Cambridge, MA: MIT Press.

Rackham, H. (1934). *Aristotle:* Nicomachean Ethics. Translation. 2nd edition. Cambridge, MA: Harvard University Press.

Rahe, P. (1992). *Republics Ancient and Modern: Classical Republicanism and American Revolution*. Chapel Hill: University of North Carolina Press.

Raphals, L. A. (1992). *Knowing Words: Wisdom and Cunning in the Classical Traditions of China and Greece*. Ithaca, NY: Cornell University Press.

Raphals, L. A. (2000). "Gendered Virtue Reconsidered: Notes from the Warring States and Han," in Li, C. (ed.), *The Sage and the Second Sex: Confucianism, Ethics, and Gender*. La Salle, IL: Open Court, 223–47.

Raphals, L. A. (2002). "Gender and Virtue in Greece and China." *Journal of Chinese Philosophy* 29, 3: 415–36.

Raphals, L. A. (2013). *Divination and Prediction in Early China and Ancient Greece*. Cambridge: Cambridge University Press.

Raphals, L. A. (2018). "Human and Animal in Early China and Greece," in Lloyd, G. E. R., & Zhao, J. J. (eds.). *Ancient Greece and China Compared*. Cambridge: Cambridge University Press, 131–59.

166 Bibliography

Raymond, C. (2017). "Shame and Virtue in Aristotle." *Oxford Studies in Ancient Philosophy* 53: 111–62.

Reddy, W. M. (2001). *The Navigation of Feeling: A Framework for the History of Emotion.* Cambridge: Cambridge University Press.

Reding, J-P. (2004). *Comparative Essays in Early Greek and Chinese Rational Thinking.* Aldershot: Ashgate.

Reeve, C. D. C. (1992). *Practices of Reason: Aristotle's* Nicomachean Ethics. Oxford: Clarendon Press.

Reis, B. (ed.). (2006). *The Virtuous Life in Greek Ethics.* New York: Cambridge University Press.

Riesbeck, D. J. (2016). *Aristotle on Political Community.* Cambridge: Cambridge University Press.

Robins, D. (2011). "The Warring States Concept of *Xing.*" *Dao: A Journal of Comparative Philosophy*, vol. 10: 31–51.

Roetz, H. (1993). *Confucian Ethics of the Axial Age.* Albany: State University of New York Press.

Roget, P. M. [1852]. (1998). *Roget's Thesaurus of English Words and Phrases.* London: Penguin.

Roochnik, D. (2015). "Courage and Shame: Aristotle's *Nicomachean Ethics* III. 6–9." *Etica & Politica / Ethics & Politics* 17, vol. 2: 200–218.

Rorty, A. O. (ed.). (1980). *Essays on Aristotle's Ethics.* Berkeley: University of California Press.

Rorty, A. O. (1984). "Aristotle on the Metaphysical Status of 'Pathē.'" *The Review of Metaphysics* 37, no. 3: 521–46.

Rorty, A. O. (ed.). (1996). *Essays on Aristotle's* Rhetoric. Berkeley: University of California Press.

Rosaldo, M. (1984). "Toward an Anthropology of Self and Feeling," in Shweder, R. A., & LeVine, R. A. (eds.), *Culture Theory: Essays on Mind, Self and Emotion.* Cambridge: Cambridge University Press, 137–57.

Rosemont, H. (2000) "State and Society in the *Xunzi*: A Philosophical Commentary," in Kline III, T. C., & Ivanhoe, P. J. (eds.), *Virtue, Nature, and Moral Agency in the Xunzi.* Indianapolis, IN: Hackett Publishing, 1–38.

Rowlands, M. (2012). *Can Animals Be Moral?* Oxford: Oxford University Press.

Russell, D. C. (ed.). (2013). *The Cambridge Companion to Virtue Ethics.* Cambridge: Cambridge University Press.

Ryle, G. (1968). *The Thinking of Thoughts: What Is "Le Penseur" Doing?* University Lectures, no. 8. Saskatoon: University of Saskatchewan.

Salkever, S. G. (2005). "Aristotle's Social Science," in Kraut, R., & Skultety, S. (eds.), *Aristotle's Politics: Critical Essays.* Lanham: Rowman & Littlefield Publishers, 27–64.

Salkever, S. G. (2009). "Reading Aristotle's *Nicomachean Ethics* and *Politics* as a Single Course of Lectures: Rhetoric, Politics, and Philosophy," in Salkever, S. G. (ed.), *The Cambridge Companion to Ancient Greek Political Thought.* Cambridge: Cambridge University Press, 209–42.

Sanders, E. (2014). *Envy and Jealousy in Classical Athens.* Oxford: Oxford University Press.

Sanders, E. & Johncock, M. (eds.) (2016). *Emotion and Persuasion in Classical Antiquity.* Stuttgart: Franz Steiner Verlag.

Sandis, C., & Cain, M. J. (eds.). (2012). *Human Nature.* Royal Institute of Philosophy supplement. Cambridge: Cambridge University Press.

Santangelo, P. (2007). "Emotions and Perception of Inner Reality: Chinese and European." *Journal of Chinese Philosophy* 34, no. 2: 289–308.

Santangelo, P., & Guida, D. (eds.). (2006). *Love, Hatred, and Other Passions: Questions and Themes on Emotions in Chinese Civilization.* Leiden: Brill.

Santangelo, P., & Middendorf, U. (eds.). (2006). *From Skin to Heart: Perceptions of Bodily Sensations and Emotions in Traditional Chinese Culture*. Wiesbaden: Harrassowitz.

Sato, M. (2003). *The Confucian Quest for Order: The Origin and Formation of the Political Thought of Xun Zi*. Sinica Leidensia, vol. 58. Leiden: Brill.

Saunders, T. J. (1995). *Aristotle: Politics. Books I and II*. Translated with a commentary. Oxford: Clarendon Press.

Saxonhouse, A. W. (2006). *Free Speech and Democracy in Ancient Athens*. Cambridge: Cambridge University Press.

Scheff, T. J. (2000). "Shame and the Social Bond: A Sociological Theory." *Sociological Theory* 18, no. 1: 84–99.

Scheidel, W. (2018). "Comparing Comparisons," in Lloyd, G. E. R., & Zhao, J. J. (eds.). *Ancient Greece and China Compared*. Cambridge: Cambridge University Press, 40–58.

Scheidel, W. (2019). *Escape from Rome: The Failure of Empire and the Road to Prosperity*. Princeton, NJ: Princeton University Press.

Scheer, M. (2012). "Are Emotions a Kind of Practice (and Is That What Makes Them Have a History?) A Bourdieuian Approach to Understanding Emotion." *History & Theory*, 51, no. 2: 193–220.

Schnell, R. (2015). *Haben Gefühle eine Geschichte? Aporien einer History of Emotions*. 2 vols. Göttingen: Vandenhoeck and Ruprecht.

Schofer, J. W. (1993). "Virtues in Xunzi's Thought." *The Journal of Religious Ethics* 21, no. 1: 117–36.

Schofield, M. (2006). "Aristotle's Political Ethics," in Kraut, R. (ed.), *The Blackwell Guide to Aristotle's Nicomachean Ethics*. Malden: Blackwell Publishing, 305–22.

Schumacher, J. (1993). *Über Den Begriff Des Nützlichen Bei Mengzi*. Schweizer Asiatische Studien. Monographien/ Etudes Asiatiques Suisses. Bern: Peter Lang.

Scott, D. (2020). *Listening to Reason in Plato and Aristotle*. Oxford: Oxford University Press.

Scott, S. (2020). "Loving and Living Well: The Importance of Shame in Plato's Phaedrus," in Candiotto, L., & Renaut, O. (eds.), *Emotions in Plato*. Leiden: Brill, 270–84.

Sedley, D. (1991). "Is Aristotle's Teleology Anthropocentric?" *Phronesis* 36, no. 2: 179–96.

Sedley, D. (2010). "Teleology, Aristotelian and Platonic," in Lennox, J. G., & Bolton, R. (eds.), *Being, Nature, and Life in Aristotle: Essays in Honor of Allan Gotthelf*. Cambridge: Cambridge University Press, 5–29.

Segal, C. (1970). "Shame and Purity in Euripides' *Hippolytus*." *Hermes* 98, no. 3: 278–99.

Seok, B. (2015). "Moral Psychology of Shame in Early Confucian Philosophy." *Frontiers of Philosophy in China* 10, no. 1: 21–57.

Seok, B. (2017). *Moral Psychology of Confucian Shame: Shame of Shamelessness*. Mary Land: Rowman and Littlefield.

Shankman, S., & Durrant, S. W. (2000). *The Siren and the Sage: Knowledge and Wisdom in Ancient Greece and China*. London: Cassell.

Shankman, S., & Durrant, S. W. (eds.). (2002). *Early China/Ancient Greece: Thinking through Comparisons*. Albany: State University of New York Press.

Shao, X. 邵顯俠, & Chen Z. 陳真. (2010). *Rong ru si xiang de zhong xi zhe xue ji chu yan jiu* 榮辱思想的中西哲學基礎研究. Beijing: Ren min chu ban she 北京 : 人民出版社.

Shen, V. (ed.). (2014). *Dao Companion to Classical Confucian Philosophy*. Dordrecht: Springer Netherlands.

Shun, K-L. (2001). "Self and Self-Cultivation in Early Confucian Thought," in Mou, B. (ed.), *Two Roads to Wisdom? Chinese and Analytic Philosophical Traditions*. La Salle, IL: Open Court, 229–44.

168 Bibliography

Shun, K-L, & Wong, D. B. (eds.). (2004). *Confucian Ethics: A Comparative Study of Self, Autonomy, and Community*. New York: Cambridge University Press.

Shweder, R. A., & LeVine, R. A. (eds.). (1984). *Culture Theory: Essays on Mind, Self and Emotion*. Cambridge: Cambridge University Press.

Sim, M. (2007a). *Remastering Morals with Aristotle and Confucius*. Cambridge: Cambridge University Press.

Sim, M. (2007b). "Virtue-oriented Politics: Confucius and Aristotle," in Goodman, L. E., & Talisse, R. B. (eds.), *Aristotle's Politics Today*. Albany: State University of New York Press, 53–76.

Simpson, P. (1998). *A Philosophical Commentary on the* Politics *of Aristotle*. Chapel Hill: University of North Carolina Press.

Sivin, N. (1995). *Medicine, Philosophy and Religion in Ancient China: Researches and Reflections*. Aldershot: Variorum, Ashgate.

Skinner, Q. (1978). *The Foundations of Modern Political Thought*. Cambridge: Cambridge University Press.

Slingerland, E. (2003). *Confucius:* Analects. With selections from traditional commentaries. Indianapolis: Hackett Publishing.

Slote, M. (2020). *Between Psychology and Philosophy: East-West Themes and Beyond*. Cham: Palgrave Macmillan.

Smid, R. W. (2009). *Methodologies of Comparative Philosophy: The Pragmatist and Process Traditions*. Albany: State University of New York Press.

Smith, T. W. (2015). *The Book of Human Emotions*. London: Profile Books.

Snell, B. (1953). *The Discovery of the Mind: The Greek Origins of European Thought*. Translated by T. G. Rosenmeyer. New York: Harper & Row.

Sokolon, M. K. (2006). *Political Emotions: Aristotle and the Symphony of Reason and Emotion*. Dekalb: Northern Illinois University Press.

Solomon, R. C. (1995). "The Cross-Cultural Comparison of Emotion," in Marks, J., & Ames, R. T. (eds.), *Emotions in Asian Thought: A Dialogue in Comparative Philosophy*. Albany: State University of New York Press, 253–300.

Solomon, R. C. (2001). "'What Is Philosophy?' The Status of Non-Western Philosophy in the Profession." *Philosophy East and West* 51, no. 1: 100–104.

Solomon, R. C. (2008). "The Philosophy of Emotions," in Lewis, M., Haviland-Jones, J. M., & Barrett, L. F. (eds.), *Handbook of Emotions*. 3rd edition. New York: Guilford Press, 3–16.

Song, B. (ed.). (2021). *Intelligence and Wisdom: Artificial Intelligence Meets Chinese Philosophers*. Singapore: Springer.

Sorabji, R. (1993). *Animal Minds and Human Morals: The Origins of the Western Debate*. Cornell Studies in Classical Philology, vol. 54. Ithaca, NY: Cornell University Press.

Sorabji, R. (1996). "Rationality," in Frede, M., & Striker, G. (eds.), *Rationality in Greek Thought*. Oxford: Clarendon Press, 311–34.

Sorabji, R. (2000). *Emotion and Peace of Mind: From Stoic Agitation to Christian Temptation*. Oxford: Oxford University Press.

de Sousa, R. (2001). "Moral Emotions." *Ethical Theory and Moral Practice* 4, no. 2: 109–26.

Spalding, K. J. (1937). "A Chinese Aristotle," in Hughes, E. R. (ed.), *The Individual in East and West*. Humphrey Milford: Oxford University Press, 58–86.

Spalding, K. J. (1947). *Three Chinese Thinkers*. Nanking: National Central Library.

Spatharas, D. (2019). *Emotions, Persuasion, and Public Discourse in Classical Athens. Ancient Emotions II*. Berlin: De Gruyter.

Stalnaker, A. (2006). *Overcoming Our Evil Human Nature and Spiritual Exercises in Xunzi and Augustine*. Washington, DC: Georgetown University Press.

Stearns, P. N. (2017). *Shame: A Brief History*. Urbana: University of Illinois Press.

Steiner, G. (2008). *Animals and the Moral Community: Mental Life, Moral Status, and Kinship*. New York: Columbia University Press.

Sterckx, R. (2002). *The Animal and the Daemon in Early China*. Albany: State University of New York Press.

Striker, G. (1996). "Emotions in Context: Aristotle's Treatment of the Passions in the *Rhetoric* and His Moral Psychology," in Rorty, A. O. (ed.), *Essays on Aristotle's Rhetoric*. Berkeley: California University Press, 286–302.

Striker, G. (2006). "Aristotle's Ethics as Political Science," in Reis, B. (ed.), *The Virtuous Life in Greek Ethics*. New York: Cambridge University Press, 127–41.

Strohm, P. (2013). *Conscience: A Very Short Introduction*. Oxford: Oxford University Press.

Sun, W. 孫偉. (2015). *'Dao' yu 'xing fu': Xunzi yu Yalishiduode lun li xue bi jiao yan jiu* "道"與"幸福"：荀子與亞里士多德倫理學比較研究. Beijing: Peking University Press 北京：北京大學出版社.

Sung, W. (2012). "*Yu* in the *Xunzi*: Can Desire by Itself Motivate Action?" *Dao: A Journal of Comparative Philosophy* 11, no. 3: 369–88.

Susemihl, F., & Hicks, R. D. (1894). *The* Politics *of Aristotle*. A revised text, with introduction, analysis and commentary. London: Macmillan and Co.

Suzuki, Y. (2018). *Methods of Moral Enquiry in the Earliest Chinese Texts: A Comparative Analysis with Socrates in Plato's Dialogues*. PhD dissertation. University of Hong Kong.

Swan, K., and Vallier, K. (2012). "The Normative Significance of Conscience." *Journal of Ethics & Social Philosophy* 6, no. 3: 1–21.

Swanson, J. A. (1992). *The Public and the Private in Aristotle's Political Philosophy*. Ithaca, NY: Cornell University Press.

Tang, Junyi 唐君毅. (2005). *Zhong guo zhe xue yuan lun - yuan xing pian* 中國哲學原論 - 原性篇. Beijing: China Social Sciences Press 北京：中國社會科學出版社.

Tangney, J. P., & Dearing, R. L. (2002). *Shame and Guilt*. New York: Guilford Publications.

Tanner, J. (2009). "Sino-Hellenic Studies and Comparative Approaches to the Classical World: Ancient Greece, Early China: A Review Article." *Journal of Hellenic Studies* 129: 89–109.

Tarnopolsky, C. H. (2010). *Prudes, Perverts, and Tyrants: Plato's Gorgias and the Politics of Shame*. Princeton, NJ: Princeton University Press.

Taylor, C. C. W. (2006). *Aristotle: Nicomachean Ethics. Books II-IV*. Translated with an introduction and commentary. Oxford: Oxford University Press.

Taylor, G. (1985). *Pride, Shame, and Guilt: Emotions of Self-Assessment*. Oxford: Clarendon Press.

Tomkins, S. S. (1963). *Affect, Imagery, Consciousness. Volume II—The Negative Affects*. New York: Springer.

Trott, A. (2014). *Aristotle on the Nature of Community*. Cambridge: Cambridge University Press.

Tu, W. (1989). *Centrality and Commonality: An Essay on Confucian Religiousness*. A revised and enlarged edition. Albany: State University of New York Press.

Van Norden, B. W. (2000). "Mengzi and Xunzi: Two Views of Human Agency," in Kline III T. C., & Ivanhoe, P. J. (eds.). *Virtue, Nature, and Moral Agency in the Xunzi*. Indianapolis, IN: Hackett Publishing, 103–34.

Van Norden, B. W. (2002) "The Emotion of Shame and the Virtue of Righteousness in Mencius." *Dao: A Journal of Comparative Philosophy* 2, no. 1: 45–77.

Van Norden, B. W. (2007). *Virtue Ethics and Consequentialism in Early Chinese Philosophy*. New York: Cambridge University Press.

Vander Waerdt, P. A. (1985). "The Political Intentions of Aristotle's Moral Philosophy." *Ancient Philosophy* 5.1: 77–89.

Bibliography

Virág, C. (2014). "Early Confucian Perspectives on Emotions," in Shen, V. (ed.), *Dao Companion to Classical Confucian Philosophy*. Dordrecht: Springer Netherlands, 203–226.

Virág, C. (2016). "The Intelligence of Emotions? Debates over the Structure of Moral Life in Early China. *L'Atelier du Centre de Recherches Historiques* 16. https://doi.org/10.4000/acrh.6721.

Virág, C. (2017). *The Emotions in Early Chinese Philosophy*. New York: Oxford University Press.

von Erffa, C. E. (1937). *Aidōs, Und Verwandte Begriffe in Ihrer Entwicklung von Homer Bis Demokrit*. Leipzig: Dietrich.

Wallach W., & Allen, C. (2008). *Moral Machines: Teaching Robots Right from Wrong*. New York: Oxford University Press.

Wang, B. (2012). "The Development of Education and the Flourishing of Scholarship," in Yuan, X., Yan, W., Zhang, C., & Lou, Y. (eds.), *The History of Chinese Civilization*, vol. 1. Translated by David. R. Knechtges. Cambridge: Cambridge University Press, 477–551.

Wang, K. 王楷. (2011). *Tian ran yu xiu wei: Xunzi dao de zhe xue de jing shen* 天然與修為：荀子道德哲學的精神. Beijing: Peking University Press 北京：北京大學出版社.

Wang, K. 王楷. (2018). *Tian sheng ren cheng: Xunzi gong fu lun de zhi qu* 天生人成：荀子功夫論的智趣. Beijing: China Social Sciences Press 北京：中國社會科學出版社.

Wardy, R. (1993). "Aristotelian Rainfall or the Lore of Averages." *Phronesis* 38, no.1: 18–30.

Wardy, R. (2000). *Aristotle in China: Language, Categories and Translation*. Needham Research Institute Studies, 2. Cambridge: Cambridge University Press.

Warren, J. (2021). *Regret: A Study in Ancient Moral Psychology*. Oxford: Oxford University Press.

Watson, B. (2003). *Xunzi: Basic Writings*. Translation. New York: Columbia University Press.

Watson, B. (2003). *The Complete Works of Zhuangzi*. Translation. New York: Columbia University Press.

Weber, R. (2013). "A Stick Which May be Grabbed on Either Side: Sino Hellenic Studies in the Mirror of Comparative Philosophy." *International Journal of the Classical Tradition* 20, no. 1–2: 1–14.

Weber, R. (2014). "Comparative Philosophy and the Tertium: Comparing What with What, and in What Respect?" *Dao: A Journal of Comparative Philosophy* 13, no. 2: 151–71.

Weingarten, O. (2015). "'Self-cultivation' (修身 *Xiu Shen*) in the Early Edited Literature: Uses and Contexts." *Oriens Extremus* 54: 163–208.

Wierzbicka, A. (1999). *Emotions across Languages and Cultures: Diversity and Universals*. Cambridge: Cambridge University Press.

Williams, B. (1993). *Shame and Necessity*. Berkeley: University of California Press.

Wong, D. B. (1996). "Xunzi on Moral Motivation," in Ivanhoe, P. J. (ed.), *Chinese Language, Thought, and Culture: Nivison and His Critics*. La Salle, IL: Open Court, 202–23.

Wray, D. (2015). "Seneca's Shame," in Bartsch, S., & Schiesaro, A. (eds.), *The Cambridge Companion to Seneca*. Cambridge: Cambridge University Press, 199–211.

Xu, F. 徐複觀. (2001). *Zhong guo ren xing lun shi* 中國人性論史. Shanghai: Shang hai san lian shu dian 上海：上海三聯書店.

Xu, K. 徐克謙. (2009). *Xun zi: zhi shi de li xiang* 荀子：治世的理想. Shanghai: Shang hai gu ji chu ban she 上海：上海古籍出版社.

Yack, B. (1993). *The Problems of a Political Animal: Community, Justice, and Conflict in Aristotelian Political Thought*. Berkeley: University of California Press.

Yu, J. (1998). "Virtue: Confucius and Aristotle." *Philosophy East and West* 48, no. 2: 323–47.

Yu, J. (2005). "Human Nature and Virtue in Mencius and Xunzi: An Aristotelian Interpretation." *Dao: A Journal of Comparative Philosophy* 5, no.1: 11–30.

Yu, J. (2007). *The Ethics of Confucius and Aristotle: Mirrors of Virtue*. New York: Routledge.

Yu, J. (2010). "The Practicality of Ancient Virtue Ethics: Greece and China." *Dao: A Journal of Comparative Philosophy* 9, no. 3: 289–302.

Bibliography 171

Yu, J., & Bunnin, N. (2001). "Saving the Phenomena: An Aristotelian Method in Comparative Philosophy," in Mou, B. (ed.), *Two Roads to Wisdom? Chinese and Analytic Philosophical Traditions*. La Salle, IL: Open Court, 293–312.

Yuan, X., Yan, W., Zhang, C., & Lou, Y. (eds.). (2012). *The History of Chinese Civilization*. 4 vols. Translated by Knechtges, D. R. Cambridge: Cambridge University Press.

Zhang, L. (1992). *The Tao and the Logos: Literary Hermeneutics, East and West*. Durham, NC: Duke University Press.

Zhang, L. (1998). *Mighty Opposites: From Dichotomies to Differences in the Comparative Study of China*. Stanford, CA: Stanford University Press.

Zhang, L. (2015). "Cross-cultural Translatability: Challenges and Prospects." *European Review* 23, no.3: 369–78.

Zhang, W. (2023). "Sino-Hellenic Studies: A Survey." *Museum Sinicum* 西方古典學輯刊 5: 228–95.

Zhao, J. J. (2018). "Shame and Moral Education in Aristotle and Xunzi," in Lloyd, G. E. R., & Zhao, J. J. (eds.). *Ancient Greece and China Compared*. Cambridge: Cambridge University Press, 110–30.

Zhao, J. J. (Forthcoming). "Humility: Ancient Greek and Chinese Perspectives," in Steinberg, J. (ed.) *Humility*. Oxford Philosophical Concepts. Oxford: Oxford University Press.

Zhou, C. 周熾成. (2009). *Xun, han: ren xing lun yu she hui li shi zhe xue* 荀，韓：人性論與社會歷史哲學. Guangzhou: Sun Yat-sen University Press 廣州：中山大學出版社.

Zhou, Y. (2010). *Festivals, Feasts, and Gender Relations in Ancient China and Greece*. Cambridge: Cambridge University Press.

Zhou, Y. (2018). "Helen and Chinese Femmes Fetales," in Lloyd, G. E. R. & Zhao, J. J. (eds.), *Ancient Greece and China Compared*. Cambridge: Cambridge University Press, 234–55.

Zhu, W. 朱旺力. (2004) "Cong 'fa zhi' dao 'fa zhi'—xun zi he ya li shi duo de de fa lü si xiang bi jiao." "從'法制'到'法治'-荀子和亞裡士多德的法律思想比較." *Journal of Hebei University of Science and Technology (Social Sciences)* 河北科技大學學報（社會科學版）4, no. 3, 31–33, 42.

DATABASES

Chinese Text Project (中國哲學書電子化計劃). Sturgeon, D. (ed.). https://ctext.org

Perseus Digital Library. Crane, G. R. (ed.). Tufts University. http://www.perseus.tufts.edu

Index

For the benefit of digital users, indexed terms that span two pages (e.g., 52–53) may, on occasion, appear on only one of those pages.

agency, 29–30, 29n.16, 38n.42, 109–10, 111n.50

AI. *See* artificial intelligence

aideisthai, 39–40, 50–51

aidēmōn, 49–50, 95–96

aidōs

   aischunē and, 10–13, 16–17, 21, 31–32, 38–40, 46–53, 59–60, 80–81, 97–98, 102, 107–8, 139–40, 145–46

   aretē and, 95–96

   civic courage and, 66, 68, 95–96, 100

   epithumiai and, 106–7

   fear and, 46–48, 80–81, 92, 96–97, 100–1, 107–8, 114–15, 126–27, 132–33, 143

   habituation process and, 91

   hoi polloi and, 132–33, 143

   honour and, 39–40, 46–47, 66, 91, 92, 95–97, 100–2

   to kalon and, 95–97, 102

   lianchi and, 59, 88–89

   logos and, 80–81

   in moral development, 31–32, 46–47, 52–53, 68, 98, 100–1, 132–33

   in moral education, 32–33, 78n.64

   as *pathos*, 48–49, 50, 95–96, 97–98

   social relations and, 125

   timē and, 39–40

   virtue and, 95–98

   women and, 127–28, 131

   xiu, chi, ru and, 10–13, 16–17, 21, 139–40

   young people and, 98, 106–7, 145–46

to aischron, 32–33, 49–50, 52–53, 59–60, 68, 99–100, 101

aischunē

   aidōs and, 10–13, 16–17, 21, 31–32, 38–40, 46–53, 59–60, 80–81, 97–98, 102, 107–8, 139–40, 145–46

   as a genus, 48

   pathos and, 42, 45, 60, 97–98, 143–44

akratēs, enkratēs and, 108

Alexander the Great, 26–27, 27n.6, 143

Analects (Confucius), 21, 27n.7, 34, 142–43

   on self-reflection, 111–12, 113–14

   on shame, 36–37

   Xunzi and, 20–21, 37–38, 113–14

   on *zheng* (edicts), 134, 135–36

animals

   ants and bees, 83

   ape, 84, 84n.84

   Aristotle and Xunzi on, 63, 70–71, 77–78, 86–87, 88–89

   birds and beasts, 71, 74–76, 84–85

   dog, 73, 75n.53, 89, 89n.101

   dog and boar, 72–75, 72n.44, 75n.53, 88–89

   dogs and horses, 75n.53

   horses and oxen, 81–82, 83

   humans and, 63–65, 66–67, 70–71, 72–75, 77, 79–82, 83–84, 86–91, 116–17, 144–45, 146–47

   morality and, 88–91

   'political', 79, 116–17

   shame and, 88–91, 89n.101

174 Index

animals (*cont.*)
  Xunzi on, 71, 72–76, 77, 81–82, 83–84
  anthropocentrism, 62n.3, 89n.101
Antiphon, 39–40, 53n.50
aretē, 31–32, 39–40, 95–96
artificial intelligence (AI), 146–47
audience, 30–35, 42, 143
Augustine, 12–13, 113–14
Axial Age, 25

Barnes, Jonathan, 16–17
Bekoff, Marc, 90–91
Benedict, Ruth, 6–7, 7n.25, 9
bian
  as 'differentiation', 23, 63, 77–78, 84–
    87, 85n.88
  as 'argumentation', 23, 63, 77–78, 85–
    87, 85n.88
Book of Rites, 85
bridge concepts, 12–13, 12n.44
Brindley, Erica, 29–30, 29n.16, 37–38n.42
Burnyeat, Myles, 33n.28, 34–35, 100–1

Cairns, Douglas L., 9, 52–53, 101, 106, 140–41
Carr, E. H., 18
Charmides (Plato), 46n.20
chi (shame, disgrace), 10–13, 16–17, 21, 33–34,
    53–59, 97–98, 139–40, 143–44. See also
    lianchi
Chinese School (BBC documentary), 8–9
Christianity and Judeo-Christian tradition,
    9, 25, 113–14, 122–23, 140–41
Chunshen (lord), 29–30
Cicero, 127n.29
comparative philosophy, 4n.13, 16–17, 17n.59
conceptual maps, conceptual clusters, 9, 10–
    12, 13–14, 22–23, 59–60
Confucianism, 1–3, 9–11, 20–21, 35–
    36, 126–27
Confucius, 34–37, 38–39, 116, 135. See also
    Analects (Confucius)
conscience, 53–54, 113–14, 140–41
consequentialism, 122–23
Constitution of Athens, 26
contemporary society, 2n.4, 7–8, 7n.26, 9–
    10, 139–40, 146–47
courage, 23, 65–68, 72–74, 144–45
  civic, 65–66, 68, 95–96, 100–1, 102, 132–33
  spirited, 65–67, 100, 132–33
  true, 65–66, 68

Cua, Antonio, 10–11, 104n.34, 105n.37, 109–10

Daoist, 117–18
Darwin, Charles, 90–91
de (virtue/ virtuosity), 103, 104–5, 103n.32,
    134, 135–36
De Anima (Aristotle), 31–32, 106–7
definitions
  for 'emotions', 5, 11–12, 43–44, 45
  in Greek and Chinese traditions, 45–46
deliberation, 87, 110n.49
  in Aristotle, 80–81, 107n.39
  in Xunzi, 69–70, 109
democracy, 7n.26, 26
desire, 106–14, 113n.55, 115, 120–23
  as *orexis*, 106–7
  as *yu*, 102, 108–10, 122–23
  See also *epithumia*
de Waal, Frans, 89–91
dikē, aidōs and, 39–40, 78–79, 78n.64
disgrace, 13–14, 24, 122–23, 138. See also *ru*
disorder, 120–23, 124, 136–37
disrepute (*adoxia*), 47–49, 100–2, 107–8
Dodds, E. R., 6–7, 39–40

emotions, 1–4, 13–14, 19–20, 24
  animals and, 63, 90–91
  children and young people, 68, 106–8
  'emotional turn', 1
  'positive' vs. 'negative', 9–10
  social, 90–91
  See also *phusis*; *qing*
epithumia, 64–65, 67, 98–99, 99n.20, 106–7
ethics
  relationship with politics, 116, 116n.3, 119–
    20, 124–25, 145–46
eudaimonia, 64–65, 91, 94–95, 116–17, 144–45
Eudemian Ethics (Aristotle), 30–32, 64–65
Euripides, 39–40, 127–28
Eurocentrism, 1–3, 113–14

face, 6–7, 53–54, 54n.54
fa (law, standard), 24, 135–37, 135n.47, 144–45
fen (social divisions), 81–82, 82n.76, 83, 84–
    85, 116–17
Fraser, Chris, 85–86, 85n.88
Frevert, Ute, 8–9, 13–14
friendship, 57, 99–100, 100n.21, 105–6

Gaozi, 93–94

Gauthier, R. A., and Jolif, J. Y., 46–47, 47n.23
Geaney, Jane, 75–76, 126–27
god
in Aristotle's taxonomy, 64–65, 64–65n.13
God-like machines, 146–47
good life, 1–3, 9–10, 17–18, 91, 103, 116–17, 121n.13, 139–40, 141–42
worship of, 78–79
See also *eudaimonia*
Goldin, Paul R., 15–16, 36n.37, 58n.67, 62n.3, 135n.47
Graham, A. C., 43–44
Grimaldi, William M. A., 46–47, 50, 51–52
Guanzi, 57–58, 58n.68, 129
guilt, 9, 9n.35, 16, 53–54, 53n.52, 106, 140–41
guilt culture, 6–7, 7n.25, 9, 16, 24, 140–41

habituation, 24, 32–33, 61–63, 68, 71, 91, 93–94, 116, 117–18, 132–33, 143
hai (harm), 55n.56, 103, 104
Han Fei, 35–36
Harbsmeier, Christoph, 45
heart-mind. See *xin*
Herodotus, 62n.7, 127–28
Hesiod, 39–40, 78–79, 78n.64
Hippolytus (Euripides), 39–40, 127–28
History of Animals (Aristotle), 79, 128–29
hoi polloi, 132–33, 143
Homer, 39–40, 125–27
honour, 140–41
aidōs and, 39–40, 46–47, 66, 91, 92, 95–97, 100–2
benefit and, 104
courage and, 95–96, 100
friendship and, 99–100
love of honour (*philotimia*), 99
as object of party strife, 133
as *rong*, 54–56, 59–60, 103–5, 123–24
of rulers and state, 123–24
shame and, 6, 7–8, 9, 92, 95–97, 99, 112–13, 114–15, 117–18, 131
superficial *versus* true, 104–5
as *timē*, 39–40, 59–60
yirong (honour that derives from inner disposition), and *shirong* (honour that derives from force of circumstances), 37, 54–56
young people and, 99–100, 107–8
hubris, 46, 131

human communities, 116–18, 144–45
qun and, 77–78, 81–82, 81n.75, 83, 116–17
social distinctions and, 77–87
human nature, 61–63, 64–77, 139–40. See also *phusis*; *xing*
shame and, 61
Xunzi on, Aristotle and, 61–66, 70–71, 88–89, 93–94
Xunzi on, Mencius and, 37–38, 68–69, 70–71, 76–77, 93–94
Xunzi on human nature as bad, 69, 71–72, 77, 93–94, 122–23
humans and human being
animals and, 63–65, 66–67, 70–71, 72–75, 77, 79–82, 83–84, 86–91, 116–17, 144–45, 146–47
Aristotle on, 64–68
equal potential of, 64–65, 65n.16
as *politikon zōon*, 61–63, 77–78, 79, 116–17
Xunzi on, 68–77
humiliation, 6–7, 8–9
humility, 125–27
'Hundred Schools of Thought', 29
Hutton, Eric L., 56.n57, 82n.76, 82n.77, 84n.82, 85n.88, 104n.36, 110–11, 135n.50, 136n.56

individualism, collectivism and, 24, 145–46
insult, 54–56, 58–59, 89n.101
internalisation of values, 106–14, 140–41
itinerant scholars (*youshi*), 29–30, 119–20

Jaspers, Karl, 25
jiaohua (personal transformation), 94–95
Jimenez, Marta, 46–47, 50, 100–1, 102n.29
jiu (guilt), 53–54, 53n.52
Jixia Academy, 29–30
junzi (gentleman), 56, 110–11, 130–31
phronimos and, 93–94, 115, 131, 144–45

to kalon, 32–33, 59–60, 94–97, 101–2
Kaster, Robert A., 5, 126n.26
Knoblock, John, 65n.16, 84n.84, 85, 85n.88
Konstan, David, 3, 5n.16, 43n.4, 46–47, 50–51, 52n.47

laws. See '*fa*'; '*nomos*'
Laws (Plato), 39–40, 137–38, 142–43
le (happiness, willingness, pleasure), 57
'Legalist' School, 35–36, 36n.37
legislator, 24, 27–28, 34–35, 120n.11, 132–33, 138, 143

176   *Index*

legislation, 119–20, 133, 133n.42, 137–38, 142–43
  vs. 'ritual', 137–38, 136n.56
Lévy-Bruhl, Lucien, 14–15
Lewis, Mark Edward, 7–8
li (benefit), 55–56, 120–22
  hai (harm) and, 55n.56, 103, 104
  yi (propriety) and, 55n.56, 72–73, 104,
    114–15, 120–21, 138
li (ritual), 24, 28, 120–23, 131–32, 134–38,
    142–43, 144–45
lianchi (sense of shame), 12, 57–58, 97–99
  aidōs and, 59, 88–89
  wu lianchi (shameless), 57–59, 72–74,
    112–13, 143–44
Li Si, 35–36
Liu Xiang, 30–31
Lloyd, G. E. R., 14–15, 16–17, 17n.59, 19–
    20, 61–63
logos, 63, 77–78, 79–81, 86–87, 144–45
Lucretia, 127n.29
Lyceum, 27–28, 30–31, 143

magnanimity (*megalopsuchia*), 59–60
magnanimous person
    (*megalopsuchos*) 96–97
Mencius, 20–21, 37–38, 54n.54
  Aristotle and, 70–71, 97–98
  on ethical education, 116
  on humans and animals, 74–75, 85
  Xunzi and, 34–38, 61–63, 68–69, 70–71,
    76–77, 85–86, 93–94
Mencius, 21, 34, 36–37, 69–70, 74–75, 93–94,
    130–31, 142–43
modesty, 125–28, 125n.24, 127n.29
monarch, 21–22, 27n.6
monarchy
  Chinese, 28, 28n.10, 29–30
  Greek, 26–27, 26n.4
moral development, 31–32, 46–47, 52–53, 68,
    98, 100–1, 132–33
moral education
  aidōs in, 32–33, 78n.64
  Aristotle and Xunzi on, 17–18, 21, 23, 93–
    95, 118–20
  the ideal and, 93–95
  internalisation of values in, 106
  political nature of, 116–27, 138
  shame and, 6, 9, 21, 36–37, 100–1, 102,
    124–25

moral virtues, 10–11, 94–95
motivation
  for actions, 16, 39–40, 66, 74–75, 97n.15,
    100–1, 106, 112–13, 114–15, 140–41
  of authors, 16–17

Needham, Joseph, 63n.9, 87–88
nemesis, 78n.64
Nemesius, 47–48
Newmyer, Stephen. T., 89–91
Nicomachean Ethics (Aristotle), 30–32
  on *aidōs*, 46, 47–48, 49–51, 66, 95–98,
    100, 132–33, 143
  on *aischunē*, 47–48, 49–51
  on audience, 32–33
  on *epithumia* and *thumos*, 67
  on *eudaimonia*, 64–65
  on legislators, 119–20
  on pleasure, 80–81, 106–7
  on politics, 124–25
  on virtue, 87–88
  on young people, 98–100
Nisbett, Richard, 14–15
nomos, 131–32, 137–38, 144–45
nonhuman animals. *See* animals

Odyssey (Homer), 125–27
Orientalism, 15–16

paideia, 94–95
pathos and *pathē*, 21, 31–32, 33–34
  aidōs as, 50, 95–96, 97–98
  aischunē and, 42, 45, 60, 97–98, 143–44
  persuasion, 16–17, 22, 31–32, 33–35, 142–43
  qing and, 42–46
Phaedra, 127–28, 128n.31, 131
Philip (king), 26–27
Philosophy
  in China, 1–3
  comparative (see *comparative philosophy*)
  contemporary, 1–3
phronimos, junzi and, 93–94, 115, 131,
    144–45
phusis, 61–63, 139–40
plants, 64–65, 64–65n.13
Plato, 46n.20, 78–79
  Aristotle and, 26–28, 38–40, 43, 45–46,
    137–38, 142–43
  on *pathē*, 43, 45–46

Index   177

pleasure, desire and, 106–14, 115. See also *le*
  (happiness, willingness, pleasure)
Pliny, 89
Plutarch, 89
polis, 79, 99, 116–17
Politics (Aristotle), 26–27, 30–31, 79–80, 119–
  20, 124–25, 128–29, 133, 145–46
politikon zōon, 61–63, 77–78, 79
prohairesis, 67, 87–88, 98–99
Protagoras (Plato), 39–40, 78–79
Puett, Michael, 15–16, 43–44
punishments
  in Aristotle, 132–33
  in Xunzi, 134, 137–38
pursuit of goods, shame and, 95–106

Qin, State of, 28n.13, 29n.15,
  35–36, 143
qing (emotion, disposition), 33–34, 42–46,
  108–9, 145–46
qun (form community), 77–78, 81–82,
  81n.75, 83, 116–17

rationality, 87–88
respect, 53n.50, 56, 59, 75–76, 105–6, 125n.24,
  126–27, 127n.29
Rhetoric (Aristotle), 21, 30–32, 58–59, 60,
  98–100, 128–29
  on *aidōs* and *aischunē*, 46–48, 51–52
  on *pathē*, 33–34, 42, 43–44
rong (honour), *ru* (shame, disgrace) and,
  54–56, 59–60, 103–5, 123–24
Rowlands, Mark, 90–91
ru (shame, disgrace)
  in relation to ranking (*yi*) propriety and *li*
    (benefit), 120–21
  rong and, 54–56, 59–60, 103–5, 123–24
  xiu, chi and, 10–13, 16–17, 21, 33–34, 53–59,
    139–40, 143–44
  yiru (disgrace that derives from inner
    disposition), *shiru* (disgrace that
    derives from force of circumstances)
    and, 37, 54–56, 104–5

scala naturae, 64–65n.13, 87–88
self-reflection
  neixing, 53–54
  zixing, 53–54, 109–11, 112–14
Seok, Bongrae, 10–11

sexuality
  and shame, 127–28, 127n.29, 129, 131
shame
  Analects on, 36–37
  animals and, 88–91, 89n.101
  cross-cultural comparisons of, 4–14
  defining, 5–6
  disgrace and, 13–14, 24, 138
  fear and, 134
  guilt *versus*, 9, 9n.35, 16, 106, 140–41
  honour and, 6, 7–8, 9, 92, 95–97, 99, 112–
    13, 114–15, 117–18, 131
  metaphors, 126–27
  moral education and, 6, 9, 21, 36–37, 100–
    1, 102, 124–25
  moral virtue and, 10–11
  negative connotations of, 6–7, 6n.20,
    7n.26, 9–10
  politics of, women and, 127–31
  prospective and retrospective, 9–10
  pursuit of goods and, 95–106
  as social emotion, 24, 61
  universality of, 13–14, 141–42
  virtue and, 100–1
  vocabulary of, 11–13, 22–23, 59–60, 139–42
shame culture, 6–8, 7n.25, 9, 16, 24, 39–40,
  53–54, 140–41
shamelessness, 58–59, 128–29
  as *anaischuntia*, 58–59, 95–96
  as *wu lianchi*, 57–59, 72–74, 112–13, 143–44
shaming, 6–9
shan (good, goodness), 37–38, 68n.29,
  87, 105–6
shi ('scholar-official') stratum, 29, 29n.14
Shuowen jiezi, 54–55
Sima Qian, 29–30
Sivin, Nathan, 17n.59
Skinner, Quentin, 16–17, 17n.58
Smid, Robert. W., 4n.13
social divisions. See *fen*
social institutions, norms and, 131–
  38, 144–45
Socrates, 45
Song Xing (Songzi), 54–55, 69–70,
  108–9
soul, 64–65, 64n.11, 87–88, 91, 94–95, 98–
  99, 106–7
Stalnaker, Aaron, 12–13, 12n.44, 113–14
Sterckx, Roel, 45–46, 75–76

178 Index

Stoics, 89

taxonomy, 23, 45–46, 61, 63, 64–65, 71, 77, 88–89, 146–47
Theognis, 78–79
theōria, 64–65, 64–65n.13, 95n.7
thumos, 66, 67–68, 133

Van Norden, Bryan. W., 1–3, 97–98, 102n.31
virtue
  aidōs and, 95–98
  aretē as, 31–32, 39–40, 95–96
  friendship and, 105–6
  human community and, 116–17
  of *megalopsuchia*, 59–60
  prohairesis and, 87–88
  of rulers, 34–35
  shame and, 100–1
virtue ethics, 1–3, 9–10, 146–47

Warring States period, in China, 21–22, 25–26, 28–30, 34–36
way (*dao*), 84, 109–10
wei (artifice), 69–70, 120–21
Williams, Bernard, 9, 106, 140–41
women
  politics of shame and, 127–31

xin (heart-mind), 35n.36, 69–70, 87–88, 108–11, 112–13

xing (nature, disposition), 37–38n.42, 43–44, 68–70
  phusis and, 61–63, 139–40
xiu (ashamed), *chi* (shame, ashamed, disgrace) and, 56–57, 97–98
xue (learning), 71, 94–95
Xunzi
  Analects and, 20–21, 37–38, 113–14
  audience for, 34–35
  as counsel to rulers, 122–24
  nature of the text, 30–31
  Rhetoric and, 33–34

Yack, Bernard, 118
yi (propriety), 37–38, 61–63, 69–70, 71, 81–83, 87–89, 144–46
  li (benefit) and, 55n.56, 72–73, 104, 114–15, 120–21, 138
  li (ritual) and, 120–23, 135–36, 142–43
young people, 32–33, 39n.48, 98–101, 102, 103n.32, 103n.33, 105–8, 145–47
Yu, Jiyuan, 70–71, 77, 19n.62

zheng (edicts), 134–36
Zhuangzi, 19–20, 28n.10, 30–31, 35n.36, 69–70, 117–18, 118n.7
Zi Si, 35–36
zixing. See self-reflection

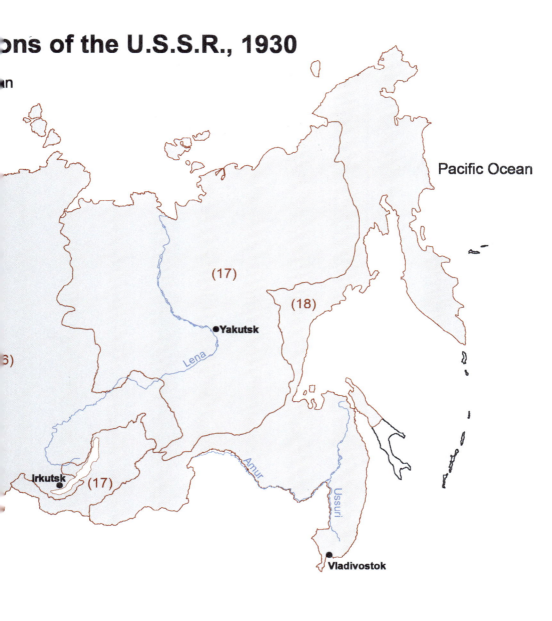
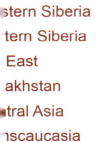
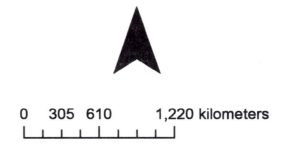